AMERICAN DREAMER

AMERICAN DREAMER

My Story of Survival, Adventure, and Success

ROBERT HALMI SR.

WITH DAN GABBAY

FOREWORD BY ISABELLA ROSSELLINI

INTRODUCTION BY PATRICK STEWART

Guilford, Connecticut

An imprint of Rowman & Littlefield

Distributed by NATIONAL BOOK NETWORK

British Library Cataloguing in Publication Information Available

Library of Congress Cataloging-in-Publication Data

Halmi, Robert.
  American dreamer : my story of survival, adventure, and success / Robert Halmi, Sr., with Dan Gabbay ; foreword by Isabella Rossellini ; introduction by Patrick Stewart.
    pages cm
  Includes index.
  ISBN 978-1-4930-0908-4 (hardcover) — ISBN 978-1-4930-1793-5 (e-book) 1. Halmi, Robert.
2. Television producers and directors—United States—Biography. I. Title.
  PN1992.4.H25A3 2015
  791.4502'32092—dc23
  [B]
                        2015006746

♾™ The paper used in this publication meets the minimum requirements of American National Standard for Information Sciences—Permanence of Paper for Printed Library Materials, ANSI/ NISO Z39.48-1992.

To Caroline, Kevin, Kim, Robi, and Billy:
Thank you for your tolerance and patience,
letting me live my life.
—Robert

To Deborah and Alex, who together have made my story a happy one.
—Dan

CONTENTS

FOREWORD BY ISABELLA ROSSELLINI

I met Bob Halmi for the first time a year or two after my mom, Ingrid Bergman, died. Bob wanted to make a TV film about her life, but in the family we thought this was a dreadful idea. We would rather have just maintained our privacy. But we were advised by mother's agent Kay Brown that since Mamma was a public person, anyone could make a film about her. She said it would be better for us to meet with Robert Halmi and negotiate so we might have at least some say in the film.

When I met with Bob, I was full of diffidence and disdain. It took five minutes for me to be totally charmed by him. First of all, he was a friend of Bob Capa, the great war photographer whom my mom had loved. Capa and Halmi were both Hungarians, and it seemed to me they had the same crazy sense of adventure. Now, his nationality seems irrelevant, but some years after we met, I accompanied Bob to a dinner at the United Nations in his honor. The great journalist Walter Cronkite introduced Bob by saying, "We have all wondered when aliens would come to our planet. They have. They are the Hungarians, and one of them is here tonight and being honored. Robert Halmi."

Bob and I ended up not doing the film about Mamma, but we worked together on many other productions: *Merlin, Don Quixote, The Odyssey*. We both love animals, and we did a film—*Ivory Hunters*—about the plight of the elephant, which is being exterminated for its ivory. One day we were filming some wild elephants when they started to charge us. We could have been killed, but I was with Bob, who, like a cat, has many lives. He can survive anything. He survived Nazism that condemned him to death. He survived Communism that condemned him to death, and he even survived strapping dynamite to himself and exploding it to get a great picture for *Life* magazine.

With Bob I did things I wouldn't have dared do with anyone else. He gives me the sense that life should be lived in full and in the moment and that death isn't to be feared, just ignored.

I was with Bob in Borneo attempting to organize a film about Biruté Galdikas, the conservationist who has studied the lives of orangutans for many years. We ended up being surrounded by wild orangutans in the forest. They could have easily killed us, but they didn't because I was with Bob. When you're with Bob, you have nothing to fear! Bob just sat on a log, looking at the orangutans with great enchantment. He told me to relax and sit next to him. "This is a truly exceptional sight," he said. "This is a wonderful day."

INTRODUCTION BY PATRICK STEWART

I first met Robert Halmi in the doorway of his suite at the Beverly Wilshire Hotel. I had gone there to try and persuade him I could be Captain Ahab in his upcoming new TV film of *Moby Dick*. My expectations were not high, but I was determined to make a fight of it. When the door opened, he saw me and immediately pulled me into the room. With an arm around my shoulder, he punched me in the chest with his other hand and emoted, "Patrick, this is going to be f***ing marvelous; you are Ahab." Of course you have to imagine the Hungarian accent to truly feel the impact of the man. He put a glass of champagne into my hand and launched into a description of how it was all going to be. I was overwhelmed, nodding my head fatuously and, I guess, grinning from ear to ear. So began an awesome and exciting journey, not just through *Moby Dick*, but through years of collaboration and fun: *A Christmas Carol*, *Animal Farm*, *King of Texas*, *The Lion in Winter*. Each film was a fresh and bold exploration of an established—and in the case of Dickens's great work—much-beloved classic.

My then wife and producing partner at the time, Wendy Neuss, was most instrumental in bringing three of these productions to Robert's attention, but *Animal Farm* was a straightforward offer from Robert to play Napoleon, the farm pig who at first supports the animal rights movement, which leads to the farm animals overthrowing the incompetent, drunken farmer and turning him off his land. Napoleon, at first collaborative and democratic but with the taste of power in his snout, becomes a cruel despot and the imaginative source behind the slogan All Animals Are Equal . . . But Some Are More Equal Than Others. One of the joys of voice-over for animation is the liberation it gives an actor—wacky, huge, grotesque, broad—and most of all for me, the opportunity to be comic or absurd. As Napoleon I snorted and grunted, belched and roared, and sucked whiskey right out of the bottle. In the recording studio it must have been a truly offensive sight, but I loved every moment.

I was, however, unaware that Robert had a plan to bring me face-to-face with Napoleon. At the press conference promoting the movie,

Robert and I sat side by side not far from a curtained-off platform area. At some point Robert announced that we were lucky to have an additional cast member joining us, and with that the curtains whisked back and there he was . . . Napoleon himself, blinking in the lights and looking suspiciously around at the assembled media. Well, can you blame him? Even animatronic creations might have reason to squirm under the gaze of TV writers and critics. Robert, always a showman, invited the journalists to question Napoleon, and as might be expected, he answered cautiously but always caustically and contemptuously: a dictator to the last bristle on his snout.

Of course the photographers wanted only one photo: Napoleon and me, my arm around him, and as the flashes blazed, he muttered in my ear unrepeatable obscenities.

A Christmas Carol was a delicious experience, although it was not the *Christmas Carol* that director David Jones and I had pitched to Robert. I had had some success with a solo stage version of the book, and we wanted to film that, but Robert convinced us that a more conventional treatment would be better; that is what we went with, and it is lovely. It was filmed at Ealing Studios in London, and it is filled with brilliant and legendary British character actors: Elizabeth Spriggs, Liz Smith, John Franklyn-Robbins, Richard E. Grant, Saskia Reeves, and the glorious Trevor Peacock. But an Anglo-American slant was given to the piece by the inclusion of the brilliant Joel Grey as the Ghost of Christmas Past, a piece of casting I feel inclined to take credit for—but I could be wrong.

For me the lasting satisfaction is that the BBC has made it what seems to be an annual Christmas movie event: It's played every year.

King of Texas I can take some credit for. I have always loved Shakespeare's play *King Lear*, but back in the '90s I saw little chance of me playing the role. So why not take the story and rewrite it for another time and another place like, say, the American West? I was having dinner with Robert one evening, and we met at his Manhattan town house for a glass of wine. As the bottle was being opened, I decided to plunge ahead with my pitch–the cowboy *King Lear*. Before barely a sip had been taken, Robert was on his feet: "My God, brilliant, we'll do it." And that was that. I seem to remember that the very next day, I received a draft contract. And that is one of the things that sets Robert Halmi apart and makes him such a stimulating colleague. If a pitch appeals, if it excites him, he just goes for it. There is no committee, no focus group, just Robert saying, "Dammit, we'll do it."

One day while filming in a somewhat remote part of Mexico, I had to call him to say we needed more money for a suddenly expanded scene that the director and Wendy and I thought would be exciting. Robert sighed and grumbled and gave me a lecture about keeping within the budget and then . . . he gave us the money.

The Lion in Winter was Wendy's passion, and I wasn't sure, but when Robert charmed Glenn Close into playing Eleanor of Aquitaine (she won an Emmy and a Golden Globe), I was not going to miss such an opportunity. We filmed in the winter in Hungary, and it was delightful to find how many doors Robert Halmi's name opened.

But back to *Moby Dick*. We filmed in Victoria, Australia, and from start to finish the twelve weeks were unforgettable: a great novel and a very good script, as well as an outstanding cast—notably Ted Levine as a passionate, brooding Starbuck.

We were in the last week of filming when the day arrived to shoot Ahab lashed to the back of the white whale. We were in a tank beside the Tasman Sea. It was cold, and a steady drizzle was falling. At the start of the shot, I was underwater with a regulator, which I passed to a diver stationed nearby when we got the signal for action. Then the whale moved on tracks through the water and up, then dove again. It had not been anticipated how the force of water over the whale's smooth sides would try to sweep me out of the ropes. (And, I constantly reflected, under the wheels of Moby Dick.) It was a technically very difficult shot, and we did it again and again. At last I could take no more, and I signaled to the director I was done. "We haven't got it," he groaned, "we need one more take." "I can't," I protested. "I'm exhausted and I'm afraid something will happen." Robert, sitting on the bank in a heavy-duty parka, under an umbrella, with a hot drink in his hand, had this conversation relayed to him. "Patrick," he yelled. "Don't worry. If anything happens to you, I'll take care of your family." So I did another take. Not because I didn't believe something would go wrong, but because if it did, Robert would keep his word. I love him.

PROLOGUE
BURSTING ONTO THE SCENE

The story begins in darkness. There is the barest trace of light up ahead, and we are moving toward it. But where are we? And where are we going?

Suddenly we break out of the darkness and leave it behind. A man on horseback bursts out of a canopy of trees and into the light. We don't see his face; we are trailing behind him as he rushes away from us at full gallop across a great expanse of shallow tidal pools reflecting a purple sky. His objective appears to be an island in the middle distance, but before he reaches his destination, we cut to an old man, his face filling the screen.

He is wrinkled and timeworn with white hair and a beard. The old man is troubled, haunted even, a hint of madness in his red-rimmed eyes—eyes as reflective as those tidal pools. This is a man who has seen too much. He has been through hell, and now, as time closes in on him, he is compelled to share what he knows before it's too late. His whole life has come down to the story he says he has to tell.

The old man talks directly to us. He chooses his words carefully; he needs to be clear: This is *not* a fairy tale, but it does have elements of one. "It has magic," he says. "In my day magic was much more commonplace." But where to begin? he asks. At the beginning, of course. "In the terrible years of darkness. . . . Death came so easily then."

The man is Merlin. He is a character in the miniseries of the same name, which I conceived and brought to term in 1998. Appearing on two successive nights on NBC, *Merlin* was one of the last of its kind—a dramatic television event targeting a large, cross-generational audience. Television used to be *big* and still can be, but for the most part it's getting smaller. Except for the Super Bowl, there isn't much room left on television for spectacle. Watching television used to be a shared experience. Now we all go our own way. Before long, not only will we each have our own TV, we'll each have our own channel.

But I've always been a storyteller. Whether I'm speaking to an audience of one or one million—through the lens of a camera, a television screen, or simply sitting around the dinner table—I've always got a story to tell. I look back on my life and I see one story followed by another: comedy, drama, tragedy, horror, adventure. . . . And back in the mid-'90s, even as television got smaller, I was still thinking big. I couldn't help myself. I didn't want to make small pictures and small talk, I wanted to make *Merlin*. Somehow I managed to pull it off. Pulled it out of my hat is more like it, because getting that cast together was quite a trick.

Sam Neill, John Gielgud, Isabella Rossellini, Helena Bonham Carter, Rutger Hauer, Miranda Richardson, Martin Short—these were top stars who commanded top money. But I wasn't Disney. I didn't have an unlimited budget. When I make a picture, I have to be creative in all sorts of ways, telling stories to the bankers too. So how did I get this incredible cast together, get them all on the same page? I'll let you in on a deep, dark, dirty little secret: There's more to this movie business than money. Usually the way it works, once a producer has decided who he wants to star in his movie, he has his assistant call the star's agent's assistant; the two assistants then attempt to synchronize schedules and egos and the tides of the moon and somehow arrive at a time when the producer's assistant can once again call the star's agent's assistant, whereupon they can be put on hold, and finally, miraculously, with a scientific precision worthy of a space shuttle launch, producer and agent are connected. Scripts are sent, lunches are arranged, numbers are crunched—a complex dance with one simple question at its core: *how much?*

I had a different idea. Pick up the phone, call the stars themselves, and ask them for five minutes of their time. Instead of talking money, I told them a story—my vision of *Merlin*. I wasn't in a position to appeal to their pocketbooks, so I appealed to what got them into acting in the first place. No one in his right mind becomes an actor for the money. You become an actor to tell stories, to create an illusion that is more real than reality. You become an actor for the same reason I became a producer: to put on a show. And I told them they would not only be in the show, they would be in on its creation, writing lines, shaping scenes, developing characters. In exchange for a smaller salary, they would receive creative input. The idea of it thrilled them, but I doubt it pleased their agents.

A few years before, Sam Neill had been battling dinosaurs for Steven Spielberg. Now he would be taking on the legendary magician's demons for me. I couldn't have dreamed up a more perfect Merlin. Sam's gentle, intelligent face mirrors the spirit of the man—a spirit I could easily imagine bringing souls together, which is what the movie is all about. Merlin is a transitional figure, a bridge between the dark and chaotic ancient times ruled by myth, magic, and murder, and Camelot, an age of enlightenment and reason, presided over by men in shining armor with laws and social contracts. But Merlin knows that a world without magic is not a world worth living in. His challenge is to escape the dangers of the old world but bring the magic with him into the new.

How do you grow old while at the same time holding on to your youth and spirit? For Merlin, the answer, the true magic of a man's life, is borne on the love of a woman—and it is at the nexus of love and magic, danger, and storytelling that the world turns. Or at least *my* world.

The rider on the horse, we come to learn, is the magician at a younger age—a simple but clever spirit, a vigorous man of nature who is also a man of action. Merlin is riding out of the darkness of the past and toward the dawn of the future. It's no accident that I have chosen Merlin's story to start my own. I have lived through the horrors of Europe's darkest days. I have raced away across the ocean to create a new life on an island in the new world. And I like to think that I have brought a little magic with me.

Some five decades before bringing *Merlin* to the screen, I walked out into the middle of a field in New Jersey, grabbed my Leica and a stick and a half of dynamite, climbed into a wooden box about the size of a coffin, lit the fuse, and blew myself up.

It was 1952, I was twenty-eight, I'd been in America for a little over a year, and I was struggling like hell to make ends meet—and make a name for myself. Hungarian by birth, I came of age in a country that had experienced a thousand years of isolation, invasion, and betrayal—one crushing defeat after another. Hungarians are nothing if not masters of survival, with both a deep-rooted sense of being alone in the world and an ability to laugh at almost any situation. After all, if you've got to go through hell to get to heaven, you better have a sense of humor. And I am Hungarian to the bone.

I did have one advantage over the average Hungarian, though: my mastery of the English language. I had learned it at a young age—my father saw to that, sending me to an elite 450-year-old school in the hills outside of Budapest where the classes were conducted in English. This fact was literally pounded into my head by one professor with an Oxford English Dictionary—removing one of my teeth in the process—when I failed to complete an essay on Lord Byron. I may have lost a tooth, but I gained the world, because I spoke the *language* of the world.

I spoke English, but better yet, it was English with an accent. It was thick with European culture, mystery, and charm—stuff Americans can't get enough of—and it gave me access to people and places that I might not otherwise have had. Which is all very nice, but that hardly explains what I was doing leaping into a box of dynamite out there in that vacant lot in New Jersey. It certainly wasn't my accent that put me there. It was my hunger.

At the time I was shooting photos for my supper, and *True* was my meal ticket. And *shooting* is just the right word for it. The magazine's offices were on West 44th Street next to the Algonquin Hotel—but they may as well have been in Tombstone, Arizona. *True* was the Wild West of the publishing world—unruly and untamed—and the photographers were the hired guns. Photos of bear hunters, hero cops, ballplayers, UFOs, and Nazi spies with a Vargas pin-up thrown in now and then for spice—anything to boost male testosterone and *True*'s circulation. It was not exactly the pinnacle of photojournalism, but it was definitely a lot of fun—and certainly an education.

The editors were eager for photos—the wilder the better—and I was just as eager to get them pictures for both the exposure and the money. I was willing to go to the ends of the earth—or on this particular day to Danbury, Connecticut—to find them. New York City was New York City; the Danbury Fair was America.

Here, one carnival act in particular commanded my attention—as it did the attention of every man, woman, and child at the fair. A guy crawled into a box rigged with dynamite, then blew the box to kingdom come. He walked away a little mussed, as if climbing out of his girlfriend's bed, but none the worse for wear. It was one hell of an act, and I wanted in on it. With my camera.

I buttonholed the man and asked him if it was possible for me to do the trick. He said, "Well, sure it's possible, but it's also possible you could get hurt." I arranged to meet him at his next show—a fair in Paterson, New Jersey, where he promised he would give me the opportunity to, as he put it, shake hands with the dynamite.

He explained the gimmick to me. It was all a matter of physics and timing. A stick and a half of dynamite in a closed space creates a vacuum a foot and half away. Leap in at the proper moment and position yourself in that vacuum and, boom, you're home free. And I'm thinking, if this scrawny little piece of human shrapnel in his worn dungarees could do it, then so could Bob Halmi. You have to take your science on faith. A stick and a half of dynamite a foot and a half away—not one stick or two, not twelve inches or twenty-four. One misstep or miscalculation, of course, and this story would have ended right there. But I didn't think that way. All I thought about was, how was I going to get the shot?

I had already been condemned to die twice, first by the Nazis, then by the Communists—and now the idea of escaping death had become second nature to me. Or part of my nature. Sure, I fear death. And I don't believe in an afterlife. When it's done, it's done. This is why I cram as much as I can into this life. There's one thing I fear more, and that's boredom. So on a warm and lovely summer evening, under a high blue sky and in the shadow of the Paterson silk mills, I strapped a camera to my chest and lit a fuse.

It was a simple matter of physics. And ambition and showmanship and, well, okay, stupidity, too, which is to say, the ability to leap before you look. The evidence—that I am sitting here recalling the events of that day—suggests that I got the physics and numbers and calculations right. I walked away with limbs attached and a photo that no one had ever gotten before. I don't know, maybe it wasn't physics at all. Maybe it was magic.

In the end the only difference between the guy at the fair and me was our reach. I was thinking *audience share* before I knew such a phrase even existed. From *True* to *Sports Illustrated* to *Life*, from Alaska to Africa to Hollywood, from a stick of dynamite in a box to the magic of Merlin on the screen, I was that guy who'll risk everything in the name of entertainment and do anything to get the shot.

CHAPTER ONE

Hungarian Rhapsody

On my sixteenth birthday my mother took me to the opera—opening night of a new production of *The Tales of Hoffmann*—and I remember it like it was yesterday. I remember sitting in the taxi as it pulled up in front of the magnificent Hungarian State Opera House in Budapest, when my mother, leaning in close, making sure the driver couldn't hear, whispered in my ear:

"Bobi. Tonight don't tell anyone you're my son."

I can still see the Myrna Loy twinkle in her eye, catch the smell of her expensive French perfume—a touch of lavender—always the best for my mom. I also remember the little thrill that went through me—the thrill of being invited to join her masquerade, to enter into this conspiracy of two. Far from being confused or disturbed by her surprise request, I was intrigued—found myself breathing more sophisticated air. I had been liberated, though I had no clue from what. My mother had brought me to the opera and ushered me into adulthood—or at least had brought me to the starting gate.

My mother's reasons for denying her maternity that night were far more complicated than I could make sense of then—or now, for that matter. That doesn't mean I don't understand it. For while I was turning sixteen, my mother was on the verge of turning forty—a twice-married woman who, though still capable of a Myrna Loy wink and smile, had seen the sharp Myrna Loy twists and curves she had possessed in her twenties start to soften and fade.

Six years before, on the occasion of her second marriage—I was ten at the time—my mother had sent me off to live with my father. For her, to be freed suddenly from the everyday appearance of motherhood had been a chance to regain a purchase on her youth. Now, six years later, to thrust a sixteen-year-old son into the picture would have been like hurling a grenade into a carefully crafted house of glass. After all, she was an actress who became a playwright, and as far as she was concerned, the line "All the world's a stage" was not a metaphor—it was a way of life. And on *her* stage, at her stage in life, there was simply no room or role for a sixteen-year-old son.

As for me, on that night at the opera, my mother's whisper in the backseat of the taxi took me aback. It stunned me and frightened me but also excited me. It raised a question that could in itself cause an opera to break out: *If I'm not my mother's son, then who the hell am I?*

The way I saw it, if she could be whomever she wanted to be, well then, so could I. Whether by intention or by accident, she had planted the seed of an idea in my sixteen-year-old brain that night: I was not bound by my past in creating my future. I could write my own story and my own ticket. Granted, it took a while for me to figure that out. In fact, it's a lesson I've never stopped learning. But the notion of inventing—and reinventing—myself has served me well throughout my life. I'm a fish that has to keep moving to breathe. I guess I am my mother's son after all.

And my father's too. But there's a reason I choose to start my memoir in this place, in the shadow of Mozart, Verdi, Puccini, and the rest. And that is this: Everything I need to know about life, I learned at the opera. The power of love, and the tragedy that sometimes goes with it. The power of laughter, and the danger behind it. The backstabbing, betrayal, and deception. The courage and sacrifice. The loudmouths and heaving breasts. I learned that death can come knocking at your door without warning, that romance and revenge are blood brothers, and that even the ugliest dwarf in the room can walk away with the prettiest girl on stage. I discovered that the most powerful tool on the planet is the human voice, and finally, that life is nothing if not a performance.

In 1924 in Hollywood, Metro Pictures, Goldwyn Pictures, and the Louis B. Mayer Company merged to form MGM. In Munich, Hitler went on trial for treason. In Washington, J. Edgar Hoover was appointed head of the FBI. And on January 22, in a fourth-story room of a five-story white stone house on the corner of Kecskeméti Street and Kalvin Square, in one of the most storied districts in Budapest—a lovely, labyrinthine neighborhood built atop the accumulated ruins of Celts, Romans, and Huns—one more Hungarian made his entrance on stage, crying his lungs out. I had arrived.

I doubt my birth created much of a stir, except, of course, in the lives of my mother and father. Sarah Deri, a twenty-four-year-old beauty with dark eyes and full lips, born in 1900 on Christmas Eve, pushed me out into the world that day—sixteen years later she would push me a little farther out. And my photographer father, Bela (pronounced BAY-la) Halmi, with a high, intelligent forehead, aquiline nose, and fierce sense of honor and ambition, was born in 1892. While it was my mother who brought me into this world, it was my father who would set out to prepare me for it.

But what exactly was this world I had gotten myself into? What was this *Hungary*? For though I am American by choice, I am Hungarian by birth, and the country is in my blood, my bones, my DNA. You can't begin to know yourself—or anyone else for that matter—until you know where you're from. Me, I'm from this place where history is myth—a country of storytellers and fabricators, consummate artists and con artists. My homeland is one of the greatest stories ever told, featuring assorted pagans, saints, sorceresses, sultans, beautiful maidens, beautiful maiden–impregnating birds of prey, armies of the dead, armies of the soon-to-be-dead, emperors, kings, queens, princes, and pretenders to the throne, with a special flashback cameo appearance, in the fifth century, by the one and only Attila the Hun.

But how did all this get started? Legend has it that twin brothers, Hunor and Magor, sons of the mighty hunter Nimrod and great-great-grandsons of Noah, set out one morning on a hunting trip in pursuit of an ethereal white stag. While Hunor and Magor never did find the stag, they did find a couple of lovely ladies, the daughters of Dula, King of Alans. Whether by the force of their charm or simply by force, the brothers carried the two maidens away and married them, the offspring of the two marriages producing the Huns and the Magyars—the two sides of the Hungarian coin.

Typical Hungarians. They go off in search of one thing and end up finding something completely different that, for better or worse, turns their lives upside down. Serendipity. It has certainly played a role in my life—and my career. And I've always been a hunter, but I've never let predetermined goals get in the way of landing bigger game.

The Huns and Magyars have rolled merrily along throughout Hungary's long, violent, volatile, and visionary history. Stephen I, crowned Hungary's first Christian king on the first day of the year 1001, is revered as the kindhearted and benevolent creator of the nation. Thirty years later, in 1031, in a struggle for the throne, Stephen had his nephew blinded and molten lead poured into his ears. Welcome to the family. Welcome to Hungary.

Hungary has always been a land of paradox, beset by a multiple personality disorder—invaded by the Turks, dominated by the Germans, used and abused by the Russians, admired by the British, disrespected by the French, and ultimately ignored by them all. It is a nation that has won many great victories in battle—but has not won a single war. In every war of significance, Hungary's greatest enemy has always been itself. In the lost war of revolution of 1848, one Hungarian aristocrat put it this way: "The King of Hungary had declared war on the King of Croatia while the Emperor of Austria remained neutral, and these three monarchs were one and the same person."

This thousand-year-long reign of confusion begs the question: Who are we Hungarians *really*? The bloodthirsty, human-flesh-eating Huns of lore? Or the cultured, music-loving saviors of Western civilization? Turns out, we're a bit of both. And so am I. I love music, but I've had my moments of bloodthirst as well. Otherwise I never would have made a single movie. Not a good one, anyway. Creativity is a very destructive thing. To create something new and different, you have to both love civilization and be willing to rip it apart. You can't build a road through rock without dynamite and a bulldozer, and if you want to make a good movie, bring some charm, bring some money . . . and bring some dynamite and a bulldozer.

Speaking of destruction—ten years before I was born, on June 28, 1914, in the name of a united Yugoslavia, Gavrilo Princip, the

4

nineteen-year-old son of a Serbian postman, emerged from a delicatessen in Sarajevo and fired two rounds. The first severed the jugular vein of Archduke Franz Ferdinand of Austria, presumptive heir to the Austro-Hungarian throne. The second penetrated the abdomen of his wife, Sophie, Duchess of Hohenberg. Princip got off a third shot, intending to kill himself, but when it came to blowing his own head off, his aim was not so true. He survived to later die in a prison cell. The archduke and his wife, however, died within minutes. The rest, as they say, is history—and once again Hungary ended up on the wrong side of it.

The Great War was on, which turned out not to be so great for Hungary—or for my parents' families. The peace agreement—the Treaty of Trianon—effected vengeance upon Hungary by mandating its vivisection. Great slabs of Hungarian territory were lopped off and reattached to neighboring nations. Overnight Hungary lost its access to the sea, and all four of my grandparents became foreigners to me. Twelve million people went to bed Hungarian and woke up Czechoslovakian or Romanian or Transylvanian. I did later learn in school—as all young Hungarians did—that on the day the treaty was signed, black flags went up all over Budapest, traffic stopped, and funerals were held in churches. The country does not lack for drama.

There is irony in the fact that if America—the country that I now call home and that I have come to love—had not been instrumental in defeating the land of my birth in two world wars, it is highly unlikely I ever would have come here. I suspect that that is true of millions of other immigrants over the last hundred years. It is one of the amazing things about America: It will beat you to a pulp in a fight, but once the fight is over, it will reach down, lift you up, and invite you over.

⚊⌣⚊

So there I was, in a fourth-story room on the corner of Kecskeméti Street, crying my little eyes out and letting everyone within earshot know: Attention must be paid. Little did I know that this ground from which I had sprouted, this Hungary, was a land obsessed with its own defeat and made paranoid and delusional by it—and that the seed of my leaving it had already been planted.

Budapest in the 1920s was rife with conspiracy and skullduggery committed by Communists, right-wing terror groups with names like the Double Cross Blood Union, and the secret police alike. But what did I know? I was just a kid, and to me Budapest was a playground—a world of profound beauty, unlimited possibility, and endless discovery. And just as I didn't have a clue that I was the product of a broken country, neither did I know that I was the product of a broken family. My parents divorced when I was two, so I had no sense of them as ever having been together. My family simply consisted of two independent islands, each with its own climate, culture, and landscape. I spent time on one island, then moved on to the next—nothing broken, nothing in need of repair. That was simply the way life was.

As for my family history, I have none. It was all lost in the war and in the peace that followed. My parents had come to Budapest from the country at an early age, seeking to make better lives for themselves, and were ultimately cut off from their families.

I never met my grandparents on my mother's side. I don't even remember her ever talking about them. I like to think that there was some great scandalous truth she was concealing—that she was a runaway Gypsy or the illegitimate offspring of royalty or Enrico Caruso's secret lover.

As for my father's parents, I did meet them—once. And what that brings to mind is cheese. Smoked cheese. Incredibly delicious smoked cheese. I must have been about four at the time. They had come down to Budapest from their dairy farm on the Arva River, in the shadow of the Carpathian Mountains, land that, in 1920, had been turned over to Czechoslovakia. They had made the journey across the border to visit their son and meet their grandchild—me.

The afternoon of their arrival—my father busy upstairs working in his studio—I sat across from my grandfather at a table in the courtyard, not quite sure what to make of his big ears, bushy mustache, light blue tie, and stiff white collar. He didn't smile much, but he had a pleasant way of looking at me, as though happy simply to have me for company. Perhaps I reminded him of my dad when he was still in short pants.

My grandfather asked if I was hungry. As I had decided to nod yes to everything he said, I nodded yes. Anticipating my answer, he had already reached down into the satchel at his feet and pulled out a package wrapped in paper and string. To me, with all the patience of a four-year-old, it seemed to take the better part of the afternoon to get the damn thing open. What delightful, delectable treasure had this bushy-faced man brought me from his faraway farmland? Ice cream? Cake? Candy?

Cheese. I can't say if my grandfather saw the disappointment in my face, but if he did, he pretended not to notice. From the inside pocket of his jacket, next to his watch chain, he pulled out a pocketknife. He sliced off the rind, then cut two pieces of the cheese, one slice for each of us. Although I was more interested in the watch chain and the knife, I politely took the cheese and, after watching him take a bite, I dutifully followed his example. I have dined in some of the finest restaurants around the world, but I don't know that I have ever tasted anything quite so good as that first bite of my grandfather's smoked cheese. Proust had his cookie. I have my cheese, the memory of which is as distinct today, eighty-five years later, as the taste of it was that afternoon in the courtyard.

Although our lives begin at birth, our conscious lives begin with our first memories. That moment in the courtyard was a point of departure. My story can be measured by the four great pleasures I have taken in life: the importance of work, the company of women, the value of family, and the taste of good food. Three out of the four—family, work, and food— were wrapped up in that package of my grandfather's. The company of women part would come later.

As much as I loved my grandfather's smoked cheese, that was how much my father hated it. Not the taste of it. What he despised was the idea of cheese—of spending his life surrounded and imprisoned by it. By the time my dad was in his early teens, he already knew that there was more to life—more to *his* life—than making curds and whey. He had a talent for drafting and drawing and saw himself as an artist. And Rembrandt didn't milk cows.

There was a time, of course, when leaving the family farm was unthinkable. But new markets opened up to my grandfather, and by 1910 his cheeses were showing up in shops in Strasbourg and restaurants in Vienna. My grandfather was a landowner and a businessman as well as a farmer, and he could imagine, and even welcome, a life different from his own for his son. So he agreed to finance his son's escape from the family business.

Wasting no time, my father lit out for the Academy of Fine Arts in Munich, one of Germany's most prestigious art schools. Being a smart guy, he learned pretty fast he wasn't a very good painter. Disappointed but in no way defeated, he turned his sights back on Hungary, not to the farm but to Budapest, a place he had never visited. He immersed himself in the cafes and the conversation in a place where his artistic ambitions could come to fruition. My father was able to realize his vision not with a paintbrush but through the lens of a camera.

Barely twenty, he found work as an assistant in a photography studio near the center of the city. Twentieth-century Hungary has produced visionary photographers—Moholy-Nagy, Brassaï, and Capa to name a few—but the photographer my dad went to work for was decidedly *not* one of them. Born around the time the daguerreotype was invented, the old fellow had yet to bring his studio into the new century—and saw no need to. A wooden box, a bulb, and some emulsion, and he was set. As my father put it, his boss was not in the business of producing art, he was in the business of producing money. And the money was in portraits.

Pre–World War I Hungary was a land of countless counts and barons. You could get a title the old-fashioned way, by being born into it; by buying one if you had the cash; or simply by taking on a job in the government like running a post office or collecting taxes. And every single count and baron worth his salt needed a framed picture of himself showing off his mustache and medals and shiny leather boots.

Working twelve-hour days—a hard worker who worked cheap—my father took to the business like the son of a cheese farmer who never wanted to go back to the cheese farm. And not only did he hone his skills as a portrait photographer and businessman, he began to make the connections that would change his life—and ultimately make mine possible.

One morning in the winter of 1915, my father arrived at the studio, unlocked the doors, and went to work the same way he did every other day. Except this day, the owner's houseboy, who typically brought the old man his lunch, brought the news of his death. The old photographer had no sons or wives who wanted anything to do with the studio, and so my father took over. At twenty-three, he set out to expand the client list beyond counts and barons, to politicians, military officers, and theater people. And as luck and politics would have it, he landed the most prestigious account of the time. Once again, death took a hand.

On November 21, 1916, Franz Joseph I, emperor of Austria, king of Bohemia, king of Croatia, apostolic king of Hungary, king of Galicia and Lodomeria, and grand duke of Cracow, died. Three days later, coincidentally, Mai Manó, court photographer to the Habsburgs, also passed away.

Hungary's annual budget had to be signed into law and validated by the sovereign by the end of the year. There would be no budget unless a new emperor was crowned by December 31. And royal families being as conscious of image as Cadillac or Mercedes-Benz, there could be no coronation without an official court photographer to record it. For reasons that are too byzantine to go into, a Hungarian photographer had to be chosen. All eyes turned to Budapest, where the politicians, barons, and military all had their portraits hanging over the fireplace, thanks to one photographer. All agreed: Bela Halmi was the man for the job.

On December 30, 1916, my father recorded for posterity the last great pageant of the royal family: the coronation of Emperor Karl I, with the dark-eyed Queen Zita and the golden boy, six-year-old crown prince Otto at the new emperor's side. My dad had been invited to the final coronation, the last time the thousand-year-old Crown of Saint Stephen would be used for its essential purpose. It was the beginning of the end of the empire.

From that moment on, my father was a Royalist—a fact that would both safeguard and endanger him for decades to come. His friendship with Otto, the crown prince, would last a lifetime, and his connection to the Habsburgs remained strong. But in times of crisis—and in Hungary that was every minute of every day throughout the twentieth century—to rely on the protection of the Habsburgs was tantamount to having a parachute that you couldn't be sure would open until you've already jumped out of the plane.

For better or worse my father would always be "the last court photographer of the Royal Habsburgs," and professionally it proved a boon. From the 1920s through the '30s, every dignitary, opera singer, and movie star who passed through Budapest put my father's studio on their itinerary. Even Pope Pius XI invited my old man, son of a cheese farmer, to take his portrait in the Vatican. But for all the faces and figures who sat before my father's cameras, there is one that stands out.

A spring day in 1921, my father leaned forward to press his eye to the camera and saw a striking, young, dark-eyed actress staring back at him. I might not have been conceived in that instant, but the possibility of me certainly was. Three years later, one floor down from the studio where he took a picture of that actress, the possibility became flesh, combining in some uncertain measure his rebellion and ambition with her theatrical, self-creative force.

I was their only child.

My mom didn't cook much for me, but my idea of happiness on a summer afternoon was a bowl of her sour cherry soup. They don't make sour cherry soup like that anymore. Or childhoods. After my parents divorced, I lived with my mother for eight years, and my memory of her love for me is concentrated in those bowls of soup. A little sweet, a little sour, cold yet comforting, and in the moment, completely satisfying.

I don't remember sharing a single intimate moment with my mother— with the exception of that quick whispered conversation in the taxi on my sixteenth birthday. Perhaps it's a failure of memory, but more likely, it was just who she was. She didn't know what I needed or wanted from her, so she gave me cherry soup. And I was perfectly happy.

From the ages of four to six, I spent my days in kindergarten. The school was run by a German, meaning that if I knew what was good for me, I'd learn to speak German, which I did. After kindergarten, until I was ten, came what we in Hungary called preschool. At the end of each day I'd come home, where some young women hired by Mother would feed me and put me to bed, my mom off doing whatever it was that show business people did all night. Later, of course, becoming one of those show business people, I found out for myself what they did all night.

My first experience of show business came at Városliget, the enormous city park with its zoo, amusement park, ice-skating rink, and permanent circus. I loved the place and the fact that in the middle of the city, a short ride from my home, there existed this island of enchantment populated with elephants, clowns, daredevils, and fire-eaters. I marveled at the scope of it all and wondered if I could be a part of it. I remember thinking no, I couldn't just join the circus; you had to be born into it. What I didn't realize at the time was that it *was* in my blood. I was born to be in the circus—or at least to produce them.

The first real turning point in my life came at age ten—a turning point precipitated by two events, both stage-managed by my mother. Event #1 was my first paying job in show business. Appropriately enough, it came to pass at the Hungarian State Opera House. My mother was thick as thieves with the entire ensemble and knew all their tricks.

In the worlds of sports, politics, and the arts, there is no one more insecure, competitive, and cutthroat than an opera singer. Adulation is what they feed on, and back then in Budapest, they paid kids to give it to them, passing out the Hungarian equivalent of a quarter to each of us per performance. We'd sit in the highest tier in the last row, where we couldn't even see the stage, receiving a signal at the appropriate moment to rise and applaud. A different group of us would rise to applaud a particular solo, depending upon which performer had put the quarters in our pockets. Being kids, of course, each group would try to out-applaud the last. We were performers, too, part of the opera—we were the clappers, and I loved being a part of it all.

The second event that led to the turning point began in a hot bath, some eight hundred kilometers west of Budapest. Every summer, my mother took me with her on holiday—more her holiday than mine, as she would always go someplace, the mountains or on the Adriatic, where there was a camp for kids, which was where I would spend the balance of the holiday. My favorite part of these holidays was the train rides, watching the world go by outside the window.

In the summer of my tenth year, we went to a new place, the spa at Baden-Baden, on the edge of the Black Forest. My mother told me she wanted to take the hot springs for her health, but as I learned on the train back to Budapest, there was more to this journey than thermal pools and skin treatments. When we were a few miles out of Budapest, my mother told me she'd met a very nice man recently, a banker, and she had run into him in Baden-Baden. I was old enough to realize that there was nothing coincidental about their meeting. She went on: The man had asked her to marry him, and she had already talked it over with my father. They had agreed it would be a good idea if I went to live with him for a while.

When my mother said "for a while," what she really meant was *forever*. But it was okay by me. Whenever I was with my dad, he let me work with him in his studio. By the age of six, I was loading plates into his camera, and by this time I'd learned how to develop, print, and retouch photographs. I was an independent kid anyway, and a parent was someone I saw for a few hours on the weekend, if that. I would simply be living with my father now rather than my mother. And he didn't know what to do with me either.

I can't blame him. He was a bachelor, used to working all day in his studio and playing all night in the clubs and cafes. What the hell was he going to do with some bright-eyed ten-year-old kid? Simple. He was going to turn him into a man. And I mean that in the best sense. My father never talked down to me, never hid the truth from me, always treated me as though I was worthy of his honesty and respect. When I wasn't off at boarding school or summer camp, he set about to build my character, using my blood, sweat, and tears for bricks and mortar.

The fun and games began at 6:30 in the morning in the gym with boxing lessons, knocking some sense into me first thing every day. After breakfast I sat down with my father for an hour and a half of chess, giving my brains cells a chance to go a few rounds. Then, finally, came fencing, ending my morning workout behind a mesh mask with a saber in my hand, learning to thrust and parry. I worked hard and felt good, as though I was in training for something—which, of course, I was. The skills and discipline I developed those mornings have paid dividends throughout my life—whether in a prison cell in Budapest, a bank in Manhattan, or a studio in Hollywood. I still wake up every morning ready to mix it up, knowing at any moment I might have to take a body blow to the gut or deliver a right cross to the chin.

I spent afternoons in my dad's studio learning how to take pictures. The eight-hundred-square-foot studio took up the entire top floor of our building, complete with changing rooms, darkrooms, and enormous sky-lights. There were painted backgrounds and velvet curtains on rollers with as many as twelve assistants running around at any given time. The photography was a far cry from today's point-and-shoot. You had to know a bit of chemistry, physics, geometry, and engineering just to get the image from your eye into the camera and ultimately onto paper. It didn't hurt to know a little psychology as well.

Like the time Tarzan came by the studio to have his portrait taken. I, of course, was in awe, but Johnny Weissmuller was in a foul mood, arriving with a couple of bodyguards and looking as though he'd just come from a wrestling match—which he may well have, seeing as how he was mar-ried at the time to the Mexican actress Lupe Vélez. The two of them were renowned for their nightclub slap fights and running around hotel lobbies in their pajamas cursing at each other. Weissmuller was in no shape to have his portrait taken, and sizing up the situation, my father had some food and wine brought up to the studio. Within an hour they were joking and laughing, and Tarzan, makeup applied, was ready for his close-up.

The whole business of my father's studio had a touch of alchemy about it—and I was the sorcerer's apprentice, learning not only how to see images but how to design and shape them. From manipulating special effects (those velvet curtains on wheels) to managing people in front of and behind the camera, I look back on those years as my introduction to the experience of film production. Half a century after watching my dad tame Tarzan, I would try to work a similar magic on a host of literary characters, from Odysseus to Lear to Gulliver.

Back then, though, most of my spare time was spent in the company of Sultan, my German shepherd. Late in the afternoon, my father figur-ing his business could survive without me for a few hours, he would send me on my way. The rest of the day into the evening, I was on my own. For four years, from the time I was age ten to fourteen, my father sub-scribed to Kárpátia—a nearby restaurant and Budapest landmark where Gypsies played violins and I ate dinner, my dog at my feet. Every night, I sat and studied the menu, carefully weighing my choices . . . and every night I ordered the same thing: Wiener schnitzel with raspberry sauce and potato salad for me, and a pail of bones for Sultan.

After dinner I'd round out the day with a book, getting lost in a fantasy by Jules Verne or an adventure by Edgar Rice Burroughs (Tarzan again) in German translation. Occasionally, a rare treat, I set out to one of the city's movie houses, which was where I got my first taste of America—a land where giant apes climbed tall buildings clutching half-naked women in their paws, and gorgeous funny dames in evening gowns and high heels were spun around the city streets by skinny men in tuxedoes. Of course I knew it was all make-believe, but I wondered what it was really like there, in America. With its lovelorn apes, impossibly tall buildings, and beautiful breezy dancers, it appealed to me in the same way the circus did. America was a strange, wonderful, out-of-this-world place that I couldn't imagine ever being a part of.

⁓

The next phase of my education began the same year I moved in with my father, 1934, in a small town rich in culture some three hours out of Budapest. It's called Sárospatak—otherwise known as the Athens of the River Bodrog, a fortress of learning in Hungary since 1531 when the Reformed Church College was founded there. In 1934, at the age of ten, I became the member of an exclusive club: one of only ten Hungarian boys my age selected to participate in an exclusive eight-year high school program at Sárospatak. But as exceptional as the quality of my education was, it would never have come about if not for an apparently random encounter one evening at a Monte Carlo roulette table in 1927.

The man with all the chips in his hand that evening was Lord Rothermere, the Rupert Murdoch of his day, pioneering steward of London's *Daily Mirror* and *Daily Mail*. Aside from tabloid journalism, Rothermere had two passions—gambling and pretty women. And he had the money to indulge both. Which he did that day in Monte Carlo, introducing himself to the beautiful and highly intelligent Princess Stephanie Julianne von Hohenlohe. It wasn't long before the lovely Steph had Rothermere's ear, and she steered their pillow talk toward one of *her* passions: Hungary.

The motives behind the princess's fervent advocacy of Hungary remain something of a mystery. Austrian by birth, she didn't speak a word of Hungarian and had never even set foot in the country. What is known is that, half Jewish on her mother's side, she was awarded in Berlin the status of "honorary Aryan," an honor bestowed upon her with the blessing of her very good friend, Adolf Hitler. Was it a chance encounter that brought her together with Rothermere, or did the German Nazis take a hand? Certainly it was a stroke of good fortune for the Führer to have a lady friend in bed with a lord of the British press.

Within a few months of meeting the princess, Lord Rothermere wrote and printed a series of full-page articles in his newspapers with titles like "Hungary's Place in the Sun" and "Europe's Powder Keg," decrying the injustices visited upon Hungary by the Treaty of Trianon. While Rothermere's controversial defense of Hungary brought him condemnation in London, it made him a hero in Budapest, where in 1928 there was a plan afoot to have the lord's young son crowned king of Hungary. That never got off the ground, but several of Rothermere's other schemes flourished—one of which was to create and fund a college in Sárospatak.

The college that Rothermere built was modeled after Britain's beloved Eton. Each year, ten Hungarian boys who were ten years old out of the total entry of thirty-five would be selected for the exclusive English class, and I was lucky enough to be one of them. All thirty-five students sat in on the same classes in history, algebra, and so on, but while the other twenty-five students were off studying Greek or Latin, the languages of Homer and Plutarch, we ten were having our brains soaked in the language of John Milton and Mae West—taught to us by professors brought over from England.

So I spent the years from 1934 to 1942 in the company of Shakespeare, Swift, Byron, all the great and usual suspects of English literature, sometimes having their words literally pounded into my head—as when Gyula Svabo, the dean of the school, brought the Oxford English Dictionary down on my skull for not finishing an assignment on time.

Our education was not confined to the classrooms. Those of us in the English college had our own dormitory, laundry service, and fancy uniforms. At night we put our shoes in the hallway outside our room, and by the morning they'd be shined. We had a billiard room, library, and gymnasium—a school dedicated to the fitness of mind and body. And, of course, fencing. Hungarians love to draw swords, live for the sound of metal against metal. Just look at the Olympics and the scores of medals Hungary has brought home in the event. Between the crossing of the swords, the shining of my shoes, and the weight of the English language coming down on my head, it was at Sárospatak that I came into my own.

❧

On holidays from school I'd head back to Budapest, where I'd spend time with my cousin Paul and close friend Almási. Four years older than me and extremely athletic, Paul was always challenging me to one physical contest or another. In the summer we'd go rowing on the Danube, and in the winter he'd take me up into the mountains to ski—excursions that invariably turned into heated contests, fighting the river currents or flying down the slopes as if we were chased by demons.

With Almási, the challenge was not so much physical as it was psychological. More than a friend, Almási became my cohort and accomplice. His parents died when he was fourteen, and my father gave him a job in the studio. We found we had similar interests, which for the most part consisted of doing stupid things. The two of us went out looking for trouble and were very adept at finding it—crashing parties, getting into fights, taking the measure of the world and ourselves.

Between my adventures with Paul and Almási, I made a discovery: For whatever reason—some mysterious combination of foolishness and hard-headedness—I had little fear of physical injury or personal consequences. I refused to back away from a challenge—even if it made all the sense in the world to do so. I've always moved in one direction (forward) and at one speed (fast). That has never changed—another trait I attribute to my father.

He never walked away from a fight in his life. Just as my mother loved a good opera, my dad, like all of Hungary, loved a good scrap. Hungarians have long had the worst tempers in all of Europe. For years dueling was a core principle of Hungarian politics, parliamentary debate an excuse to draw weapons. The newspapers reported the schedule and outcome of duels in the back pages, like baseball box scores in American papers. Up until 1914, when the "first blood" law was enacted, politicians were regularly pointing and shooting guns at each other in the name of good governance. After 1914 duels were fought with sabers, and the duel was done at the sign of first blood. And the more cuts you had, the bigger a man you were.

My father was no politician, but he was Hungarian—and the moment someone disrespected him or a woman in his company, the Attila the Hun in him came out swinging. And there was blood. One time someone at a restaurant spilled red wine on my father's girlfriend. Dad calmly signaled a waiter, ordered a bottle, and poured the entire contents over the offender. Satisfaction was demanded, and they met at dawn, spilling blood instead of wine.

The year I turned sixteen, my father took me to my first duel, appointing me as his second. I had gone with my father and his female companion to the Gellért thermal baths and swimming pool. Gellért was, and continues to be, a lovely spot in the heart of Budapest and the site—according to the Turkish occupiers of the sixteenth century—of a magical healing spring. We were all sunning by the pool, my father, his lady friend, and I, when a rather large and careless stranger stepped on my father's hand. Push came to shove, and the big fellow ended up tumbling into those magical healing waters. When order was restored, arrangements were made for a duel. It was all very civilized . . . until we reached the gymnasium the next morning.

My father's enemy, it turned out, was a cavalry officer, and he was so certain of victory that he had brought along his friends and family to watch his great triumph. I could see the veins popping out of my father's neck at this insult, and I said to myself, *Oh shit, he's going to do something stupid.* Sure enough, before the referee had a chance to signal the duelists to come forward, my father rushed his opponent, who was a good head and shoulders taller than him, and jumped on him, pummeling the man's skull with the butt end of his saber. The poor cavalry officer didn't know what hit him, blood pouring down his face. What began as a matter of honor, a piece of high drama, ended up an act of low comedy. Somehow it all made sense. Duels were part of history. In a country and a continent about to go straight to hell, there was no room left for chivalry and honor.

⌣

I graduated from high school with honors in 1942 and returned to Budapest, where my real education began. For eight years, the three-foot walls of

Sárospatak had shielded me from the real world. Sure, we knew a war was on, but we had no concept of what that meant. We were too busy fencing and parsing dead poets. We had nothing to worry about. Until we got home.

My father did all he could to keep me out of the war, enrolling me in the University of Budapest to study international economics. I hated every minute of it. I never have been very good with money, and a career in economics was clearly not in my future, if I had any future at all. Nazi soldiers were in our streets, young men were disappearing, and we wondered if the end was coming. There was a group of five of us, students from the university, who began holding clandestine meetings to discuss what we could do to get the Nazis out. But they were part of the most powerful military machine in the world. What could we do? And even if we did have a plan, the authorities would most likely hear about it; the city was full of informers.

At the same time I had another encounter that would both test my courage and haunt me throughout this war. Her name was Klâri.

I had known women before, and I had known love. But I hadn't put them together until I saw Klâri—at one of those parties I crashed with Almási. I'd cooked up a lot of trouble, but Klâri was something altogether different. I knew I was risking my life in making myself an enemy of the Nazis. But this was risking my heart—which seemed to me to be far more frightening and dangerous.

I had never seen anyone so beautiful in my life—so lovely to look at and to be with. Klâri made me laugh and made me crazy. She was my Fay Wray, and I'd carry her up the side of a building if I had to. On occasion we even managed to get away from the city and from the war at a resort on Lake Balaton.

The last time we got away was in August 1944. Returning to Budapest early in the evening on a Monday, I walked Klâri home along the promenade of the Danube, the sun reflecting off the river. For once it actually looked blue, reflecting our mood that night. She told me it was a beautiful evening and we should spend it together. But as much as I wanted to, I told her I couldn't. I had to meet my friends.

Why? she wanted to know. What was so important about my friends? Of course I couldn't tell her. All I could say was that I was obligated. Klâri pouted, and I promised to meet her for a late-night dinner. I took her the rest of the way home, and she went in without looking back. I fought the urge to follow her in. Our group counted on one another. It was all or nothing—if one of us didn't show up, the rule was, there'd be no meeting. I just hoped tonight's meeting wouldn't last too long. I would make it up to Klâri later.

But I wasn't able to keep my promise to her that night. The war intervened, and I wouldn't see Klâri again for six months.

CHAPTER TWO

And the White Horse You Rode in On

Let me back up a few years and set the stage for that summer night in August 1944—back to when I was still at Sárospatak boning up on my Shakespeare and getting my shoes shined. While we were shielded from the unfolding horrors of war, outside the school walls the ground was shifting and churning and turning all of Europe inside out.

In March 1938, responding to a probably bogus invitation from Austrian National Socialists, the 8th Army of the German Wehrmacht marched into Austria greeted by flowers, flags, and Nazi salutes. The entire nation, like a rat in a snake, was swallowed whole.

In September 1939, after Hitler signed the Treaty of Nonaggression with Stalin, the German war machine ripped into Poland from the west. The Red Army brought down the hammer and sickle in the east. Squeezed from both sides, Poland was lost.

For as long as we could remember, Hungary had Austria sitting on our western frontier and Poland perched on the eastern. Now we had a new pair of neighbors—Germany on one side, the Soviets on the other. Not a very comfortable place to be.

In March 1941, despite signing a pact of eternal friendship with Yugoslavia three months before, Hungary's head of state, Miklós Horthy, agreed to join with the Germans in their attack on Yugoslavia. In return, Hungary would regain territories lost at Trianon.

A week later, Hungary's prime minister, Count Pál Teleki, committed suicide and was succeeded by Nazi sympathizer László Bárdossy. After first concealing the nature of Teleki's death, the government admitted to the suicide but attributed the cause to anxiety over the economy and his wife's heart condition. What they didn't reveal was the contents of a letter left behind by the prime minister addressed to Horthy: *We have become breakers of our word—out of cowardice. . . . We have placed ourselves on the side of scoundrels. . . . We shall become the despoilers of corpses, the most abominable of nations! I did not restrain you. I am guilty.* The government feared that if Hitler got wind of the letter, he'd doubt Hungary's loyalty to him and refuse to give back to the country the territory it had lost at Trianon. Hungary had made a deal with the devil and was doing everything in its power to hold up its end.

Four days after Teleki's funeral, the German army drove across the border into Yugoslavia. And Hitler kept his word. Hungarian units occupied the lost territories. At the time it must have seemed the smart move—Hungary was a bump in Hitler's road, and he was going to roll over Yugoslavia whatever Hungary did.

On June 22, 1941, some 3.9 million troops of the Axis powers poured across the border into the Soviet Union. Having Yugoslavia for an enemy was one thing; taking on the Soviets was another thing entirely. Nazi Germany had already taken possession of Hungary's soul. With Operation Barbarossa, the Reich would demand that the flesh and blood follow. But Hungary resisted, backing Germany in word but not in deed, vowing to refrain from joining the war.

The vow lasted until June 26. After planes identified as Soviet bombed the city of Kassa, the military in Budapest, overwhelmingly pro-German, demanded satisfaction. Two days later Hungary officially declared war on the Soviet Union. That the planes were in all likelihood stolen, piloted by and under the command of the German Luftwaffe, was beside the point. Hitler was exactly what Hungary was waiting for, the man on the white horse, the symbol of nationalism and victory—the trick of the aircraft the culmination of a thousand years of illusions and delusions.

We all heard the story in school. When Prince Csaba, the youngest son of Attila the Hun and our great warrior hero, was killed in battle, our enemies swooped down upon Hungary laughing at our weakness and mocking us: "Who will protect you now?" What our enemies didn't know was that Csaba possessed a magic herb that had the power to bring him and his warriors back to life. The prince on his white horse led his armies down across the Milky Way to massacre our foes, and Hungary had the last laugh. Now Hitler had fallen from the sky to save Hungary from those enemies who had ripped into the country at Trianon.

Unfortunately, as Hungary would soon learn, Hitler had no magic herbs, and when he sent Hungarian soldiers to fight and die on the eastern front, they stayed dead.

The last dominoes fell. On December 13, 1941, under pressure from Berlin, Hungary declared war on Great Britain and the United States. In January 1942, in and around the city of Novi Sad, in the Yugoslavian territory that Hitler turned over to Hungary, Hungarian troops rounded up some four thousand "undesirables"—Jews, Serbs, Gypsies, men, women, and children. The soldiers herded many of their prisoners to the banks of the Danube, where they opened fire, then turned their guns on the river ice to break it, shooting at the drowning victims. Teleki's suicide note haunted the proceedings: *We shall become the despoilers of corpses, the most abominable of nations!*

———

This is where I come into the picture. School was out, and reality was setting in. I'd have to shine my own shoes from now on. Everything I knew about life came to nothing in the face of this war.

First and foremost was the question of survival. Looking back, I recognize that my survival depended not on any smart choices I made, but rather on dumb luck. For instance, there was my decision to make an enemy of the most feared and most powerful military machine in the world.

There were five of us. Karoly was the oldest and most serious in the group, rarely smiling, the weight of the world sitting on his shoulders. A graduate of the school of economics that I had walked away from, Karoly had settled into a position at a Swiss-Hungarian bank. Gyula was the son of a doctor, tall, strapping, and athletic. He liked to challenge us to wrestling matches and then pin us to the ground until we said uncle—a boy who always had something to prove. Jenō was the brains of the operation, a student of all the twisted history, convoluted politics, and palace intrigue that had led to this mess. And there was György, who fancied himself a poet. More important to us was that, through his literary friends, he had access to a printing press. A small fellow with a big heart, György didn't talk much about himself—and for very good reason, as we later discovered. Finally, there was me, the most impulsive—some might say reckless—of the bunch, and for better or worse, the group's ringleader.

We were joined together by our common belief that the country was on the wrong course and that we were the ones to right the ship. It had been a little over a year since the prime minister committed suicide, and as far as we were concerned, by throwing in with Hitler, all of Hungary had put a gun to its head. And it was just a matter of time before the Great Dictator reached out and pulled the trigger.

The five of us met, talked, and argued. We strategized, conspired, and quietly tried to draw friends over to our way of thinking. We worked late into the night and early morning, conceiving and writing and printing hundreds of copies of our manifestos—*the truth* as we saw it. The dangerous shadow looming over the land. The evil trickster in Berlin pulling the strings. We laid it on pretty thick. For the most part, our youthful idealism—our infinite enthusiasm and passion for the cause—were met with one long, great national yawn.

Not to say that we were alone. Throughout Hungary, and especially in Budapest, groups and individuals were quietly resisting the country's alliance with Nazi Germany. But as our efforts fell on deaf ears, we couldn't get any traction. In the summer of 1942, the general response in Budapest to the war was apathy. There were no bullets or bombs flying here—the only thing booming was the economy, Hungary's farms and factories growing rich and fat from the demand to feed and oil the German war machine. Hungary had put all its eggs in the German basket. And why not? The Wehrmacht was having its way with Europe and now Asia.

If the Germans and Russians wanted to spend their summer killing each other off, that was their business. Have at it, the Hungarians said. Meanwhile, in Budapest the dance floors were packed, the cafes abuzz, and the tennis courts booked solid. The newspapers and newsreels screamed of the great Axis victories to the east and west; why bother with the cheap, inflammatory pamphlets written by some anonymous group of boys just out of school and distributed in the dark of night? Hungary had all its lost territories back; it was winning the war and barely had to lift a finger.

Behind the scenes, though, the seeds of Hungary's devastation had already been sown. In January of 1942 German Foreign Minister Ribbentrop paid a visit to Budapest and presented the Nazi bill to Hungary for the return of the lost territories: warm bodies for the eastern front. Thus began the mobilization of the Second Army of Hungary. But *army* is too strong a word—they were raw recruits who used bicycles and horse-drawn carriages. The first time most of the soldiers saw a tank was when they were emerging out of the Russian mists rolling toward them. Nevertheless, by the end of that summer, after six weeks of training—without actual guns or artillery to train with—some two hundred thousand Hungarian young men and boys had been packed onto trains headed east . . . into a buzz saw.

All the while, my fellow conspirators and I continued to press our point. Hitler was not our savior; he was our enslaver. But no one was listening, and I grew increasingly frustrated, several times nearly coming to blows with some young Arrow Cross bullyboy spouting off in a nightclub. Technically, the Arrow Cross Party—the Hungarian Fascist movement—had been banned by the Hungarian government, but its members had simply gone underground to bide their time. They were not hard to spot, and getting into fights with them—and thus getting into their crosshairs—was not the smartest thing for me to do. But I am my father's son, and I've never been one to keep my opinions to myself.

I have to admit, in that summer of surreal calm, false hope, and fragile prosperity, I was not immune to the temptations and illusions of peace. I was a young man in love, and Klâri and I spent many hours taking pleasure in each other's company—sunning along the banks of the Danube, finding shady, secluded spots in the great Városliget Park. This, of course, was a whole different kind of circus. On those afternoons and evenings with Klâri, the war might as well have been on the moon. Like all of Budapest, for one idyllic summer, we were carried away by an illusion of peace.

Then came the fall. And winter.

We first heard the news in Jenő's closet. Jenő had carved out a nice private space for himself in a small, oddly angled upper room of his family's home—a sanctuary where he could sleep, read, and write our political tracts in peace. It was also a place where we could escape to reality. Jenő had gotten hold of a shortwave radio—an offense punishable by arrest—that he kept hidden under a pile of laundry in his closet.

On November 9, 1942, the five of us huddled around that shortwave, mesmerized, energized, and little bit agitated—as if stirred by the sound of distant thunder. The Americans and British had landed in North Africa, establishing a beachhead and seizing several airports. A crack in Hitler's armor. Perhaps we weren't alone after all.

Had the tide turned? No. But the worm had. On the sands of Morocco and Algeria, the Allies lit a match in a dark world—and lit a fire under us. Budapest was our beachhead, and words were our weapons. We printed more leaflets, extolling the Allied victories in Africa, condemning Hungary's friendship with Nazi Germany, and urging opposition to the current government. *If the Allies win*, we wrote, *we will lose; but if the Germans win, we will be lost.*

Over the next two months, through December, several times a week I would stuff leaflets under my overcoat and late at night wander the city. I'd leave them on church steps or at deserted tram stops and insert them between the pages of phone books in phone booths, my heart pounding for fear that I'd be spotted and taken in for interrogation.

I never told my father what I was doing, but he knew where I stood on the German question and how passionate I was—and whatever I was up to, he wanted me to stop. Go back to university, he urged me, and lie low. History will take care of itself; it doesn't need your help. But I was as stubborn then as I am now, and I suspect that if I had given in to my father and stopped fighting for what I believed in, in his heart of hearts he would have been disappointed. I continued to spread our message, my cohorts and I determined to save Hungary from itself.

But by the end of that winter of 1943, any twinges of doubt over Germany's defeats in Africa metastasized into a cancerous spasm of fear and loathing. In January Hungary's Second Army, which the German high command had "invited" to the eastern front to participate in the final victory of the Axis powers, did indeed play a critical role in the victory—of the Soviets. The Red Army, in a counterattack in defense of Stalingrad, annihilated the Hungarians at the Don River. Of the two hundred thousand Hungarian soldiers and fifty thousand Jewish Hungarian slave laborers deployed to the front, some forty thousand returned to Hungary—the rest either killed or captured. And those who did return did not come bearing tidings of good cheer.

You could spot them in the beer gardens, young men my age but looking twenty years older, some in uniforms, others not, but all with a hard, angry edge about them. I'd buy them drinks and draw them out, stories pouring out like blood from a bayonet wound.

I spent an afternoon drinking beer in the sun with one veteran of the battle. He sipped through a straw, his fingers a casualty of the Russian winter, and talked about the corpses along the roadsides, their eyes frozen open. He laughed and said, "We Hungarians, you have to kill us in order to get us to open our eyes." And he said *his* eyes were open now—vowing to commit suicide before fighting alongside the Germans again. Why, he asked, are we going to war against the Bolsheviks? Bolsheviks, Nazis, he said, they could all go to hell. I went home that evening and cried. I couldn't sleep, thinking how that soldier, maybe twenty years old, could easily have been me. It was some of that pure dumb luck that I wasn't the one sipping beer through a straw.

Hungary, on the other hand, was clean out of luck. The bloody disaster on the Don was a slap in the face to the whole country. More people were willing to listen to us now. The resistance was growing, and we were a small but passionate part of it. But just as our message began to get through, it became considerably more dangerous to deliver it.

That spring and summer of 1943, resistance groups came out of the Hungarian woodwork. The Democratic Citizens Alliance. The Independent Smallholders. The Social Democrats. The National Peasant Party. The Catholic Social People's Movement. Royalists, Communists, and every other kind of *ist* imaginable. Suddenly Budapest was filled to capacity with revolutionaries, revisionists, and fire-breathing anarchists. But the five of us had no interest in revolution. We simply wanted Hungary back.

Fueled by discontent and expanding in all directions, the Hungarian resistance was in chaos. We didn't trust a soul, the city lousy with spies, traitors, and informers. Hitler had eyes and ears everywhere—and heard all the same rumors we did. The talk of guns stockpiled in Budapest basements in preparation for a government coup. Stories about Hungarian envoys on secret missions to Ankara, Istanbul, Washington, and London, and their attempts to negotiate a separate peace with the Americans and British. Whispers about Miklós Horthy Jr., the regent's son and an avid Anglophile, urging his father to sever Hungary's ties to Germany. Every day there were new rumors of Hungarian resistance and rebellion, and we ate them up like kids sneaking snacks from a cookie jar.

In July the Allies took Sicily, and Italy—recognizing which side its bread was buttered on—gave Mussolini the boot. The news hit us like a jolt of electricity. The Americans were coming! In fact, we used to watch them. Afternoons we'd sit on the promenade of the Danube, our eyes turned to the southern horizon. Most every day waves of American bombers, planes filling the sky, would fly overhead bound for targets in Germany. Crowds gathered to watch the show, waving and sometimes even cheering. How long could it take for the Americans to march up the Italian peninsula and into Hungary? Soon we'd be buying them drinks in the beer gardens.

But Hitler had other ideas. He began pouring money into the Arrow Cross Party in Budapest. He led us to the cliff with a carrot—the promise of land—and now he'd push us over it with a stick: the Arrow Cross. The party consisted for the most part of young thugs whose primary talent lay in torturing cats. Now they were marching around the city in black boots and black jackets with green shirts and green ties. A gang of sadists in ugly uniforms beating up on Jews and anyone else deemed an enemy of the Nazi cause.

Needless to say, this was not an auspicious time to be badmouthing National Socialism. But we did nonetheless, quietly, carefully, watching our backs, condemning the Arrow Cross clowns and their ringmasters in Berlin. But we knew now that the Allies were not going to save us. It was all on us. The worst of Hungary had come out. The demons were walking our streets, the fires were beginning to burn, and the inferno was coming. But first the devil himself would pay us a visit.

——•——

1944. Hungary reaps the whirlwind, and I get swept away.

On a gorgeous spring day in March, a Sunday, I got out of bed early and went by Klári's house. We made it a habit to have breakfast in one of the cafes along Andrássy Avenue. I was on my third pastry, Klári still nibbling on her first, and we were talking about how to spend our afternoon. A small argument. She wanted to go to the movie theater, but I thought going to the movies on a date was a waste of time. I preferred to be alone with her, not sitting in a crowd staring up at a screen. A walk in the park, I suggested. But we never did resolve the issue, our conversation—and our lives—interrupted by a marching band.

We heard them before we saw them. The big bass drums, the bold brass instruments, the sound of soldiers singing. The Germans were marching into Budapest, occupying Hungary, barely a shot fired. Their arrival was a foregone conclusion. Watching the column of soldiers march past us, I felt a chill up my spine. No longer were we simply in Germany's sphere; now we were under its boot.

Strangely, though, what struck me that morning—the terraces and streets packed with Hungarians coming out to watch the spectacle unfold—was how glorious these soldiers looked. Strong, handsome young men with proud, beautiful faces, smiling at us like mischievous older brothers as they went by. These soldiers were victory personified, a magnificent, polite, flirtatious killing machine. That's what the devil does. He surrounds himself with beautiful, powerful things. Because not only does he want you to fear him, he wants you to love him. And these sharp young men, marching in perfect step into the heart and soul of Hungary, were here to be feared and loved. They were well cast in the role of conquering heroes.

My father, with his friends in high places, filled me in later on how the takeover came about, the whole business making his veins pop from anger, fear, and desperation. Mostly, though, he worried about what it meant for me, his voice breaking as he spoke.

Hitler's spies had told him all about the Hungarian government's "secret" flirtation with the American OSS, and his solution was simple: Change the Hungarian government. What none of us knew at the time, though, was that the Americans were playing Hungary—and Hitler—too. The Allies knew that whatever they said to the Hungarians would end up being whispered into Hitler's ear. Hungary was an Allied diversion, reinforcing Hitler's fear that they'd come at him from the south, through the Balkans, and diverting the Wehrmacht's resources from France and the beaches at Normandy.

My dad took it for granted that my name must be on some list in Gestapo headquarters, and that it would only be a matter of time before they checked it off. He wanted me to get out of the country. He said he could get me to Portugal. But I was as stubborn as he was. I told him I couldn't survive on a seafood diet. He didn't see the humor. Anyway, I wasn't going to leave him. I wasn't going to leave Klâri. And I wasn't going to leave my friends in the resistance. At least not by choice.

That summer, the Americans did indeed come to Budapest, but not to visit our lovely beer gardens. Those bombers we used to cheer filling the skies as they headed north now sent us running for cover. Occupied by Germany, we were fair game—no longer a transit point, we were a target. And these Americans pilots were not very good shots—targeting industrial areas but often dropping their loads onto residential neighborhoods.

More bad news that summer: Our already tiny resistance group of five was reduced to four.

Denunciations in those weeks and months following the German occupation were as common as cold sores. If you coveted a man's house or job or business, all you had to do was research his ancestry—and if you uncovered a single drop of Jewish blood in him, you'd present your evidence to the authorities and wait for them to take him and his family away. Then you'd move into his house, take over his business, steal his life. And that's exactly what happened to György, the quiet one in our group. His grandfather was Jewish. His father had tried to protect his family, Magyarizing their name and converting to Christianity, but the elephant never left the room. You could change your name, but you couldn't expunge the records.

Within days of the German occupation, Adolf Eichmann—a lieutenant colonel in the Nazi SS and a prime mover behind the Holocaust—arrived in Budapest to deal with "the Jewish question." That summer, Jews were ordered into designated Yellow Star Houses—several Jewish families to a room, some sleeping on bare floors. They were only allowed to leave those houses for a couple of hours each afternoon, and their food was rationed—a starvation diet.

We did what we could for György and his family, smuggling meat, butter, and tea to them—knowing that we risked imprisonment bringing food to them, and that they risked death for taking it. One afternoon György's father whispered a request to me: Could I get him any sleeping pills? I stole some from my father's room that night and slipped them to György the next day. There was a great demand among the Jews in Budapest for sleeping pills. They hoarded them, forming suicide pacts in the event that they were ordered to board trains going north.

I don't know whether György ever had to take those pills, because I don't know what happened to him. But unless he was among the several thousand Jews saved or shielded by Raoul Wallenberg—the Swedish diplomat serving in Budapest who issued protective passports to those in danger—I suspect that an overdose of sleeping pills was the best possible fate that my friend could have met.

August was brutally hot. Klári and I had just returned from Lake Balaton, and we walked along the Danube. I kissed her good-bye, promising to meet her later for dinner. The four of us—György gone now—were meeting in the basement of the printing press. We wanted to talk about the possibility of forging documents and identity cards—see if we could help a few "undesirables" get out of Budapest. But within minutes the four of us would be counted among those same undesirables.

I was the last to arrive, bathing in sweat, and I barely had time to shake hands with the others when six Hungarian policemen and one man in plain clothes—he had Gestapo written all over him—burst into the basement. I don't know whether we had been denounced or if our time had simply come. It didn't matter. The police put our hands in cuffs and knocked us around a little. Then they shoved us into the backseats of two cars and drove us away from our lives.

It's odd how the mind works. Of course I was scared, but strangely, my greatest concern in the backseat of that car was that I would be unable to keep my word to join Klâri for dinner. Would she ever forgive me? I asked the police where we were going and got the back of one of their hands for an answer. I didn't ask again.

The answer, it turned out—I could have saved myself a bloody lip if I'd just waited a couple of minutes—was the Royal Hotel. A real classy joint, which was why the German police had taken it over. They occupied the city in five-star style.

The four of us were officially handed over to the Germans at the hotel, the basement turned into a makeshift jail. The Germans never questioned us or made any accusations against us. We just sat there for close to thirty-six hours, dying from the heat and stink, wondering if they had simply forgotten us.

Our stay was temporary. The jail was also a distribution camp, and on the morning of our second day there, a ruddy German officer accompanied by a couple of toadies with clipboards came into the basement, pointed out the four of us as well as a dozen or so more young men our age. We were escorted in our handcuffs and at gunpoint out of the hotel to a waiting truck, which took us to a train, which took us on an eight-hour ride north through what used to be Czechoslovakia to some forgettable village on the Polish border. From there another truck drove us deep into the wilds of the Carpathian Mountains, where we were just able-bodied enough to clear a path of trees and build a road for the Wehrmacht to move their trucks and tanks to the eastern front. Or to retreat from it.

To this day I don't know if we were arrested because of our resistance activities or in spite of them. I wonder if we were just part of a quota of young Hungarian men turned over to the Germans to be sent to labor camps. The whole world had turned arbitrary on us. That was our true enemy: the randomness of it all, of life, death, love, and labor. It's like asking a simple question and getting slapped in the face.

It had come to this: I was a slave. A piece of cattle. A spoil of war. There were some seventy-five to eighty of us at this labor camp, Hungarians,

Slovaks, and Austrians. Karoly, Gyula, Jenõ, and I stuck together. In a camp like this, there were bound to be rats and snakes—the human kind in addition to the rat and snake kind—and the only way to steer clear of them was to steer clear of everyone. Needless to say, we counted ourselves lucky to have each other.

Our days began at five o'clock in the morning, rousted from the barn where we slept in flea-infested hay. For breakfast, along with a chunk of hard, dry black bread, we were served from a giant copper kettle—a mess of a stew with just enough unidentifiable protein to keep our strength up for the day. Then it was off into the forest to clear trees for their road. We were city boys; we had never held a saw in our hands, and it was tough, hard work. A German officer in the engineer corps oversaw the operation, but we rarely saw him and his retinue of soldiers. Every few days they'd come by for an hour or two, check out the progress of the clearing, and vanish. My guess is that they settled into a house or inn in some small village nearby, eating, drinking, and finding young local girls to keep them company.

The Germans left us in the care of Polish guards, young, middle-aged, and older men—the fathers, brothers, and husbands of those girls back in the village—men who delighted in pushing us around, waving pistols at us, and yelling out commands. As soldiers, though, they had no discipline at all. In the warmth of the September afternoons, while we were cutting down and hauling away giant firs and stands of beech trees, it was not unusual for our guards to wander off and catch a nap in the thick under-brush of the forest. They must have assumed that, like them, we were too afraid of what the Germans would do to us if we tried to run.

Karoly, Gyula, Jenõ, and I talked about escape all the time. But as I said, we were city boys, and this was a wilderness a thousand miles from home. As the days turned into weeks, we did all grow stronger—physically and mentally. I had learned a great deal in my school days at Sáro-spatak—the power of the imagination, the importance of discipline, the need for intellectual freedom. But the lessons learned here in the Car-pathians were just as vital—and just as formative of the person I would become. The narrative of who I am took a sharp turn in those mountains.

Here, for the first time, I realized that I could face and overcome hardship. I loved my father, I loved Klâri, I loved the good life. But here

I discovered that I could endure backbreaking labor and survive on stew until I found my way back home. At Sárospatak I learned how to use my mind. In the Carpathians I learned how to live by my wits.

Three and a half weeks into our stay, the monotony was broken. As was a Hungarian boy's leg. I didn't know his name, but he was a kid, no more than seventeen. He had no friends and was scared all the time. I'd wake up in the middle of the night and hear him crying. But there was nothing we could do to comfort him. We were all lonely and scared.

The accident happened early in the morning when a giant tree limb, cut but not properly secured, came crashing down on the boy's leg. His scream was chilling. We rushed over to lift the limb off him and saw that the bones in his leg had been crushed and mangled. I didn't speak Polish, but the guard in charge understood a little German. I told him they had to get the boy to a doctor. Take him to the nearest village. Take the boy to the German officers, I said, and they would bring him to a field hospital.

I didn't know I had been yelling until the guard put his pistol in my face and told us all to move back. He said he would take care of it. He had a horse-drawn cart brought out, and they lifted the boy, barely conscious, onto its bed. The guard and the cart disappeared into the forest. We watched and waited all day long for the guard to return. Finally, near dark, we returned to the barn and saw the horse and cart, and the guard who had driven it away using the cart as a table to eat his dinner. The other guards were in the barn to get their suppers. I walked over to the guard—Karoly, Gyula, and Jenő close behind me. I asked where the boy was, and he didn't even look up. He took out his pistol, held it next to his plate, and said he had taken care of it. Without thinking, I reached back and smashed him as hard as I could in the face. We jumped on him, pounding him with our fists.

It was done in minutes—and our choice was made. We ran into the woods, running as hard as we could for thirty minutes, stumbling wildly in the moonlight. Finally we all fell to the ground, gasping for breath, trying not to breathe too loud, listening for footsteps. Nothing. I suspect that the reason they didn't follow us was in Jenő's hand. He had grabbed the guard's pistol. The Poles might work for the Germans, but they weren't going to die for them, not if they could help it. They weren't going to rush blindly into the forest to face a bullet. We lay there trying to be quiet but couldn't help ourselves, laughing like schoolboys in a church. We were all going crazy.

We were fugitives, outlaws, hiding out in the forest by day, raiding farms at night for fruit and vegetables, one pistol between us to hold off the German army. A black 9 mm–caliber Polish Vis. At least that's what it said on the barrel. None of us had ever shot a pistol before, and as there were only eight bullets in the magazine, we figured it would be imprudent to practice. We'd find out if we could shoot when the time came, taking turns lugging the thing around, a kind of Russian roulette: Who would be holding it when the time came to blast our way through a German patrol?

After a few nights—we were moving south, figuring we'd find our way home sooner or later—our hunger made us brazen. We took a risk, picking out isolated farmhouses, knocking on doors, offering to work for our supper. We were close enough to Hungary now that communication wasn't a problem. And it was astonishing how much these old farmers—all the young men gone—wanted to help. They gave us food, literally gave us the clothes off their back, sometimes even a soft place to sleep for a few hours. Out in the countryside, we learned, the Third Reich didn't have many friends.

Still, this was not a good time or place to be playing mouse to the German cat. Soldiers were everywhere. The German lines to the east were in danger of collapsing, and the Wehrmacht was pouring reinforcements in from the west—right into these hills and valleys along the Hungarian frontier where we were hiding. We did all we could to make a nuisance of ourselves.

We urged farmers to hide their food and livestock where German soldiers couldn't get their hands on it. We scouted out temporary bridges thrown across streams and returned at night to rip them apart. One morning in late September, lounging in the shade of some trees bordering on an open field of sugar beets, we heard what sounded like an approaching patrol and nearly jumped out of our skins. We all fell to the ground, making ourselves as small as possible. I looked over at Karoly and saw him pull the pistol out from under his shirt, clutching it at his hip. I slowly lifted my head to see what we were up against. The patrol consisted of a string of a dozen donkeys led by their herder, a boy no more than eleven or twelve.

Rising up and wiping the dirt from my clothes, I moved out from the cover of trees to stop the boy and ask him where he was taking the donkeys. Into the foothills, he answered, to a camp. I ascertained that the boy had been paid by a German soldier to take this motley supply train to a camp. This German didn't know the boy from Adam, so if the donkeys didn't make it to camp, well, that was fine by him as long as he could keep the coins the German had given him.

We all agreed that the boy could keep the coins, and with his help, we set about cutting the donkeys loose and sending them on their way. Or trying to. After about a half hour of pushing and pulling and yelling and sweating and slapping their stubborn behinds, the donkeys stood spread out in an area about the size of a football field dining happily on sugar beet leaves. We had to do something. If we left them here, they would be rounded up and brought to the camp. If we stripped them of the supplies, the boy might be accused of stealing. Finally we came up with a solution: Perhaps it would be best for the donkeys to continue on to the camp after all.

We'd been hearing about others like ourselves, sabotaging rail lines, blowing up supply trucks, and raising Cain behind the German lines. We knew that we were part of something bigger than ourselves. And that it was time *we* did something bigger. We had a pistol. We had eight bullets. And now we had a dozen donkeys. This was our chance.

Another half hour of rounding up and wrangling and we headed for the camp. The idea was to see how well it was guarded, and if we could figure out a way of doing it, free at least some of its laborers. Our Trojan horses—the donkeys—would be our ticket in. As we began our ascent into the foothills, Karoly handed me the pistol. As mastermind of this plan, I'd been elected ringleader of the band as well.

Just before dusk we spotted the camp, over a hill, in a clearing alongside some railroad tracks that cut through a long valley. We were too far away to make out what kind of camp it was, coming upon a sentry a good five hundred yards out. The donkeys did the trick, and I caught the sentry off his guard, pointing the pistol at him before he knew what was up. He was a local fellow, and I thought I could reason with him. Convince him of the justness of our cause. Sometimes I talk too much, and he took the opportunity to suddenly fall to the ground, grab the rifle he had dropped there, and blindly fire it into the air. I shut my mouth and pulled the trigger, winging him in the shoulder. But it was too late. I should have clobbered him over the head when I had the chance. Now the hills were alive with the sound of gunfire.

We could have run, but we would have died, and surrender was the more prudent course. We might have died anyway, but by throwing up our hands we hedged our bets. We were surrounded by soldiers. German soldiers with loud, angry voices. And lots of guns. They threw us to the ground.

As it turned out, this wasn't some tree-clearing camp. We had stumbled onto an ammunition depot, supporting the buildup of German forces in the area. I understood now why the sentry hadn't seen things my way. He knew what would happen to him if he betrayed his German bosses.

The soldiers shoved us forward toward the camp. When we reached the perimeter, one of them put a machine gun to my chest and told me to stop. The three others looked back at me as they were pushed on ahead. With as much courage as I could muster, I nodded at the fellows, thinking that, in one way or another, for good or evil, I'd rejoin them shortly. But I was mistaken. I never saw nor heard of any one of them again. I don't know who among them, if any, survived the war. I don't even know if they survived that night. From the moment we threw up our hands in the forest that night, we were lost to each other.

I believed that because I was the one who shot the sentry, they were taking me off to be executed, and my mind went off in a thousand different directions. To my mother at the opera and my father in his studio. To Sárospatak and Shakespeare. To the Danube with Klári at my side. Why had I been so stubborn? I should have listened to their advice, lain low, let the war play itself out with me hiding out in a basement somewhere. Either I was going to faint or my head was going to explode. I only came to my senses when I realized where they were taking me: into the officers' quarters.

Because I had led this brazen assault on the arms depot, they assumed I must be some kind of big shot in the Hungarian resistance, and they figured to score some points by turning me over to the Gestapo. I was their prize pig, and they fed me, cleaned me, and dressed me—preparing the hog for slaughter.

They were drinking wine and in good spirits, talking and joking with me. If I had shot another German, I'm sure it would have been a different story, but the sentry was Hungarian. I asked one of the officers why they needed a donkey train to come here in the first place, seeing as how they sat right next to a railroad line. He said the officers refused to settle for army-issue food and had several weeks' worth of cheese and wine and other local delicacies brought up from a nearby village. We Germans are as good at living, he joked, as we are at killing.

In the morning, in shackles, I was put on a train heading east, in a car reserved for special prisoners like me, an armed guard at each end. The remainder of the train was packed with starving, hollow-eyed laborers bound for the front to dig trenches. From the looks of them, the journey amounted to a death sentence.

My destination was a Gestapo camp on the Ukrainian border, where, I assumed, I would be interrogated about what I knew, who I knew, and what our plans were. I spent my time on the train making up stories—of my great exploits, of grand conspiracies, of my contact with British spies, whatever I could think of. If I told the Gestapo the truth—that I'd distributed leaflets in phone booths, then had escaped from a tree-cutting camp—I figured I'd be dead in an hour. The trick would be to engage them, get them worked up so they'd want to hear more. Like Scheherazade putting the king to sleep each night so she'd live another day.

I had plenty of time to concoct my tales of derring-do. Although traveling no more than a few hundred miles, the train crawled along at a snail's pace or not at all. Bombed-out tracks had to be repaired as we went along, and at night, as bombers flew overhead, we had to stop altogether. But unlike the train, the war was moving fast.

It took nearly three days to reach the camp, and by then—the beginning of October—the entire calculus had changed. It was as if I had gotten on the train in one war and gotten off in another. The Gestapo had vanished from the camp altogether, leaving it in the hands of an anxious trio of Ukrainian Nazis. To them I was just another prisoner to be chained up in the cellar of their abandoned farmhouse. There were nine other prisoners already there—Russian partisans recently caught behind German lines.

That night, in the pitch black, one of the Ukrainians opened the door to the cellar, letting in a sliver of light. He shouted something, tossed half a dozen shovels and pickaxes down onto the cellar floor, and closed the door. I asked one of the Russians what the Ukrainian had said. He told me that in the morning we would be taken out into the fields to dig our own graves. The Ukrainians intended to leave behind no witnesses, to bury all the evidence.

I sat awake all night, listening to the Russians snore and the sound of distant artillery, planes flying overhead. I was numb from the cold—and from the thought of dying. I had no papers to identify who I was, no means of communicating my fate. I wasn't just going to die; I was going to cease to exist.

The night's black turned to morning gray. And I waited. We all did, glancing up at the door, the portal to hell. One hour. Three hours. Nothing. A frightful silence—even the artillery had stopped. Then, late in the afternoon, the dead world came to life. Heavy footsteps, voices. The Russians jumped to their feet, straining against their chains, shouting. The door, padlocked, shook and was smashed open. Soldiers. Liberators. The Red Army. Like magic, the Ukrainian guards had disappeared, and we were still alive.

The enemy of my enemy is my friend. So the saying goes, and it was in that spirit that I managed to survive over the next few months. That I had been arrested by Nazis and imprisoned with Russian partisans put me in good with the Red Army officers. Also, it didn't hurt that I spoke a little Russian, played a decent game of chess, and could hold up my end in a discussion of Chekhov or Tolstoy.

One officer in particular—elegant, handsome, soft-spoken—named Lieutenant Rostov took an interest in me. He told me he had been a schoolteacher in Moscow and was profoundly curious about Western culture. His curiosity was not something he could share with fellow officers, as you never knew who was reporting to the NKVD, but as I was from the sophisticated city of Budapest, he assumed I must have some unique insights into Lauren Bacall, Benny Goodman, and cheeseburgers. As a gesture of goodwill, he scared up some clothes for me as well as some wool socks and boots—no small gift in that fall and winter of mud, snow, and ice. But this was not a time or place to strike up long-term friendships. After a few days the good lieutenant vanished into the fog of war, and I never saw him again. But the boots lasted me a good deal longer.

A receding tidal wave of misplaced and displaced persons moved westward behind the advancing Soviet army toward the heart of Europe. I was a single drop within it, trudging across rough, wooded country back toward the Carpathians. I made my way through farms and villages burned to the ground by the retreating Germans, bodies strung up in the trees. Across fields filled with countless smashed German and Russian tanks. Past roofless houses and small towns inhabited by mothers and children in rags, all the men either dead or gone. I bathed when I could in freezing streams, breaking the ice and wading in. I depended on Russian soldiers for food or scratched around on the abandoned farms for carrots or potatoes left behind. I walked, hitching rides on carts full of hay or sugar beets.

On occasion Russian soldiers would stop me and order me to strip to my waist and raise my arms. The SS made a practice of tattooing blood types on their underarms in the event they needed a blood transfusion. I saw SS men attempting to hide in plain sight shot down on the spot, their tattoos a death sentence. Still, we moved forward inexorably, the German army evaporating before the Russian onslaught.

One evening, anxious to get closer to home, I decided to walk through the night. At dawn I came into a clearing, which I recognized as an abandoned horse pasture. But I had moved too fast. There were several explosions, and suddenly artillery shells began to fly over my head in both directions. I had walked into the middle of a battle. I fell to the ground and belly-crawled into a stable, waiting for the storm to pass by, my heart beating so hard I thought I'd break a rib. Finally the Russians took the pasture, and I scurried back behind their line.

Some time in the middle of November—one day blending into the next—I crossed the border into Hungary. After weeks of fighting, the

Red Army had overrun Debrecen, but at a high cost; the German resistance was stiffening, and the Soviet advance stalled. The battle raged on and the killing continued, but all movement seemed to stop. The war froze in place.

I just wanted to get back to Budapest, to my father, and to Klâri. Patience has never been one of my virtues, but I had no choice but to wait. Hitler and Stalin were about to dig in their cloven hooves and send Budapest straight to hell. My problems didn't amount to a hill of beans.

Christmas Eve, 1944. Stalin orders one million soldiers encircling Budapest to take the city at any cost. Hitler orders a hundred thousand soldiers inside Budapest to defend it to the last man. Christmas Day. It begins to snow; all of the pent-up fury and terror of the age is about to be unleashed, and nothing can stop it.

I waited in a riverside village a dozen or so miles northeast of Budapest. The Soviets had turned the village into a command post for the artillery now pounding Budapest, every tree and telephone pole in the town cut down for the wood. I dug ditches. The Russians had freed me from the Nazis and brought me this far; the least I could do was dig some holes to lay mines for a German counterattack that never came.

The Russian soldiers' work ethic was like nothing I'd ever seen. The soldiers would rise at dawn and work without complaint until midnight, like ants on a farm. Of course, there was occasional dissension in the ranks. Once I saw a group of soldiers huddled around a magazine—a copy of *Esquire*. Most of the equipment used by the Soviets came from America, and the magazine had turned up in a crate of artillery shells or tins of ready-to-eat meals. The soldiers weren't gawking at the Vargas pin-ups, but at the advertisements: the shiny cars, refrigerators, and wing-tip shoes. Perhaps it dawned on them that they'd been handed a bill of goods—Soviet Communism wasn't all it was cracked up to be. At least when set side by side with a pair of Florsheims.

Their grumble of a rebellion didn't last long. Everywhere the Soviet army went, the NKVD was sure to follow. These secret police were the worst-kept secret behind Russian lines, standing out like sore thumbs in their heavy cologne and fur caps. Their task was to maintain loyalty—a nice word for fear—in the ranks. And they were very good at it. The sight of a single fur cap could silence entire battalions.

The Germans defended Budapest house by house, digging into the cellars and sewers. Meanwhile I watched train after train packed with laborers moving back east, the way I had come. While they were killing Germans, the Red Army also had a quota to fill, sending slave laborers back to the Soviet Union. Getting arrested months before by the Nazis and being sent out of Budapest may have been the best thing that could have happened to me. If I'd remained in the city, I might easily have ended up on one of those trains bound for Siberia, one of the vanished.

In the middle of February, with the German army in Budapest collapsing, I finally started back to the city. Drunken Cossacks on horseback roamed the countryside shooting cattle, pigs, anything that moved. When I saw them coming, I dived into a ditch or barn and waited for them to run out of ammunition. As I got closer to Budapest, I saw hundreds of Hungarian soldiers emerging from the forests looking for Russians to surrender to. Even in surrender, there was strength in numbers. If they appeared in groups of two or three, it would be easier for the Russians to simply shoot them than to take them prisoner.

February 16, 1945. Home. Budapest. The City of the Damned. The war for Hungary was over, but the nightmare had just begun. Budapest smoldered, much of it reduced to rubble, the streets littered with the carcasses of horses and the corpses of German soldiers, frozen in the contortions of death. Most of the horses had been stripped to the bone for meat, and over the next several weeks I would have my share of horseflesh stew—it was either that or eat dust. My first evening back in Budapest, a family invited me into their cellar to share dinner; afterward their two children ran out into the street neighing and braying like horses, their Hungarian sense of humor shining through the darkness.

The next morning, I headed home—to what was now a pile of smoking rubble. The house was gone, a bombed-out shell—smashed by neither the Soviets nor the Nazis, but by the American bombers. And for all I knew, my father's corpse lay buried in the rubble. No one had seen him for months. And most of the people I asked about him just shook their head and walked away. As a friend to the Habsburgs, marked as a Royalist, my father—even the memory of him—had turned radioactive in this cold new world.

Throughout Budapest, the Hungarian bourgeoisie was busy burning documents and uniforms, reinventing themselves and eradicating any connection to the previous regime. The Soviets, having "liberated" Budapest, now proceeded to eviscerate it. The frontline Red Army soldiers were tough, disciplined men. Those that followed—the great occupying mass of young, illiterate country boys—were not. Soldiers in name only, unruly and impulsive, they were like children without parents—capable of extraordinary acts of kindness and of unimaginable cruelty—the very same soldiers whom I had embraced when I was freed from prison camp now went wild.

They'd storm into homes and drag women off at gunpoint to "peel potatoes." Daughters, wives, grandmothers—it didn't matter. Those with no place to hide learned to blacken their faces with charcoal or feign the symptoms of syphilis, a sure way to discourage the rapists. But not all escaped. For four months the Budapest National Council suspended the ban against abortion in order to deal with all the unwanted pregnancies.

Hungarians also learned, if asked for the time by a Russian soldier, not to look at their watches. Best to leave them at home, buried in the garden. The Russian soldiers would commandeer them, wearing six or seven wristwatches on each arm, like ticking bracelets. Officers set their sights higher, emptying entire houses, hauling furniture, rugs, and artwork down to the Danube, where barges were waiting to carry their loot back home to Russia.

Homeless, fatherless, penniless, I wandered through the broken city in a daze. I knew what I wanted to do, what I had to do, but this next move scared the daylights out of me. It took me several days—I don't even know how many—of meandering through the streets, scavenging for dry beans and horse meat, melting snow to drink, sleeping where I could, to screw up the courage. And suddenly there I was, standing in the shadows across the street from the house—Klári's house. The entire block miraculously stood intact, not a bullet hole or a scratch anywhere.

I was paralyzed. I wasn't even sure if she lived there anymore—or if she lived anywhere anymore, for that matter. And if she was alive, what had she been through? How would she have changed? It didn't matter; I just wanted to see her again. Walk up to her and say, "Sorry I'm late for dinner." And we'd laugh, and that would be that, as if nothing had happened. But I couldn't move. What if she wasn't there? What would I do then? Klâri was all I had. Beyond her I saw nothing, a void. Without her I might as well be dead.

Afternoon turned to evening. An old woman emerged from a house next door with a wind-up gramophone and began to waltz alone in the dim light. A man in a business suit with holes worn at the knees hauled a couple of pails of water across the street on a child's sled. A couple of drunken soldiers stumbled around the corner, and everything except for the woman dancing to the gramophone froze. They stopped for a moment to listen to the music, then moved on, barely able to stand. So the war had come to this street after all—leaving behind craziness, desperation, and fear.

I don't know how long I stood there, watching and waiting, but finally, in last light, I saw her. She came strolling down the walk, giggling, a Soviet officer holding her around the shoulders, whispering into her ear. I stepped back deeper into the shadows. They walked up the steps of her house, went inside, and shut the door behind them. It made sense now—her house untouched. Protected. Immune. Klâri had done what she had to do to survive. Just as I did. Just as we all did. Survival exacted a high price. The sun sank, and so did my heart. I walked away and never came back, never saw Klâri again. It was the beginning of one of the strangest nights—and days—in my entire life.

Leaving Klâri behind, I walked that night by the light of the moon—me just one more ghost in a city of ghosts—until I couldn't walk anymore, landing on a bench in Városliget, the same great park I used to visit as a child to go to the circus and would come to with Klâri for a picnic lunch.

It was a cold, clear night, but lying there wrapped up in my coat, I didn't feel the chill. I didn't feel much of anything. I drifted off into a shallow, uneasy sleep, waking a few hours later, sometime after midnight, when I sat bolt upright. I stared into the nearby bushes, something stirring. A woman emerged from the shadows as if from a different time and place—a beautiful young blond with too much makeup and a smear of lipstick on one cheek. She asked me if I was Hungarian, and I said I wouldn't be in this godforsaken country if I weren't.

A look of relief came over her, and she asked if she could sit down. She said she had been on a date, changing her mind at the last minute and running away. I didn't ask but knew without asking that what she had run away from made her as frightened and lonely as I was. We were both saved by the Soviet army and were now running from it. We slipped off the bench and back into the bushes to make love—both of us desperate for something to hold on to, desperation leading to desire. Afterward she told me her name: Erzsi.

In the morning desperation took a different turn. I asked Erzsi to marry me. And she said yes.

Trapped in a nightmare, beset on all sides by death, despair, and madness, we had awakened in a panic, determined to live our entire lives in a single day. Get married, have children, grow old, and die before the sun set. Our time was running out.

I was nothing if not resourceful. In a city without electricity, running water, or any semblance of civilian authority, I discovered that there were civil servants with nothing better to do who dutifully went about the business of bureaucracy—stamping birth certificates, signing death certificates, issuing marriage licenses. Even in hell, life goes on.

One particularly affable, expedient, and versatile clerk—a jack-of-all-trades—not only helped us fill out the proper forms but conducted the ceremony, acting himself as witness. Twenty minutes after walking in the door, we were declared man and wife—a Vegas-style wedding in the middle of war-torn Budapest. Did the man have the authority? Who knows? In those days the whole idea of authority was laughable, and we were all in on the joke.

My new bride took me home to her parents' house, and for the next two days straight we stayed in bed. Let the world outside go to hell, we had each other—bedridden and sick in love. Then on our third night, in the middle of the night, early in the morning, I woke in the darkness as if from a dream and learned what panic *really* was. It was as if I had been in a delirium the last few days, and now my fever had broken. Suddenly this room and this bed no longer seemed a sanctuary but another prison cell. Barely moving, not wanting to wake Erzsi, I asked myself:

What the hell did I do?

I might have been dumb, but I wasn't crazy. Or is it the other way around? Barely twenty-one and married to a stranger, I could barely keep myself alive. What good was I to her? Who the hell did I think I was? Looking back, I believe I saw in Erzsi a way out, an escape from the terror of the time. A bit of love and pleasure to ease the pain. All my buddies gone, my father missing, Klári lost to me, my gorgeous blond mirage of a wife was all I had left of the city I loved.

But here was the revelation. From the moment I had been freed from the prison camp in the Ukraine, I lived—and fought and starved and yearned—to get back to Budapest. Now, tying the knot, all I wanted to do was untie it. I wanted out of Hungary. The place was killing me.

That morning, before the sun rose, I quietly rose from the bed, slipped into my clothes, and slipped out of the room, out of the house, and out of her life. Just like that I drifted away, back into the fog of the postwar.

We all did what we had to.

I wish I could talk to her. For she had, in some strange way, saved me. I hope I did the same for her.

The war was over, and so was the honeymoon. The sun might be rising over Budapest, but even darker affairs awaited me before I could escape this city that was as beautiful, seductive, and desperate as the woman I had just left behind.

CHAPTER THREE

Curtains: 1946–1947

Late April 1946; a beautiful Budapest spring; a city rising from the ashes. The ghosts of war were still floating about, the soot and smoke in our clothes and eyes, but hope, too, was in the air. Bridges were being rebuilt, banks opening, magnolias were in bloom along the broad avenues. We were no longer forced to scavenge for horsemeat, to survive on weak tea and pickled cabbage. Two or three days a week, farmers brought their goods to market in the city squares, where stalls were piled high with potatoes, fresh vegetables, even some fruit, meat, and cheese. Budapest was alive again, awakening from its long nightmare.

Recovery was slow, and the conflict continued to claim victims every day. Malnutrition, diabetes, diphtheria, syphilis, typhoid fever, a swamp of infections and afflictions we didn't even know the name of rose up out of the sewers and alleyways unchecked. Medicine—penicillin in particular, a single dose costing seventy-five dollars on the black market—was a luxury few could find even if they could have afforded it. People would simply and suddenly disappear. You didn't know if they had been struck by some disease and had gone off to the hospital to recover or die—or if they had been hauled off in the middle of the night to 60 Andrássy Avenue, the great and once-elegant stone house converted by the Nazis into a house of torture and now in the brutal hands of the Hungarian Communists. If you were smart, you didn't ask.

It was a fact of life: We all lived in uncertainty—but we *lived*. At the end of the day, we were nothing if not Hungarians, and as the poet Antal Szerb pointed out, Hungarians have a gift for "sudden veering from rational hopelessness to irrational confidence." I'll take irrational confidence over rational hopelessness any day of the week. I never would have gotten anywhere without it, and it's what kept me going in the wake of the war in Budapest. (Three months before the war's end, Szerb was beaten to death in a Nazi concentration camp. I can't make sense of such a thing: why some, like me, escaped, while so many others didn't.)

In the spring of 1946, I was doing okay. I thought less about Klári each day and more about getting by. I even managed to open a small photography studio and start a business. I had enough money in my pockets to take care of myself and help out a few others. It was not unusual for a stranger to wander into the place and offer to wash the windows or sweep the floor, and whether or not the windows needed washing or the floor needed sweeping, if I had a little extra to give, I'd take them up on their offer, giving them the price of a pastry and a cup of tea. It wasn't charity; it was a sensible form of government under the circumstances. We had to watch out for each other.

My good fortune had come thanks in large part to the Americans— both the journalists and the generals stationed in Budapest. As a tour guide, interpreter, and driver, I possessed a commodity as valuable as Hershey bars or gasoline: my mastery of English. But whereas it was English that kept me in dollars, it was my broken Russian that kept me in business.

Around Christmas I had run into Clare Rozgonyi sipping tea in a cafe, though I hardly recognized her. The last time I'd seen her, 1940 maybe, she was an awkward teenager two years my junior, and I had always gone out of my way to ignore her. But here she was all grown up, a petite, pleasant-to-look-at young lady, whose bright blue eyes lit up when she saw me. And I'm sure my eyes lit up as well. In those days nothing was more gratifying than to catch up with someone you had known in the days before the war. It was a reaffirmation that you were alive—that your past was somehow connected to a future.

As it turned out, Clare and I had a great deal in common. Not only were our fathers both photographers, but each of them had also gone missing in the war. I told her about my studio a couple of blocks from Calvin Square. It was a ground-floor storefront, literally a hole in the wall, which I'd found empty and claimed as my own. Clare saw where I was going before I got there and agreed to come help me out in the studio. It would be nice to have a friendly face around; also she knew her way around cameras and darkrooms and could hold her own when it came to the management and manipulation of light and shadow. In other words she knew how to take a picture.

The studio was bigger than a bread box but not by much, a cozy little space lined with the spoils of war, bicycles, sacks of flour, cartons of cigarettes, typewriters—anything and everything that could be used, in the absence of a proper currency, to pay us for our portraiture. Our clientele consisted primarily of Russian soldiers, homesick young men, many of them barely literate, looking for a way to connect with their families back in the cities and steppes of the motherland.

One evening late in that April of 1946, Clare and I were prepping one such soldier for his glorification. He was a sweet, earnest young man with a shy grin and a shock of yellow hair under his cap. It's hard to fathom that, a year or so earlier, this very same young man might well have put a bullet in my head and raped Clare, but here he was talking to me about American jazz and flirting innocently with her. I put a rifle in his hand and told him to tilt his head down and look up at the camera. I glanced at Clare to see what she thought of the pose but saw that she was looking toward the door of the studio. I followed her eyes and saw that a man had stopped on the sidewalk. He looked furtively up and down the street, then paused for a moment and came into the studio.

An ill-fitting gray cloth coat hung on his thin frame, his hands hidden deep in his pockets. He had untrimmed hair and a beard to match, an old brown fedora pulled down over his forehead to protect him against the rain. It was that time of day. Hunger can chase you all day, but it's in the evening that it catches you, and I assumed that's what chased this old man into my place.

I put my hand on the soldier's shoulder to reassure him that I would only be a moment and took a step toward the stranger. If he wanted my help getting a bowl of soup, I would give it to him. But if he wanted to give me trouble, I would give him more in return. I asked the man what I could do for him. He lifted his head, and I saw a smile cross his thin lips. Then I saw his piercing eyes full of tears.

"Bobi," he said, "if you are going to be a photographer, you have to learn how to take a picture."

My father. Missing for over a year, dead for all I knew, he now stood before me, joking, weeping, a gaunt, gallant flesh-and-blood figure of a man, back from the purgatory of war. I put my arms around him and laid my head on his shoulder, and Clare came over to touch him, as though to assure herself that he was really there. And then the Russian soldier, too, gently putting the rifle down on the floor, came over and wrapped his arms around us all—the four of us crying like babies as the daylight drained away.

I held on tight to my father, trying to make sure he wouldn't get away from me again.

Toward the end of the war, even as the fighting raged in the streets and sewers, it became clear that the Nazis would soon be history, and the battle for the future began. As far as the Hungarian Communist Party was concerned, the future belonged to them, and they turned their dagger eyes on the enemy within. They came down on anyone associated with the royal family—my father, who had once served as official royal photographer, among them. They had snatched him from our family home in the dark of night and taken him to a camp in the plains of eastern Hungary, an old, isolated farm where they kept political prisoners, sorting them out, deciding what to do with them.

After a year of living off the land, out of sight and out of mind, his once-soft hands calloused and hard, my father had been released. There was no rhyme or reason to it. Others in his position had died or simply disappeared. My father, they let go. As a Royalist, he had wealthy, powerful friends in Switzerland, Italy, and France; perhaps they bought his freedom. But over time, my father said, he had made friends with his guards. The Communists must have realized that this old man wasn't going to lead any uprisings. My father had been deemed harmless, no longer a threat.

I was a different story.

Major General William Shaffer Key, the pride of Oklahoma City, an American businessman, banker, and director of various life insurance and natural gas companies, was a thirty-third degree Mason, recipient of the Order of the Falcon from Iceland, and a Knight Commander in the Order of the Bath from Great Britain. Key was, in short, a man to be reckoned with. And from 1945 to the summer of 1946, he was the Grand Poobah of Budapest, the commanding general of the US forces in Hungary and chief US representative on the Allied Control Commission—the body of Allied wartime coalition members that administered the defeated powers of the Axis. Jowly, tight-lipped, and well-fed, Key lorded over his cowering staff in his American embassy office, decorated with the cheap bric-a-brac and ugly paintings sold to him by local artists who hailed them as fine examples of the Magyar Rococo school or masterpieces of the Hungarian Renaissance.

But there was much more to the major general than so-called art and culture. Key liked to play the role of supreme commander of Allied forces, shrewdly calculating spymaster, and king of Hungary all rolled into one fine, upstanding package of civic virtue and American know-how. I later learned that his home state of Oklahoma had honored the man by erecting a prison in his name—a tribute that speaks for itself.

Key's interest in me was twofold. First, he sought relief from the gaggle of newspapermen, and he hired me to keep the correspondents occupied and away from him. Second, he saw me as his eyes and ears on the ground. The real American spies in Budapest, and there were plenty of them, were foxes in civilian clothing—agricultural attachés, oilmen, and such—and Major General Key, a vainglorious show-off of a man sure to spill any secrets that came his way, was the last man in Europe with whom they'd share any information. But that didn't stop him from trying, and I was his prime asset. The fact that I knew a few Russian soldiers and officers, and that I spoke their language, led him to believe that I had some special access and insight to the inner workings of the Soviet military mind.

I don't think I was much use to him. The only Russian maneuvers I knew about were which cafes the soldiers preferred and which streets they liked to wander in search of hookers. Although I didn't do much for him, General Key, without intending it, did a great deal for me. His request that I keep the coming invasion of American journalists out of his hair opened up new worlds of possibility for me.

My first order of business was to find the journalists a decent place to sleep. The hotels and boarding rooms were booked solid with Allied military men, diplomats, and government officials, so I had to look elsewhere. My search led me to the Sisters of Mercy convent. The convent was not immune to the economic hardship, and the mother superior agreed, for a fee, to open the convent to the pack of correspondents—who, within a few days, proceeded to break most every commandment in the book.

The mother superior looked the other way when they bought lipstick and stockings for the nuns. She closed the door and closed her eyes when she caught me giving a massage to *Vogue* correspondent Lee Miller. But the final straw came when several of the journalists came up with the idea of bringing a prostitute into the convent. This time Mother Superior didn't turn the other cheek. I had to find the newspapermen—and woman—other accommodations.

Some of the journalists left the city never to return. Lee Miller, formerly a successful fashion model, had apprenticed as a photographer with the surrealist Man Ray and during the war had covered the London Blitz, the liberation of Paris, and the horrors of the death camps at Buchenwald and Dachau. She had come to Budapest to photograph bombed-out buildings and firing squads and had turned to me not only for early-morning nude massages but as an interpreter, assistant, and chess partner. But now she was moving on, leaving Budapest for Saint Moritz, where she took pictures of beautiful people and exiled royalty. Others, like Vienna-based correspondent Sy Bourgin—tall and rangy and as American as Jimmy Stewart—kept coming back. He couldn't help himself. Budapest was like a beautiful woman who spoils you for all other women, and that spring, the city was more exciting and more alive than ever. All of Europe had been liberated, but Budapest was the most liberated city on the continent.

It was as if in that short space of time between the iron fist of the Fascists and the Iron Curtain of the Communists, we lived outside of history. God and the devil were off in London, Paris, and Rome, busy assigning guilt, repressing impulse, and restoring order. For eighteen wonderful months they forgot about Budapest, leaving us to our own devices. The gods and demons would return soon enough, but for the moment we danced and played.

On February 1, 1946, the Kingdom of Hungary ceased to exist. The country was a republic now—a republic that had an aristocracy all its own: the Americans. While the American dollar ruled, the Russian generals ran the show. In 1945 at Yalta the big three—Churchill, Roosevelt, and Stalin—had agreed that although Hungary was at war with the Allied powers, at war's end it would not be treated as a defeated enemy but as a liberated country. Consequently, an Allied Control Commission was established in Budapest, chaired by Soviet Marshal Kliment Voroshilov with representatives from both the United States and Britain. The Americans had put forth a set of proposed regulations, which Voroshilov accepted as a "basis for discussion." He promptly stuffed the regulations into his back pocket—as he did all of Hungary. The Soviets had plans for Hungary, which didn't include America or Britain. And clearly Budapest was not a priority in either London or Washington.

Say what you will about the Russians, though, they loved a good time. They loved to sing, dance, and drink. And drink some more. Cologne, aftershave, the emulsifier in my darkroom—none of it was safe from the Russian soldiers. But among the first capitalistic activities authorized by the Russian command were the nightclubs and after-hours hot spots. Nailed down and boarded up by the Nazis, the clubs threw open their doors and welcomed back Hungary's acclaimed singers and pretty young dancing girls.

Many of the girls had slipped across the border years ago, turning up—and dancing—at Karpic's club in Ankara, the Casino in Tehran, and the Kit-Kat in Cairo. For some, the war years proved to be a boon, and these girls came home with trunks full of fine clothes, arms loaded with golden bracelets, and, more than likely, heads full of more military secrets than any intelligence-gathering operation in Europe. And when they came back, I was there to greet them.

Every night around eleven, I climbed into what, next to my cameras, was my most prized possession—my 1938 blue Bugatti 57SC coupe, another gift from the American armed forces. When the US Army first arrived in Budapest, I had served as both interpreter and chauffeur, and to get around the city they had provided me with the Bugatti, which they had confiscated from the garage of a once high-ranking official of the

Hungarian Fascist Arrow Cross Party. My driving days for the Americans were over, but they seemed to have forgotten about the car, and I saw no reason to remind them about it.

Around the clubs and cafes of the city, I was called the Emperor of the Night. My realm stretched from the Miami Beach Cafe, where I kept a table for ten, paying each night for the streetwalkers to come have a bowl of chicken soup, to the Palais de Dance and the Moulin Rouge with their dull French names and hot American jazz. But the place I loved most was the Plantazs club, where Margit (Baby) Sugar lit up the stage and danced the lights out. Russian, British, and American officers and diplomats, correspondents from New York and London, and a few lucky Hungarians like me—anyone with a few Swiss francs, English pounds, or American dollars in their pocket—could come to the Plantazs and have the time of their lives. In the nightclubs it didn't matter what country you came from. Everyone got along, and we lived like there was no tomorrow.

—◦—

"The Emperor of the Night Arrested!" That was the newspaper headline the day after my reign ended.

At the time I was living and sleeping in my photography studio. I had been staying in a small, comfortable apartment with my father, but my odd hours, the company I kept, even the car I drove—none of it sat well with him. Looking back, perhaps I would have been better off listening to my father. But I regret nothing, other than the anguish I caused him. Given the chance to do it all over again, I'd do it all over again: climb into my Bugatti and race off to Plantazs.

Around 4:30 in the morning, July 19, 1946, marked the beginning of the end for me in Budapest. I hadn't been in bed for more than thirty minutes, falling dead asleep the moment my head hit the pillow, when the Hungarian Communist Party's political police smashed in my door. They could have walked right in—I didn't have a lock on the door—but these bastards liked to make an entrance.

I had known for some time that I was being watched, but I had fooled myself into thinking I was safe. I wasn't participating in political meetings or selling secrets to the enemy. I was watching dancing girls, listening to jazz, and drinking with newspapermen. Not exactly innocent, but totally harmless, I thought. But the Communists thought differently, and their thinking trumped mine. They rousted me out of bed and hauled me off to Marko Street.

Politically, the situation in Hungary was fluid and volatile. When the Soviet army took control of Budapest in January 1945, the bullet-headed Mátyás Rákosi—an exiled Hungarian Communist who called himself Stalin's best pupil, returned from Moscow, was installed as general secretary of the Hungarian Communist Party, and set about teaching Hungary the lessons he had learned at Stalin's knee. But we Hungarians have a gift for not recognizing the obvious.

Every once in a while, an election was called and ballots were cast, but all for show. In the parliamentary election of 1947, in the face of Soviet detention of opposition members, the purging of some half a million voters from the rolls, and the stuffing of the ballot boxes in their favor, the Communist Party still barely won 20 percent of the votes cast. Regardless, they continued to hold the highest offices because they had the one vote that really counted: the one cast by the man with the mustache in Moscow.

We should have known that Hungary's fate was being decided elsewhere. It always had been, and the signs were everywhere. We were having too good a time to notice, for example, that the movie theaters stopped showing American movies, replacing them with Soviet films. We just stopped going to the movies. The moment they took over the movie screens, we should have known we didn't stand a chance.

Two days before my arrest, in the middle of the afternoon of July 17, 1946, a young Hungarian man shot and killed two Russian soldiers and a Hungarian girl in a busy Budapest market. An hour later, the charred body of the young man was found in a nearby attic. In the pocket of his jacket, which was burned to a crisp, papers were found tying him to the Catholic anti-Communist underground. The papers were intact, without so much as a flick of ash around the edges. This was the act of war the Hungarian Communist Party had been waiting for. They rounded up their perceived enemies, including me.

The crackdown reduced the Marko Street prison into a hot, humid, human mess. Jammed into a cell intended for two—maybe fifteen by six feet—there could be anywhere from eight to fourteen of us at one time. We took turns on the two straw mattresses, the rest of us sleeping on the floor. Every morning, the guards brought us two pails of water, which we had to make last for twenty-four hours. Twice a day they brought us a bowl of what we came to call poison ivy soup. I couldn't tell you what was in it—and if I could, you wouldn't want to know.

Remarkably, with a few exceptions, we all got along, no fighting over the mattresses or trying to sneak extra gulps of water. Any other way and we knew we'd have torn each other apart. If my time at Marko Street taught me anything, it's that the one and only place in the world Communism and collectivism work is in a prison cell.

Aside from me, there were in my cell students who had read the wrong books, office workers who had flirted with the wrong girls, Catholics who had prayed at the wrong church, and laborers who had voiced the wrong opinion over a beer. Because the one thing there was no shortage of in Budapest was informers.

Every few days the guards would come down the corridor, call out a name, and pull some quivering twenty-year-old out of his cell. They'd shackle him, push him against the wall if he resisted, and tell him to pray to his god, because if he had a maker it was time to meet him. The guards scared the hell out of all of us. Sometimes the chosen one would cry or beg, but that only increased the brutality of the removal. But word got to us from the outside. The prisoners they came for were the ones being released, the little fish thrown back into the pond. Saying they were headed for the noose or firing squad was the jailers' joke on us, their way of showing that we were completely under their control, as helpless as dogs in a kennel.

Over the next several weeks, our numbers thinned. Instead of a dozen to a cell, there were ten, then seven. It meant more water and more space for each of us—but also more room for worry. Why wasn't *I* released? What had I done to merit this special attention? But it wasn't *what* I had done, it was who I had done it with. The guards regularly called out my name—not for release, but for interrogation.

In the beginning the interrogators would spend a few hours with me, asking simple questions about my family and friends, my work, and how much money I made. . . . They were doing a job, policemen doing what they were paid to do. They'd take a few notes, nod or shrug, and send me back to my cell. I was convinced that it was just a matter of time before they'd let me go. But at the end of my first month at Marko Street, the attitude and atmosphere changed. It was as if a red flag had gone up: Somebody somewhere had decided that I was an enemy of the state.

As my status changed, so did the identity and character of my interrogators. *These* men were not motivated by salary, but by ideology, hatred, and the desire for blood and power. They had honed their interrogating skills in small, dark rooms at the end of the war, and now, instead of having a pistol as the final instrument of their judgment, they had the entire apparatus of the state. Given half a chance, these men would rip my heart out.

They wanted to know about the Americans. What did the Americans ask me? What did I tell them? Who was their leading agent? How much did they pay me? How did the Americans corrupt me? Did I understand that moral and political corruption are two sides of the same coin? Was it true that I paid for ten prostitutes to have dinner every night? Was I procuring Hungarian women for the Americans? Why did I agree to be a spy for the enemy of the people? Wasn't I ashamed of myself?

The interrogations would go on for as long as eight hours; sometimes an entire day was spent answering the same question two or three hundred times over. They'd give me paper and a pen and tell me to write out the answer each time. If the answer deviated at all, a single word altered, a comma where before I had a dash, they'd accuse me of lying or changing my story. It was proof, they said, that I was part of a vast conspiracy led by the Americans to betray Hungary. Or they'd say nothing and just slap me across the face or burn me with a cigarette on the back of my neck.

Some days, for hours on end, they'd shine a bright light inches away from my face without uttering a single word. I couldn't see them; I could only hear them going in and out of the room. At times I wasn't even sure if anyone was there, but I was too afraid to move. They'd interrogate me five or six days in a row, then stop, nothing for weeks, until out of the blue they'd come down and call my name, take me to a room, and ask the same questions all over again. They kept telling me I had to readjust my thinking, but I couldn't decipher what that meant. It seemed problematic to me: How could they judge if my thinking had been properly readjusted if anytime I changed my answers, I'd get a knock across the skull for my trouble?

The interrogations went on for more than six months. The fact that I was in good health to begin with was the only reason I managed to hold on. I had to disengage my mind from it all—from the interrogations and from the disease around me. Even as my body weakened, I could not let my mind do the same. I'd be lost if I did. The trick was memory.

To imagine what might happen the next day, the next week, or the next year was too frightening and dangerous. The moment I started to speculate about the future, I would begin to doubt that I even had one. Consequently I focused on the past.

I'd recall and reconstruct to the smallest detail a drive through the countryside in my Bugatti. A conversation with my mother, word for word, from when I was five. The taste of the smoked cheese given to me by my grandfather. The books I read at school—entire scenes in my head from the poems of Byron, the plays of Shakespeare, the novels of Jonathan Swift. I'd replay a chess game with my father, sitting across from him in the courtyard of our home, our dog Sultan at our feet. The interrogators would ask one of their stupid questions for the umpteenth time or press the smoldering coal of a cigarette into my flesh, and I'd look into my mother's eyes, stand with Gulliver against the Lilliputians, or execute a King's Gambit and watch my father smile. The burning cigarette hurt like hell, but I removed myself from the sensation of it. They had my body; my mind and my spirit were my own.

In February 1947 I was put on trial. The guards brought me a new shirt and tie and new trousers, socks, and shoes. They led me out of my cell past the interrogation rooms and upstairs to the courtroom into a chair set between two uniformed guards. Under a series of gigantic murals of the Spanish Inquisition, I looked up into the face of the "people's court." I glanced into the gallery behind me and saw my father and my good friend Almashy. My father, through a few well-placed bribes, had kept track of me. It was only now, seeing their faces—seeing myself through their eyes—that I recognized how bad a shape I must have been in. My father tried to nod and reassure me, but his fear, his sadness, and his rage at what they had done to me were written on his face.

The judge read from his notes, the prosecutor from his, each taking turns following the script. It must have taken half an hour just to read through the charges against me: treason, conspiracy against the Republic, black marketeering, possession of foreign currency, trading in foreign currency, acting as a foreign agent, giving comfort to the enemy, moral corruption, on and on and on. Men I'd never seen before testified to the plots I had hatched with the Americans, to the words I had spoken against the Hungarian people. The notes I had taken during the interrogations were presented as evidence—confessions I'd written to the court of my own free will.

The trial lasted a day, the last words of the script read by the judge, condemning me to death by hanging. I had not been allowed to say a word in my own defense, but even if I had, I wouldn't have had any idea what to say or how to save myself. As the guards led me out, I took one last look at my father. He was staring down at his hands in his lap.

My father taught me to play chess when I was eight. Whenever I was home, often in the summer, we would sit in the sun—my father in his dark suit—and have a game. He schooled me in the strategies of initiative and defense and in the tactics of sacrifice and attack.

On the morning after my trial, it must have been about six, the guards came to my cell and informed me that I was being transferred to another jail. I had no doubt what that meant, and as they gathered me up, still in the new shirt and trousers from the trial, I recalled one chess game I had played with my father. I was thirteen, and it was the first time I had beaten him legitimately—the first time I had won without a sneaking suspicion that he had thrown the match to build my confidence.

That February morning was bitterly cold, a light snow falling as the three guards led me out through the Marko Street courtyard. I could see the bullet marks on the walls where firing squads had rendered final judgment on officials of the Arrow Cross Party. Now only the trials were for show, not the executions. The guards, triangulating around me, took me into the street and toward a nearby square. One explained to me what was happening. I was being transferred into the custody of the secret police, who would then take me on to my final destination. As much as I hated Marko Street prison, now it seemed the safest place to be—a nest of vipers, but a nest nonetheless.

I had my father's Bishop pinned in front of his King and I could see how it would all play out, moving my Knight, then my Castle into position, closing off all means of escape. We reached the square and the guards stopped; they seemed uncertain what to do next. I had neither a hat nor a coat, and my fingers felt as if they were going to fall off. On the opposite side of the square, a car idled in a side street, and the guards started forward again, leading me on. My father gently touched the King's crown and toppled it to the board. I had won, the game was over, but I tried to maintain my focus on the black and white squares of the board and not on where I was now—or where I was going. I could barely walk, hadn't eaten since before the trial, was close to collapse as I moved slowly through the middle of the square.

I tried to focus on the game, reconstruct my moves. Had I really beaten my father or had he simply been more clever than ever in throwing the game? The car was coming toward us now, picking up speed, and the guards around me stiffened. The men inside the car had rifles and were pointing them at the guards, ordering them to drop to the ground, which they did without hesitation. The back door of the car opened and one of the men inside grabbed me by my shoulder and threw me to the floor of the car, holding me down with his hand on the back of my neck. I lay there, thankful to be warm at least, but speeding toward what I assumed was some freshly dug grave outside the city.

We drove for what seemed like an eternity but must have been more like twenty minutes, every bump in the street a jolt to my body. I could tell we were in the country now, less noise, more light, and more twists in the road. The car slowed, made a sharp turn, and came to a stop. The man took his hand off my neck and opened the car door. I pushed myself up and out of the car, and in front of a small country cottage, saw my father approaching me. He took off his coat and wrapped it around me, shook the hands of the men who had freed me, and took me inside, where my first real meal in over six months and warm new clothes were awaiting me. And we talked—but not about prison or the trial or my escape. My father knew that reliving the ordeal would sap the little strength I had left. We talked about small things: how my friends were, the apartment he was living in now, the latest neighborhood gossip. It was as though I had been away on business for a few months, and he was catching me up.

After a little food—it was surprising how little I ate, unable to stomach more than a few bites—I collapsed onto the softest, most comfortable bed ever made. I slept like a baby, and my father treated me like one, too, sitting in a chair next to the bed as though to make sure I didn't stop breathing. After seven hours, darkness falling, he shook me awake. I had to go. He had bought my freedom but didn't know how much time his money would buy—a bribe begins to depreciate the moment you hand over the cash.

My father had a small pack ready for me—some food and water, a blanket, some extra socks, a small knife—and led me to the garden out back to an old green bicycle leaning against the cottage wall. He gave me directions to a farm outside Hegyeshalom, a hundred thirty something kilometers away and close to the Austrian border. He gave me a letter to give to the farmer by way of introduction, and we shook hands, embraced, slapped each other on the back. Then I climbed into the saddle and wheeled away into the cold night. I wouldn't see my father again for over a decade.

I was headed west under the cover of darkness—a pariah and a fugitive on the run, spinning silently through the rolling hills of northwestern Hungary. I had cheated death. Now the question was, could I outfox and outrun it? The stars lit the way.

At the first sign of morning, a gray light obliterating the stars in the eastern sky, I dragged my bicycle out of sight into an abandoned grove of chestnut trees. Shivering, I curled up under the blanket in a bed of dead leaves, my knife in hand. I shivered from the cold and from fear. I had come a long way in the last forty-eight hours, but I still had a long way to go. And I wasn't even sure what my destination was.

Two nights of steady pedaling, diving off to the side whenever a car approached, brought me to the place my father told me about—a white stucco farmhouse with a thatched roof set back some hundred meters off the road. It was several hours before dawn, but as soon as I turned in to the place, dogs started to bark, and the farmer came out to look me over. I handed him the letter from my father, and without reading it, he stuffed it into his pocket. He led me into the house, glancing down toward the road to make sure no one had spotted me. He told me to take a seat next to the fireplace but was clearly anxious to move the process along—to get me out of his home and away from his family.

Within an hour I was back on the road, this time lying in the false bottom of the farmer's truck, under a thousand pounds of potatoes. As I quickly discovered on the half-hour drive to the Austrian border, the small airhole in the bed of the truck had been injudiciously cut adjacent to the exhaust pipe. I lay there wondering: Was this how it was going to be? Escape the Communist hangman's noose only to die in a gas chamber hidden beneath a stinking pile of spuds? As tears streamed down my face, it was all I could do to keep from choking and coughing when the border guard checked the farmer's papers and potatoes, asked after his wife and children, commented on what a lovely day it had turned out to be. . . . At long last the guard waved him on.

A few miles into Austria, the farmer pulled off the road along a deserted stretch of the Danube and freed me from the gassy bowels of his potato truck. I rolled around on the ground for a few minutes spitting up from the carbon monoxide, then tried to explain to him the flaw in his truck. He shrugged me off. I was alive and I was out of Hungary. What was the problem? And of course he was right. I was a free man. Or would be soon, if I could make it to Vienna.

Vienna was a labyrinth of a city, a multitude of checkpoints, four armies, four bureaucracies, heavily armed soldiers scowling and demanding papers and passports in four languages. I, of course, had nothing to show, no papers or passports. I didn't have a country.

The potato farmer knew where all the checkpoints were, and by following a circuitous route, managed to avoid all but the American-controlled locations. It was clear that the soldiers had gotten word from on high to give the rusty old Hungarian potato truck free passage, and we breezed through.

Late that afternoon the driver reached the end of the road—for him at least. Strasse 92, in the heart of old Vienna. Standing there on the curb, I could smell the Danube, just blocks away, the river that ran from Budapest to Vienna and had for centuries been the rich lifeblood of the Austro-Hungarian Empire. At this pre-evening hour, when most cities were percolating with life, Vienna was deathly still. There were only a few people on the street, some peeking out from their windows, but not a soul speaking a word. This was a city of secrets, of fear and famine, but to me it was a new world opening its door and letting me in.

The farmer had brought me to the American Press Club, and the man at the top of the steps opening the door to greet me was my good friend Sy Bourgin. Now *Time*'s Vienna correspondent, he had gotten word from my father that I was coming, and he had taken care of the rest—arranged for my passage through the city's checkpoints. He smiled down at me and shook his head, as though to ask what kind of trouble I had gotten into *this* time. I was a bag of bones, forty pounds lighter since he saw me last, scars on the back of my hands and neck from the cigarette burns, my feet bloody and blistered—and Sy did what any self-respecting newspaper-man would do. He told me I needed a drink.

John Phillips, photographer for *Life*; John McCormack of the London *Times*; Joe Israel of the *Saturday Evening Post*; Irving R. Levine of the International News Service; all my old buddies from Budapest were there to greet me. The champagne was already on ice, and the boys were already three drinks to the west of me, a scouting party blazing a path to the bar. They were so thrilled by my escape, they had started the celebration without me. I did my best to catch up—though I can't say for sure whether I succeeded or not. In fact, I can't say much about that evening at all. I exercised my newfound freedom like a sailor on liberty, diving into a vat of champagne and gin. Between the food and the drink, between my old friends and the pretty young new friends they introduced me to that evening, it might have been one of the most memorable nights of my life if only I could remember it.

I woke up in a bed upstairs—a bed that would be mine for the next six months—and immediately went to work. The Press Club was a beehive, half the correspondents reporting not only to their editors back home but to American intelligence officers here. But for all the activity at the Press Club and all the information passing through it, we all knew that there were no secrets here. The assumption was that the place was wired for sound—certainly by the Soviets, probably by the Americans as well—and that the Austrians who swept the floors and the girls we dated were all on somebody's payroll.

Everyone in Vienna was paid by someone to spy on someone else. Back in Washington, Truman had just signed into law, and the Congress had provided funding for, a new organization—the Central Intelligence Agency. The Soviets had experience, wile, and a medieval capacity for brutality on their side. The Americans had money, and they poured it into Europe. In Vienna, the Cold War was in its infancy, and we were there to experience the growing pains.

I went to work as a photo reporter for Ted Kaghan at the *Wiener Kurier*, a Viennese newspaper created in 1945 and funded for the next decade by the Information Services Branch (ISB) of the US armed forces in Austria. *Wiener Kurier* was of great interest and use to the new CIA. Ted bent over backward to provide all sides to a story—even if the American side was all Hollywood movies and Cadillacs and the other side was all belligerent men in gray uniforms and long lines for toilet paper. Even so, the *Wiener Kurier* was the best and most popular news source in the city.

What my time with the newspaper got me, aside from invaluable experience as a photojournalist, was a piece of white paper. It said, simply, that I worked for the ISB of the US forces in Austria. But the paper was only good in the part of Austria that the United States controlled, which meant that Vienna was only partially safe for me. Every day I spent in Vienna was another game of Russian roulette, because if I fell into the hands of the Soviets, that piece of paper of mine would have been useless, and they would have sent me packing back to Budapest.

One evening Sy talked me into tagging along on a visit to a particularly attractive Viennese girl he was pursuing. He said she had a friend, and he didn't have to twist my arm. We parked his jeep and went up to the girl's room. A couple of hours later, as we came back down into the street, we spotted a couple of Soviet sentries guarding the jeep. I slipped into an alley, and Sy went to see what they wanted. Apparently, not only did his girlfriend have a room in this neighborhood, but so too did the MVD—the Soviet Ministry of Internal Affairs. It took Sy a good hour—and a roll of dollars—to convince them that his interest lay in romantic affairs, not Soviet internal affairs. I had already known this city was too treacherous a place for me. Hiding in the shadows from the soldiers, it hit home. My days in Vienna were coming to an end.

The Americans had built a temporary airstrip out of steel plates in their sector, and with the help of my American friends and my white paper, I hopped on a plane to my next stop. I spent Christmas 1947 in Salzburg in the American-occupied zone—and what a gift it was. I was dying to embrace America and all that it symbolized, but Hungary and the Cold War were not yet ready to let me go.

For me, getting to America was no longer a choice, it was a mission. Before I could complete that mission, however, I had to undertake another: I had to free as many Hungarians as I could from the Communists. Over the next two years in Salzburg, I would discover just how much I was capable of, and I would become exactly what the Hungarian Communist Party had accused me of being: a sworn and dangerous enemy of the state.

CHAPTER FOUR

Ginger Rogers and Fingernail Clippers

Salzburg, in the American sector of Austria

We had to wait for the electricity to come back on. There were fewer outages now than there had been in recent months, but we still lost the juice on occasion for an hour here and a day there. Nobody complained. By then we were all used to the arbitrary nature of things, whether it was electric power or our lives.

Around eight that evening, the lights came back on. A single hot, bright light hung from the ceiling, above a thick wooden table in the middle of the room—the kitchen of my apartment. A pot of water boiled on the stove, metal utensils in the pot knocking against the sides. There were three of us in the kitchen: me, Ladislas Szilegyi—my best friend from Sárospatak—and his new young wife, who sat naked under a blanket on the table, the light shining down on her. The newlyweds had arrived from Budapest a few days before, and I had invited them to stay at my place. It was either that or send them off to one of the DP (displaced persons) camps outside of town. There were worse places to be than a DP camp, but I had room, and they didn't plan on being around for very long anyway. They had their sights, and hearts, set on Australia.

There was just one sticking point. Pregnant women need not apply—a rule that complicated things for Ladislas and his new wife. So when the lights finally came on, we dealt with the problem, referring to a German medical book I had acquired on the black market in exchange for some American candy bars. But that wasn't our only resource. The naked woman lying on the table in front of us, Ladislas's wife, had recently grad-uated from medical school, and for this one evening she acted as doctor and patient, directing our every move.

Within a half hour, the problem was gone. And within a month, the Szilegyis were too—on their way to Australia. Some forty years later I happened to be filming a movie down there and I looked them up. She had become a prominent and respected doctor and the proud mother of two sons. Sometimes you have to take one step back to take two steps forward.

In Salzburg every goddamn one of us faced choices we'd have to live with the rest of our lives. In the Bible, Abraham is willing to sacrifice his son to appease his god. Now we were all about to discover what we were willing to sacrifice—how much we were willing to leave behind—to break away from our history.

I was just one displaced person among thousands. I had a leg up thanks to my American connections, but we all wanted the same thing—*papers*, the Holy Grail sought by every displaced person in Europe—a govern-ment's official recognition that we existed. My papers enabled me to move freely around the American sector of Austria, but I wanted papers that would allow me to move *to* America. Without them I had nothing. I was stuck in Salzburg.

Salzburg, in the heart of the American sector of Allied-occupied Austria, 1948, was a city where nothing was fixed and everything was negotiable—government, business, people, and values. I found myself at the crossroads of never-never land and *Casablanca*.

Salzburg is a picturesque town of pretty domes and towers, majestic castles and cathedrals, labyrinthine streets and gardens. But just about everyone in the sector existed in a state of limbo, all of us here on our way to somewhere else. There were Armenians, Poles, Slavs, Latvians, Lithu-anians, Estonians, Greeks, Czechs, Ukrainians, Russians, Hungarians, Italians, Jews, Communists, Catholics, Nazis, soldiers, journalists, spies, artists and con artists, crooks and hookers, and criminals of every stripe—Salzburg was a fairy tale town under siege and bursting at the seams.

I'd often wake up at dawn to the not-so-distant blast of explosions. But it wasn't artillery or a bombing run or the approach of an advancing army. It was the sound of American GIs on the outskirts of town, fishing. They didn't cast lines into the water; they threw live grenades or sticks of dynamite into the river and waited for the dead trout to rise to the surface. The Americans were running the show, an impossible task, which they tackled with confidence and without subtlety. For them, their job— picking Europe up and putting it back on its feet—was all about fishing with dynamite. Throw everything you have at it and see what rises to the surface.

I had landed on my feet in the American sector. In the French and Russian sectors, the DPs were begging for bread. In the state of Salzburg, the shelves were stocked like supermarkets. Gangs of venture capitalists—black marketers—turned the camps into shopping malls. Hershey bars, cigarettes, nylons, bottles of schnapps, jewelry, paintings, bicycles, typewriters, pianos, jeeps—anything could be had for a price.

My place in all of this in the spring of 1948, several months after I arrived in Salzburg, was a sublet—a couple of rooms on the third floor of a building near the old city center. The building had suffered a direct hit during a wartime bombing run and had a gaping hole where the stairs should have been. Whenever I emerged from my rooms, I confronted a drop-off into a three-story abyss. A rickety contraption put together with rope and two-by-fours was my only connection to the world below. My love life suffered as a consequence.

Not that I'm complaining. It beat living in the DP camp—a former German army barracks with thirty beds to a room divided by blankets hanging from the ceiling. An apartment, even with a mineshaft in the middle of it, was a luxury in Salzburg—a luxury made possible by my work with the ISB, who paid me one hundred dollars a month to take pictures. My job: Make America, Americans, and the American Way look good.

The ISB offices were in Markt Square, a ten-minute walk from my apartment. But when I wasn't out on assignment or hunting down stories on my own, I spent the balance of my time with other members of the ISB staff across the street at Cafe Tomaselli, sipping coffee or wine, trading stories about women, war, and whatever else was on our minds. Here I often met with my boss, the head of my division, Yoichi

Okamoto. Originally commissioned as personal photographer to General Mark Clark, the high commissioner in Austria, Yoichi was now responsible for all photographs published in and about the American occupation zone.

Yoichi was a smart man who knew how to work a room and was a savvy photographer with a subtle, steady hand. But his skills and mine were exactly opposite. He preferred to be a fly on the wall, a talent that fifteen years later earned him the position of official photographer to President Lyndon Johnson. I, on the other hand, was a bull in a china shop, and if there was a shot I wanted, there wasn't a wall I wouldn't climb, bodyguard I couldn't outwit, or law I wasn't willing to break to get it. I always had a narrative I was trying to convey through the vehicle of my shutter and lens. It was a skill set perfectly suited to the task at hand: the marketing of America.

As far as the ISB was concerned, there wasn't a cleaner, brighter, bigger place on earth than America. A chicken in every pot, a Kelvinator in every kitchen, more horsepower under the hood. America the beautiful wasn't a phrase, it was a promise made by the ISB every day to the people of Eastern Europe. The Austrians might not understand these Americans—this odd alien folk who would take a perfectly delicious piece of sautéed veal, drench it in mayonnaise, slap it between two slices of tasteless bread, and call it a sandwich—but they wanted to *be* Americans. Mozart didn't stand a chance against Bing Crosby and the Andrews Sisters.

The ISB was on the front lines of a new war—a war of words and images. America was on one side, the Soviet Union on the other—and I knew which side my bread was buttered on. To me it was a shooting war, and my camera was my cannon.

Naturally, as with any war—even a Cold War—there was a dark and dirty side to it that, over time, would leave *me* cold. One of the worst-kept secrets in our circle of journalists and photographers was who the ISB was housing at a lovely villa overlooking a lake in Gmunden, about an hour east of Salzburg: a dozen or so leading former Nazis whom the ISB had put on its payroll. Certainly the ISB wasn't the only group to compromise itself. You couldn't climb into the trenches of this Cold War without coming out infested with fleas.

Nonetheless, the American cause remained my cause. I believed when I was working in Salzburg—and still do—that the good outweighed the bad. I believed in the Marshall Plan. I believed in Eisenhower. I believed that Communism was a great lie. And frankly, I believed in a hundred dollars a month.

I also supplemented my income covering news stories for *Salzburger Nachrichten*, the local paper, whose offices adjoined those of the ISB. It was not by coincidence that they were located in the same building. A principal goal of the ISB was the development of a "free and independent" press—meaning free to portray America and its mission in a positive light. I had a third revenue stream as well. With my good pal and mentor Sy Bourgin's help, a number of my photographs landed in the pages of *Time*, *Life*, and *Esquire*.

What I didn't know at the time, but would soon come to learn, was that my connection to the ISB and *Time/Life*, these two American behemoths, was driven in part by the CIA, which had just started operation in 1947. Committed as I was to this war, I was willing to go wherever it took me, even if it meant getting my hands a little dirty. But it wasn't all work and no play. If you knew where to look, you could find a good time in Salzburg.

———

I met George at the opening of the Salzburg American Express office. I could have sleepwalked through the job—if not for the tall guy with the big head and bright white suit who somehow managed to edge his way into the frame of nearly every picture I took, ruining my shots and ruining my day. After several wasted rolls of film, I decided to take it up with him personally, resolving to reason with him or knock his block off—whatever the situation called for.

Seeing me coming, he stuck out his hand in greeting. "Name's George. George London. *Sprechen zie* American?" He went on to say that he was one of the biggest celebrities here, and that I should put his picture in the paper. He explained that he was in town in between engagements with the Vienna State Opera and attending the Salzburg Music Festival. He must have detected a hint of skepticism in my face because, eyes glowering, he stepped back, pointed his finger at me, and in a bass-baritone voice as big as he was, belted out the "Credo" from Verdi's *Otello*. I took an immediate liking to him. Ever since I had been paid quarters to stand up and cheer at the Budapest State Opera House, I couldn't resist a good opera singer.

George was in need of an interpreter and tour guide, and I volunteered to show him around. But as he wasn't interested in gardens, museums, or fairy tale castles, that evening I took him out to one of the nightclubs on the edge of town. Within seconds George spotted a pair of pretty young blonds sitting alone at a table in the back of the room. "Bobby," he said to me, "let them know who I am."

I told the two women all about George's upcoming premiere in Vienna, but they were as skeptical as I had been at first. So I headed up to the orchestra leader and promised him a nice tip if his musicians could play a little Verdi. They were happy to oblige. George stood up and brought down the house. The two young blonds were overcome with emotion, starstruck. And our evening was a huge success.

A few nights later, encouraged by our good fortune, George and I headed out to another spot. Again he zeroed in on a couple of single ladies, and I headed up to the orchestra leader to get them to play Verdi. But just as George puffed up his chest and began to sing, he glanced at me and stopped. He pointed with his eyes toward a table in the back. I looked and saw why he had cut off his solo—the very same two pretty young blonds from his opening night performance were also in attendance. Tonight, however, they didn't appear to be loving the performance. George and I beat a tactical retreat.

Back on the street, walking briskly, George said that this town was too small for him. He suggested we make a getaway; one thing led to another, and we ended up in Venice. We checked into the first cheap hotel we came across, our stay lasting a little over an hour—just enough time for George to have a bath. It turned out that the hotel had a policy against opera singers, and George's rendition in the bathtub of an aria from *I due Foscari* got us a visit from the owner. He said his guests were complaining. George, wrapped in a towel and dripping on the floor, protested that those idiot Fascist guests ought to sit back and enjoy the free entertainment. We got out of there before the police arrived.

Our stay in the next cheap hotel lasted close to three hours. After I had a chance to bathe, we went out for a long dinner accompanied by several bottles of a nice local wine. Returning to the hotel, George spotted a couple of buxom, smiling young ladies hanging out the window, and he shouted out: "Who are the two whores in our hotel?"

They were the owner's daughters.

At the Lido, we found a cafe overlooking the ocean and took a table, intending to order coffee, as that was about all we could afford. But the service was a little slow for George's taste, and when the waiter finally arrived, George asked him, "Do you know who I am?" The waiter said no, he had no idea who George was, so George showed him who he was. He stood up, unzipped his pants, and slapped down on the table the organ that he considered, after his voice, to be his second greatest asset. We didn't get our coffee.

You couldn't get more American than George—big and brash and full of himself. The Italians didn't know what to make of him, and neither did I. But I loved the guy. On a continent long repressed by Fascists, Communists, Royalists, and militarists, George London was a free man. A free man without a penny in his pocket. All we had left were our return tickets to Salzburg, so that's where we went. He went on to Vienna, and the next time I saw him—our time in Venice the beginning of a lifelong friendship—was in *Don Giovanni* at the Metropolitan in New York.

———

The joke around Budapest was, how do you make a Hungarian omelet? First, steal six eggs. . . .

Whenever someone was passing through Salzburg that the ISB wanted to photograph, I would get the call. The reason was, the ISB knew I'd *get* the shot. They knew I'd make the omelet.

I wandered through the streets with the expatriate expressionist painter Oskar Kokoschka, snapping photos of him sizing up his next cityscape. And the ISB got its portrait of the artist as a free man—run off by the Nazis, condemned by the Commies, but now back with his paintbrush in the land of his birth, breathing new life into Austrian culture.

I schussed down the slopes of Bad Gastein with Douglas Fairbanks Jr., capturing the Hollywood star and war hero at his debonair best. I wanted more than a snapshot. I wanted a story. After a run down the mountain, he, a couple of his friends, and I—skis in hand—stopped in a small watering hole for a few glasses of wine. As we left, I turned, Rolleiflex ready, and shouted "*en garde,*" coming away with a shot of the legendary swordsman fencing with skis.

I tooled around the town of Gmund with Ferry Porsche, son of the company's founder Ferdinand, then in a French prison, in a wooden box on wheels—the wooden prototype of the Porsche 356, the first car to carry the Porsche name. The ISB had the picture it was after, demonstrating that Austria was open for business again.

Tales of Hoffman was a column in the *Hollywood Reporter* written by Irving Hoffman, a close friend of Walter Winchell and J. Edgar Hoover, and a man on the payroll of every studio in Hollywood. I have no clue what he was doing in Salzburg, but there he was, this large, loose-limbed, physically imposing, fast-talking, bespectacled New York nighthawk . . . and there I was, assigned to show the press agent around.

Yoichi told me to give Hoffman the grand tour of the Eagle's Nest—Hitler's mountain headquarters at Obersalzberg. But Hoffman had no interest in the Eagle's Nest. He pointed at his thick glasses and said he wouldn't be able to see a thing anyway. "Just bring me some postcards of the place and meet me for dinner."

Hoffman was more interested in sampling the local flavors—Salzburg's respectable restaurants and not-so-respectable women. An hour after dropping him at his hotel, he met me at a restaurant I had recommended. He made his entrance with a stunning young woman, half his age, hanging on his arm. Walking over to the table, he leaned in close to me and, with a perfectly straight face, said: "So, tell me something, Bob, is she pretty?"

Thanks to men like George London, Douglas Fairbanks, and Irving Hoffman, I was getting an idea of what it was like to live in America. But it was a woman who took that idea and made it an obsession.

Marilyn Thompson's father, though living in California, had connections in the US State Department. As a college graduation gift, he had sent his daughter off to Europe and had used those connections to ensure that she would have local guides along the way. In Salzburg the job fell to me.

Marilyn was a sharp, well-educated, attractive young woman taking a tour of the Old World—as many sharp, well-educated, attractive young American women tended to do in those days. She fell for me, and I fell for her, and for the week before she moved on to the next stop on her itinerary, we lived a fairy tale in this fairy tale town.

Marilyn wasn't like any other girl I'd ever known.

For one thing, she was the daughter of a bona fide American capitalist, originally from Chicago, a self-made American who rose from piano player to businessman. I wanted to meet him. I wanted to remake myself in the same way he had. But he was five thousand miles away, and my fairy tale with his daughter was rapidly coming to an end—and there was no happily ever after.

There was nothing I could do but say "so long," kissing Marilyn goodbye in the cold Alpine air on the train platform. I could barely feel her lips, my face and heart growing numb. A few days earlier, I had received a postcard from Budapest—my mother's husband informing me that she had died. Watching Marilyn climb onto the train car, bound for Florence, Copenhagen, Barcelona, or wherever, I thought about all of them—Marilyn, Klâri, my mother—and thought that's what women do. They leave. Marilyn waved good-bye through the glass.

———

Sy Bourgin was a man who wore many hats and had his hand in many games—moving fluidly and seamlessly from the corner offices of the media in New York to the corridors of power in Washington to the hall of mirrors that was Vienna. Whether sending his reports to *Stars and Stripes*, *Time* magazine, CBS radio, or the CIA, Sy had one calling: the promotion and advancement of the American century. He was also my ticket to America. If anyone could get me my damned papers, it was Sy.

In January 1950 Sy came to me with an assignment and a proposal. On the 16th of that January, Gustav Krupp von Bohlen und Halbach, bedridden and senile, took his last breath of American-occupied Austrian air, dying peacefully in the company of his wife at Blühnbach Castle near Salzburg. During the war Krupp's company, Friedrich Krupp AG, had worked tens of thousands of slave laborers to death, trading blood for steel and steel for money. The Krupps built the tanks and artillery that put the Third Reich in Paris and then on the threshold of Moscow—and Gustav and his family made out like bandits. Now the indicted war criminal—saved from Nuremberg by his porous mental condition—lay dead in Salzburg. Fittingly enough, his body was headed for the ovens.

The Allied Control Commission wanted to get out the news of Krupp's death, but they didn't want to make a big deal out of it. They invited a few journalists, military men, and important civilians to witness his cremation, spelling out the conditions, one of which was: no pictures.

The Allies were well aware that the Nazis fed off the power of imagery, and as small a risk as it was, they were not going to take a chance that the Fourth Reich would rise from the ashes of Krupp's fiery end. Sy Bourgin disagreed. History is history, and he believed it was our duty to record Krupp's passage into the inferno on film. His editors at *Life* agreed—and Sy knew I was the man for the job. He pulled a few strings and got me onto the list of those who would be viewing the cremation. It was January. It was cold, and I wore a heavy coat—the perfect hiding place for the Rolleiflex hanging around my neck.

The assembled guests and witnesses lined up to walk past a solid metal door with a small opening that slid open, through which, one by one, we were allowed to catch a glimpse of a casket sliding into the flames. As my turn came, I saw that three-quarters of the casket had already been consigned to the fire, the remainder casting a dark shadow—a black moon eclipsing the conflagration about to consume it. I unbuttoned my coat, put my camera to the opening, and snapped the shot. No one seemed to notice or care. I got the picture. The photo of the casket along with the Nazi dream of world domination going up in flames appeared in the February 6, 1950, issue of *Life* magazine. Staring out from the cover of that issue, bathed in a soft glow, was Eva Gabor, one more Hungarian working her magic on an American crowd.

Europe lay on the operating table, cut in half, her heart removed, her brains bashed in, her guts all over the place. The two sides were divided by barbed wire, land mines, and guard towers with machine guns. But the divide was not impenetrable. There was nothing a machine gun or barbed-wire fence could do to stop a radio wave from spilling over the Iron Curtain.

That spring President Truman had announced a "great campaign of truth" to fight the great lie that was Communism. The money for Radio Free Europe came from card-carrying capitalists like Henry Ford II and millions of hardworking Americans who sent in their pennies to fight the Soviet menace. Or so the story went. The real money came from the CIA, soon to be led by the Crusade for Freedom's Allen Dulles. In August 1950, to the sound of four peals of the Freedom Bell, Radio Free Europe made its first broadcast to Hungary. Answering an invitation from Sy Bourgin, I joined in. The prospect of being present at—and a participant in—the creation of free new Hungary was too great to resist.

Between the ISB, my newspaper and magazine work, and now Radio Free Europe, I could afford to move up in the world, moving into a nice hotel room near the river. Finally a decent place with actual stairs to bring my girlfriends. Life was good. I settled in and got to work. And there was lots of work to do. And lots of secrecy to go along with it.

It was at Radio Free Europe that I met John L. Carver—a short, soft-spoken, quick-witted man who didn't actually exist. We became fast friends. How do you make friends with a person who isn't there? Smoke and mirrors. In Salzburg half of us were not who we said we were, and the rest of us were on our way to becoming someone else. We were ghosts passing through that world and bound for another. The spook calling himself John L. Carver was actually Ladislas Faragó. Hungarian like me, Laci had gotten out of Europe back in the '30s, making his way to New York and then down to Washington. As much as he wanted to fight the Germans, as a Hungarian citizen he was considered an enemy national and so was barred from enlisting in the armed forces. Instead he signed up as a civilian to work for US Naval Intelligence. By the end of the war, Laci was writing propaganda for the Navy's highest-ranking officer, Admiral Nimitz—messages that were broadcast from American ships by radio. He had a remarkable gift for psychological warfare—a phrase that he had coined.

After the war Radio Free Europe recruited him to work his magic on a Hungarian audience. The problem was, RFE did not want to be associated with spooks and spies like Laci, so they created the John L. Carver character as cover. But Laci had too many enemies inside RFE, and shortly after we met, he was sent back to the States. Laci did all right by himself, ultimately penning the books that the movies *Patton* and *Tora! Tora! Tora!* were based on.

I didn't have a good feeling about Radio Free Europe, but I wouldn't find out just how rotten certain elements of it were until I got out of Salzburg and out of Europe. I was living inside a hall of mirrors and had a hard time recognizing the true nature of things. The only thing I knew for sure was that I was ready to do anything to help Hungary get out from under the Communist regime. And RFE was the only vehicle I had.

My partner in that mission was an old friend from Sárospatak, Louis Szathmary, a bear of a man with a growl as great as his laugh. Szathmary's defining trait was his appetite. He'd cook us a meal, clean his plate, head back to the stove, and start all over again. His culinary talents were honed as a cook in the Hungarian army. Later, when Louis came to America, he brought his passion for food with him, opening Chicago's popular restaurant The Bakery. He also developed the first frozen dinners for Stouffer's and designed meals for nuclear submarine crews and astronauts.

Louis and I had an early-morning radio program that was broadcast back into Hungary. It was called *Köszönt a Szabadsag*. For those of you not up on your Hungarian—"Freedom Greets You." Our mission was to inspire popular movements inside Hungary that might one day serve as a nucleus for liberation—a mission that was a disaster waiting to happen. Six years later, in 1956, the whole thing blew up in Hungary's face. But Louis and I were still idealists. We thought we could change the world, and we forged ahead.

The primary content of our programming came from those Hungarians who had escaped across the border into Austria. We interviewed them and wrote up their narratives, embellishing where we saw fit. Sometimes to really get at the truth, you have to create character and conflict, you have to build mystery and drama that leads to a climax and revelation. In other words, tell a story.

Just *telling* stories wasn't enough, though. Louis and I wanted to be a part of the story—get in on the action. Talking about getting people out was one thing. Driving down to the border with wire cutters, standing within a few feet of Hungary, and actually helping people get out was another. I was determined to do it. I've covered thousands of news stories, produced hundreds of movies in my life, and I've never done it from behind a desk. The only way I know how to do things is on location. Getting people out of Hungary was no different, even if it meant running headfirst into the Iron Curtain.

I talked to Sy. As Henry Luce's correspondent in Vienna, he had open access to Budapest. He'd relay to us the names of people ready to get out, and it was up to Louis and me to contact and work out the details of the escape with our friends inside Hungary—a kind of underground railroad of farmhouses and truckers who ran things on their side of the Curtain. The post offices were lousy with secret police, so we couldn't communicate by letter. The safest way to make contact was by telephone.

Every few weeks Sy would give us a name, and Louis and I, borrowing a Radio Free Europe car, would grab our wire cutters, make the four-hour drive across Austria to the Hungarian border, and increase the population of the free world by one. If we couldn't bring freedom to Hungary, we'd do the next best thing: empty the place out, one unhappy Hungarian at a time.

One day in December 1950, in the early morning darkness, Louis and I delivered another package through the fence—this time a small woman wrapped in coats and cloaks and blankets to protect her against the cold. When we got into the car and the lady shed her wrappings, we realized that the name Sy had given us was an alias. For one of the few times in my life, I was rendered speechless.

On the seat beside me sat Katalin Karády. To give you an idea of what that meant, imagine you have just jumped into a river and rescued from drowning a shivering Julia Roberts or Angelina Jolie, and now, so close you can hear her breathing, she's telling you how eternally grateful she is and how she owes you her life and you don't know what else she's saying because you're too starstruck and dumbfounded to hear anything at all. Louis, who had the misfortune to be driving that day, kept looking back over his shoulder. We were lucky he didn't drive us all—including one of Hungary's most gifted, beautiful, and beloved movie stars—into a ditch.

I love to tell stories, but I also know that sometimes you have to shut up and listen. For two days we turned our microphone and our radio program over to Katalin Karády—and for two days Louis and I sat mesmerized. She spoke, sharing her memories, and it was as if all of Hungary—all of the joy and pain and love and hate and blood and tears and rage it engendered—poured out of her and flooded over us.

Katalin didn't talk about her great movies or great career. She talked about how it came to an end. About how, in 1944, she had been arrested by the Nazis as an alleged Allied spy. She tried to make a joke out of it, telling them that they must have mixed her up with Mata Hari, whom she had played in the movies. But it wasn't a joke. The Nazis jailed her for three months, torturing and nearly beating her to death, her saving grace being her lover—the head of the Hungarian secret service.

One of the first things Katalin did following her release was go to one of the detention centers where Jews were being sorted out for transport to concentration camps. She sweet-talked one of the guards into letting her take several children to have breakfast but never brought them back, hiding them in one of her apartments for the duration of the war. Then when the war was over, the Communist regime—frightened by her popularity—banned all of her films and barred her from appearing in theater. Now here she was, deprived of her work and her country—of everything she loved—speaking for the last time to the audience that loved her.

Her last words broadcast back to her homeland were "Good-bye, Hungary, may God save you . . . because no one else will." With that Hungary's greatest actress and femme fatale faded away into the world. Twenty years later, Katalin Karády was selling hats in a small shop on Madison Avenue in New York.

Louie and I, however, weren't quite ready to say farewell to arms. We put together one of the most daring—and most stupid—ideas ever conceived. But then we were all stupid then. Our stupidity was what kept us from going nuts. If we'd been smart, we all would have put guns to our heads and blown our brains out.

I was settling into Salzburg. The work was good, the air was fresh, the skiing fast. I had moved into an apartment recently with another displaced person, a pretty young girl named René, fooling myself into thinking that I could build a comfortable little nest for myself. René and I were both displaced—in the same boat—so why not drift along together?

The plan Louis and I came up with was going to take direct action into Hungary. Our spymasters at Radio Free Europe, maintaining deniability, tacitly approved our plan, and so, on the afternoon of January 2, Louis and I pulled away from the RFE offices in a small truck we had finagled for the operation from the ISB. In the back of the truck were two large barrels of red powder—the chemical used to fill the flares that parachutists fire off to signal their distress and mark their location—which an English journalist who did most of his reporting to the MI6 branch of British intelligence spirited up for us.

Two of our friends were going to meet us at the border, and just after nightfall we reached the rendezvous point—a deserted, thickly forested spot miles from any town or city. A foot of snow on the ground, we took a calculated risk that any warm-blooded Hungarian border guard, given a choice between wandering these woods in the dead of night in the dead of winter or sitting by a crackling fire in his barracks warming his feet, would choose the fire and the warm feet.

We hid the truck in a stand of trees and moved toward the border. Ten or so yards from the fence, Louis and I got down on our bellies in the snow, and I made a signal toward the other side with my flashlight. Nothing. Two minutes later, still nothing. After twenty minutes we considered revising our plan—and getting the hell out of there. Louie and I were whispering back and forth, paralyzed by indecision, arguing about nothing, when we heard footsteps in the snow and saw flashlights moving in the darkness. Not on the Hungarian side, but coming up behind us. We didn't move.

We could see that there were two of them but couldn't make out whether or not they had uniforms on. It didn't matter—we had to assume the worst. And it was too late to make a run for it. Louis and I nodded at each other and waited until they were nearly on top of us. We leaped up out of the underbrush and tackled them. We had the advantage of surprise, and I caught my man in a chokehold. Only then did I realize that we were rolling around in the snow with our two Hungarian pals. They had gotten here early, saw that the coast was clear, and cut through the fence to meet us. Then promptly got lost in the forest.

We had to get moving. The success of the plan rested on Louis and I getting into Hungary, making our play, and getting back to Salzburg for our morning radio show. The four of us hauled the two barrels of red powder out of the truck, through the opening in the fence, and across the border, my first time in Hungary in four years. I had no time to savor the moment.

We moved quickly, loading the two barrels onto another truck brought here by our friends, and drove into the darkness. An hour on the back roads brought us to the banks of the Danube, some twenty miles upstream from Budapest. A flat boat was waiting for us. The four of us managed to lift the barrels onto the raft without any of us falling in, which was a victory in itself. Fortunately the sky was clear and the moon was out, meaning we were not completely blind as we pushed out into the middle of this frigid River Styx, bearing what we thought was a vital message for the lost souls downriver.

We pried the two barrels open, overturned them, and dumped the red powder into the water. The idea, if you want to call it that, was to hightail it back to our Salzburg radio studio and deliver our early morning message: "Wake up, Hungary! The Danube runs red with the blood of Communists. Wake up and rise up!" Now all we had to do was get back to Salzburg and onto the radio before the red water passed through Budapest just after dawn. We scrambled back up into the truck and headed for Austria.

The clear sky and bright moon, our friend on the river, was now our enemy. But Louis and I, kings of the world, walked out of the woods with our heads held high and made our way toward the opening in the fence. It was then that our arrogance and stupidity caught up with us. We were ordered not to take another step.

The one Hungarian who had chosen not to warm his feet at the fire stood now at the tree line, some ten yards away, pointing his rifle at us.

We raised our hands, and my heart nearly stopped. I was sure I was dead. I would be buried in Hungary after all. The only question was, would the killing be quick and to the point—a couple of bullets to the belly, my life spilling out on the snow—or long and pointless, fifty years in some dungeon, a little bit of life bleeding out of me every day?

The question went unanswered. Our two Hungarian friends, not so cocksure as we were, had circled around to watch our backs and jumped the border guard from behind. Before I knew what I was doing, I was on top of him, getting my forearm around the man's throat. I squeezed with all my strength until he stopped resisting. But the moment I relaxed my hold, he started talking, calling us enemies of the people, traitors to our country, imperialist slaves—and now it was his arrogance that caught up with him.

As I look back, I know that the two of us—the young guard and I—had everything in common. We had simply gotten caught up on opposite sides of someone else's war, blinded by our pent-up anger and passion. His spouting off made us mad, and I shut him up again. We took off his clothes and threw them with his rifle into the woods, then gagged him and tied him to a tree. He wasn't dead when we left him, but the chances of him surviving the winter night were slight. We showed him no mercy because we had none to show.

The two Hungarians who had saved *our* lives vanished into the woods, and Louis and I ran like frightened deer back into Austria.

Perhaps in the end we had gotten away with murder after all. Or we were simply soldiers, and the young man who wouldn't shut up was just another casualty of war. Either way, the prank with the red powder had turned to blood on my hands.

It occurred to me, not right at that instant but with a growing sense of discomfort—like a cancer growing in my gut—that if the only way to save something is to kill it, then maybe it's time to stop trying to save it. At the very least it was not a job for me. We never made the broadcast back to Budapest that morning about their river running red with blood. We let the red water drift away into oblivion.

Later that afternoon, when I finally made it back to my little Salzburg apartment, I discovered that René had thrown all my things out the window into the street. I thought about trying to explain to her where I had been but realized that there was no point. René and I were strangers keeping each other warm in a cold Austrian winter. In the end, we were all so used to telling lies that there was no percentage in telling the truth. None of us knew the difference. Certainly not René. She figured I had cheated on her, and I figured I had to find a new place to live.

I chose America.

René moved on as well, ending up in South America—Santiago, Chile. There she made friends with a band of rich expatriate Germans living in hillside villas, and she wrote me letters inviting me to join her. She described the parties she gave, serving oysters and champagne to the ex-Nazis around their swimming pools. I was not tempted. My heart was set on North America, the United States. Any country that could invent fingernail clippers and Ginger Rogers dancing around bedposts had my number.

In the beginning of June, Sy Bourgin brought me the good news. The Holy Grail. My papers. He had my visa in his hands, and I could've kissed him. Maybe I did. He told me that my ship would set sail on June 6 from Hamburg, bound for New York. I had three days to get my things in order. It took me three hours. I didn't pack a suitcase, just threw a couple changes of clothes into a paper bag, grabbed my camera, and lit out.

But after all I'd done, all I'd been through, I almost didn't make it out of Europe. Why? Because for the life of me, I couldn't take a pee.

Though the Americans had beaten back the Nazis and were in a life-and-death staring contest with the Soviets, there were two things they feared more than either: TB and VD. Before you could board the ship, you had to get your chest X-rayed and you had to have your urine tested. The X-ray was easy, confirming that my lungs were clear and that I had a heart. But handed a cup and sent to the toilet, I couldn't drip a drop. I was too anxious and excited. The US Army nurse, repressing her laughter, took pity on me. She sent me off to a nearby beer garden, where I gulped down three mugs and hurried back to the clinic. I filled my cup to the brim. It was a great relief.

On the morning of June 6, 1951, a warm, overcast day—the sky a dull, dishwater gray—the US Army Transport *General S. D. Sturgis* set sail from Bremerhaven, moving up the River Weser bearing the combined weight and hopes of some 1,350 displaced persons. Ginger Rogers, here I come.

I can say from firsthand experience that the most tedious leg of any odyssey is the part that takes place on a ship. And so it went, an endless ocean of monotony and canned Spam, until, ten days into our journey, at three in the morning, on Saturday, June 16, 1951, I saw it. We all saw it. All 1,350 of us rising like the dead from our graves in the ship's bowels and scrambling to one side of the deck—the landlubber in me fearing that the big boat would capsize. It was a sight I will never forget.

A flicker of light on the western horizon. Then more lights, a skyline emerging out on the edge of the world—a million points of light, American light, pricking holes in the darkness.

I thought my heart was going to burst out of my chest. There it was: King Kong's perch, the Empire State Building rising above it all.

I thought about what—and who—we had all left behind. Mothers and fathers, husbands and wives, friends and lovers, brothers and sisters. And children too—some who might have been but would never be. I thought about the choices I had made. In an underground prison cell. In a labor camp in the mountains of Poland. On a park bench in a bombed-out city. Under a single hot lamp around a kitchen table. On the border between two countries—and on the borderline between murder and self-defense. Acts of passion, anger, fear, uncertainty, and survival.

That was all behind me now. Ahead of me was New York—fast cars, fast women, fast money, and fingernail clippers. Finally, my chance to join the circus. At twenty-seven I was about to be reborn. Homeless and alone, unencumbered by love or war, I could be whoever I wanted to be. I could reinvent myself in the shadow of the New York City skyline.

CHAPTER FIVE

Free at Last! (But No Free Lunch)

A trio of horn-tooting tugboats welcomed us to America, pulling along-side the *General S. D. Sturgis* and guiding her up the Hudson River into the docks on the west side of Manhattan. The sun was rising but had not yet scaled the skyline, the ship coming to rest in the long shadow of the city. We could see warehouses and office buildings, hear cars and trucks speeding by, smell grease frying in dockside diners and coffee shops—New York so close we could taste it. Our ten-day voyage was finally over. But our wait wasn't.

A team of public health officials and Immigration and Naturalization Service agents boarded the ship and set up a series of tables. Like well-behaved schoolchildren taught to defer to authority, we formed a series of lines, all 1,350 of us, and waited, inching patiently forward without complaint—because we had none. Every minute we stood in line brought us a minute closer to the tables—our gateway to America.

When my turn finally came, after a good three hours standing in line, I stepped up to the table with my packet of documents. Barely look-ing up at me, the agent shuffled through my papers. Where, he wanted to know, was my chest X-ray? How the hell was I supposed to know? Apparently, somewhere between Hamburg and here, the damn thing had vanished into thin air, and only now was I finding out. I expressed my frustration and annoyance; all the agent could do was shrug and shake his head. Manhattan—the Promised Land—towered over me, a stone's throw away, but I was being tossed back into the sea to another island and another purgatory.

The ferry ride from the ship to Ellis Island was a voyage of the damned—babies crying, mothers moaning, old men and women muttering and worn down. Angry young men either sat and stewed or paced back and forth like caged lions. A few had been accused of forgery. Others carried papers that contained incomplete or inaccurate information—someone back in Europe neglecting to dot the i's and cross the t's. And some had crucial documents go missing.

Ellis Island was no longer America's front door, the first step to citizenship for thousands of immigrants a day, as it had been thirty years before. Now the only foreigners passing through Ellis Island were those heading the other way—deemed too sick, poor, criminal, or crazy to walk America's streets or plow its soil. By the end of World War II, the island had become a ghost of its former self, the facility's buildings in disrepair, a trickle of misfits wandering the grim, gray halls awaiting deportation. Then, a year before my arrival, the place took on a new life. Funding came through for additional staff, plumbing repairs, and a new coat of grim, gray paint. The Internal Security Act of 1950 saw to that.

The mass of displaced persons descending on America following the war had all the appearances of an invasion and sent a shiver of paranoia through the body politic that ran straight up to and through the US Congress. Their response was the Internal Security Act of 1950, banning entry to any alien who at any time had been affiliated with any section, branch, or subdivision of any totalitarian party.

The act cast a wide and often arbitrary net, and an INS agent who did not like the look in someone's eye could pack that certain someone off—along with his wife, babies, and grandmother—for further questioning, investigation, and background checks. As a result the dormitories at Ellis Island were filled to capacity. But not just with potential subversives and firebrands, suspected Fascists and Communists. There were also idiots like me, who had traveled halfway around the world only to misplace my chest X-ray.

I had fallen into a black hole of confusion and despair, of long, inexplicable lines of Yeshiva students, Italian laborers, and Polish intellectuals filled with anxiety, anger, and exasperation. Regardless of their assurances, the island had the look, feel, and smell of a penal colony.

Monday morning, after nearly forty-eight hours of going around in circles, I decided to take the direct approach. I asked one of the guards if I could make a telephone call. He looked at me as if I had asked him for a thousand dollars. "Do you really think," he said, "that we allow spies to make phone calls?"

I tried to explain to him about my missing X-ray, but he wasn't interested. He said that they didn't waste their time here with X-rays. Out of frustration I told the guard I wanted to speak to his boss, and I stalked off, figuring that would be the end of it. I was going to rot on this island, caught in some kind of Kafkaesque nightmare, within a few football fields of the Statue of Liberty. Needless to say I was shocked when, fifteen minutes later, the guard came looking for me. His supervisor would see me now. It was my first lesson in the American way of life: Never take no for an answer.

Down the hall from the dormitories, adjacent to the dining area, were several rooms that had been set aside for interviews. It was to one of these rooms that the guard brought me. His supervisor, in a shirt and tie with the sleeves rolled up, sat at the table smoking a cigarette. He nodded at the guard, who left, closing the door behind him. He then nodded at me to sit down. The supervisor studied me for a moment through the smoke and asked what I wanted to see him about. I told him I thought a mistake had been made in my case. He shrugged with a kind of half-smile, as if to say, yes, that's entirely possible, mistakes are made here all the time. I started to tell him about my X-ray, but he put up his hand and closed his eyes. He didn't want to hear it either. It was only ten in the morning, but apparently it had already been a long day for him. He opened his eyes and asked me if I knew what time it was.

I hesitated, puzzled by the question, and glanced down at my watch. I realized after a moment that I didn't have to answer. I slipped the watch off my wrist and pushed it to the center of the table. He picked it up, looked at it, smiled his approval, and dropped it into his pants pocket. Standing up, he called in the guard and told him to let me make all the phone calls I wanted.

A Nazi policeman, a Soviet soldier, and now an American bureaucrat. I had the distinction of having a wristwatch confiscated by all three. In each case it was a small price to pay.

After an hour with a telephone and a Manhattan phone book—a string of wrong numbers, unanswered calls, and crossed lines—I finally reached someone with a sympathetic ear: the wife of Carlos Israels. I had met Carlos at the Press Club in Vienna. He was an accomplished writer and a powerful advocate of displaced Europeans—and thus an expert on the hoops one had to jump through to get into America. Even better, Carlos was also a lawyer—a lawyer and a fixer who had friends in Washington—and his wife was kind enough to give me the number of his law firm. I don't know whom Carlos called, but by lunchtime I was on a ferry to Manhattan.

Still in quarantine until my heart and lungs got the health department's seal of approval, I was met on the ferry dock by an INS agent and an ambulance driver. The ambulance, a bread truck with lights and sirens, had no windows in back, my only sense of the city coming from the honking of horns and the stops and starts of cross-town traffic.

Our destination looked to me like another prison: a block-long brick building the color of dried blood sitting between First Avenue and the East River—Bellevue Hospital.

Over the next few years, I would crawl into a box of dynamite, climb a glacier, and dangle from a helicopter in search of a good picture. But no snapshot was more valuable to me—or more elusive—than the one of my chest cavity taken that Monday afternoon in the emergency room of Bellevue by a red-eyed, sleep-deprived medical student. There, amidst the open wounds and broken limbs, hacking coughs and cries of babies—in the one hospital in New York that had never refused a patient—I had at last acquired my ticket out and my ticket in to America: a clean bill of health.

I was transported back to Ellis Island for a quick final processing and the next day boarded the first ferry to Manhattan, a free man. No INS agents or ambulance drivers were waiting for me on the other side. In fact there was no one waiting for me at all. It was just New York City and me, and I was both scared to death and thrilled to death all at once. For half my young life, this was the moment I had waited for. Now what?

I started walking.

Aside from the X-ray, there was one other piece of evidence without which I might not have made my case for coming to America: a letter from Radio Free Europe. It stated, first, that upon arrival I would be given a job in their New York office; and, second, that they owed me the sum of two thousand dollars for work I had already done in Salzburg. As valuable as the letter was, it was not going to put food in my stomach this morning, and I was hungry. As for the little bit of cash I had had back in Salzburg, I had spent most of it during my last few days there and then on my train ticket to Hamburg. Now all I had in my pocket were a few crumpled dollar bills. I had several twenty-schilling Austrian bank notes in my bag, but they were worth even less here than they were in Salzburg.

On the ferry ride over, I had struck up a conversation with a member of the crew and asked him if he could recommend a cheap place to eat in Manhattan. Without hesitation he directed me to a place on Lower Broadway several blocks from the ferry dock, a Horn and Hardart automat. Between the men in business suits, the women in heels, the office workers, delivery boys, and taxi drivers, the place was jumping.

After getting change for one of my dollars from the cashier, I set about considering all the options on the menu—a chromium wall of food choices in small glass cubbies. I walked the length of the wall and back again, watching how it was done. You put your nickels in a slot, turned the knob, and grabbed your plate, the food instantly replaced by a disembodied pair of hands on the other side of the wall. It reminded me of a joke we told in Salzburg. An American GI takes his Austrian girlfriend for a drive in his convertible and parks in a nice secluded spot. He presses a button and the radio goes on. He presses another button and the windows go down. A third button and the top goes down. A gust of wind catches the hem of the girl's dress and it flies up over her hips. "You Americans don't do anything by hand, do you?" she says.

I settled finally on a pastrami sandwich, a cup of coffee, and a slice of good old American apple pie with a wedge of cheddar cheese. A taste of democracy—no match for my mom's cold sour cherry soup, but as my first meal on American soil (not counting the dietary limbo of the Ellis

Island cafeteria), I had no complaints. I ate slowly and with great pleasure—and to my delight, I still had most of my nickels left.

My stomach full, I turned to the matter of finding shelter. I headed up Broadway. When Ladislas Faragó—Laci—heard that I was coming to America, he had sent me a letter in Salzburg telling me to look him up at the Roger Williams Hotel at 28 East 31st Street. I had tried calling him, without any luck, from Ellis Island before reaching Carlos Israels, but figured he was still my best bet for finding a place to stay in the city.

Laci was still associated in some dark, mysterious way with Radio Free Europe, which was headquartered at the Empire State Building on 34th Street, a few blocks from the Roger Williams. I figured all I had to do was make my way toward the Empire State Building and I'd find his hotel. Which I did. Unfortunately, I did not find *him*. He did in fact have a room at the Roger Williams, but the staff hadn't seen him for days and had no idea where he might be. In other words, I was on my own. I asked to speak to the manager. I had nothing to lose.

I told him my story. The manager shook his head sympathetically when I came to that part—he knew all about Faragó—and then I made my pitch. A room at the hotel was $12.50. I had five dollars left in my pocket. I promised him I was good for the $7.50 if he'd give me a room for the night. He shrugged and said what the hell, I had a trustworthy face. He even insisted that I hold on to the five dollars so I could get something to eat. My first night in America, and already I was in debt. But I felt like the luckiest man alive. Set up in a so-called cheap hotel, I had a bathroom and a kitchenette, and all the gadgets worked—luxury accommodations compared to what I was used to.

The next morning, I woke up raring to go. King Kong, Ginger Rogers, all that jazz—New York. I was ready to go out on the town, dive in headfirst, and see how deep I could go. Twenty-four hours later I landed on the front page of the *New York Post*.

My day started with a few more phone calls. I had shown Irving Hoffman around Salzburg, and he was more than happy to return the favor here in

New York. "Bobby," he said, "let me take you to dinner tonight," and he told me to come by Toots Shor's on 51st Street at nine.

I showed up at the restaurant door at 8:59 on the dot and ran into a brick wall—the doorman, a gorilla with cauliflower ears and an ill-fitting suit. He looked me over, shook his head, and put his hand on my chest. This was a respectable place, he said, and you have to wear a jacket and tie to get in. I didn't like the hand on my chest, so I knocked it off. I also didn't like the business with the jacket and tie, and, foolishly, a hothead like my father, tried to push my way past the doorman. Push literally came to shove, and the next thing I know the two of us are rolling around on the sidewalk, flashbulbs are popping, and Hoffman comes out of the restaurant with Toots Shor himself—a mountain of a man, who someone once said was half stomach, half man—to pull us apart and stand us on our feet.

The cameras still clicking, Toots made me shake hands with the doorman, then put his arm around my shoulder and gave me a kiss on the cheek. The whole thing was a big misunderstanding.

"Come into my heavenly hashienda," he said, pushing open the door, "the best joint in New York, and if you don't know it already, New York is America."

Toots led me past the great circular bar surrounded by red upholstered stools—he called it his roulette wheel—and into the dining room with its vaulted ceilings. Hoffman, a big smile on his face, followed along behind. It struck me how cold the restaurant was, the whole place air-conditioned. Toots brought us to our table and went off to bear hug someone else. Irving introduced me to our dinner companion, his pal, columnist Earl Wilson.

"Welcome to America, kid," Wilson said to me, standing up to shake my hand. Then he turned to Hoffman and asked, "How'd he do?"

"Bobby's a natural," Irving said, slapping me on the back. "He was a smash."

It turned out that the two of them had cooked the whole thing up, paying the doorman to push me around until I pushed back. The fight was a publicity stunt, and good thing for me that's all it was. I learned that the doorman was an ex-boxer, and in a real fight he could have laid me out with one punch. The photos and headline in the next day's *Post* said it all: "Toots Shor Takes Hungarian Freedom Fighter Under Wing."

Welcome to America, kid.

The deception didn't bother me a bit. There was something very New York about the gimmickry—the showmanship, invention, and stretching of the truth. It was my initiation, part of my rite of passage into this new world. The next few nights Wilson and Hoffman were the ones who took me under their wing—a couple of ringmasters giving me a peek inside the circus tent.

There was no one in the world better at public relations than Irving Hoffman. He was an artist. This was the man who had turned one client, an obscure Coney Island hot dog stand called Nathan's, into a must-see New York tourist attraction. The Prince of Wales had been in town, and Hoffman somehow convinced him to stop by and try a Nathan's hot dog. He snapped a photo, which the wire services picked up, sending a shot of the royal snack around the world.

Hoffman never stopped cajoling, convincing, and closing deals. He took me one evening to meet his father, a feeble old guy living alone in an apartment on the Upper West Side. Determined to make the old man happy, he had arranged for three beautiful young actresses to meet us there. I don't know what Hoffman told them or promised them, but we went up to the apartment, he handed his father a Polaroid camera, and the girls promptly took off their clothes to pose for him.

Most nights, we'd meet for dinner at Toots Shor's or The Stork Club. Irving was kind enough to provide me with a jacket and tie until I came up with my own—and the evening would start out with a walk through the dining room and a round of introductions. I shook hands with the likes of Joe DiMaggio, Jackie Gleason, and Frank Costello, whoever happened to be in the house that night—the young Hungarian freedom fighter in the court of American kings. I was savvy enough to know that I was a novelty act. Though standing in the presence of the great players of the American dream—whether it be baseball star or mobster—I was not yet a part of it. Whatever I had done back in Eastern Europe was part of a previous life. I had to build a new one here.

Hoffman and Wilson were always in a rush to get to the next night-club, next show, next bar—on the move until three or four in the morning.

I wanted to slow down and take in the sights and lights. I was afraid that I was missing something.

What that was becomes clear when I look back at the first letter I wrote from New York to Sy Bourgin in Vienna. I told him about one of those nights out:

> *A TV director came over and started talking about the Hungarian deportation, not knowing a thing about it. After two sentences I gave up and changed the subject. Then several sexy dames came to the table, and my first impression is that American food and women look better than the European but taste a hell of a lot worse. I couldn't tell you where I've been. Going around with Hoffman and Wilson is like being a four-year-old child dragged by his mother through a crowd.*

What I was missing was a sense of belonging. In the heart of Manhattan, I was still a displaced person with one foot—and a big piece of my heart—back in Hungary.

One night Wilson and Hoffman took me to a play at the Royale Theater on 45th Street—*Darkness at Noon* starring Claude Rains. Afterward, looking for a quote, Earl asked me what I thought of it. "It was a kid-glove jail on stage," I told him. "They don't know how to do torture." It was a magnificent play, and Claude Rains gave a remarkable performance, but all I saw was its failure to do my memories justice. Only a few days in this country and already reality was setting in. Being a "Hungarian freedom fighter" was a nice publicity stunt, but it wasn't going to keep me company at night or pay my hotel bill.

I ended that letter to Sy with a question: *I wonder how long this "Bobby in Wonderland" story is going to last?*

I didn't have a lot of time to think about, let alone answer, the question. Toward the end of my first week in New York, sometime after eleven in the morning—following another late night of carousing with Hoffman—the phone rousted me out of a dead sleep. The hotel switchboard operator said she had a long distance call for me from California and wanted to know whether to put it through. That woke me up. "Yes," I said to the operator, sitting up straight.

Ever since our time together in Salzburg, when our tour of the city had led to a love affair, the American girl Marilyn Thompson and I had maintained a passionate weekly correspondence. We had our hearts set on making those dreams come true and getting married as soon as I set foot on American soil. I had written her from Hamburg to tell her that I was on my way, and, not having a phone number for her in San Diego, I had sent her a telegram the day before with the happy news of my arrival, telling her she could reach me at the Roger Williams Hotel.

Now Marilyn called, awakening me with the news that our wedding date was set for July 15, three and a half weeks from now. She had already picked out a best man for me, purchased my tuxedo, and picked out a lovely spot up the California coast for our honeymoon. She had put a nine-page letter in the mail for me with specific wedding instructions and had also sent out invitations to family and several hundred of her best friends. "And of course," she added, "you can invite somebody too because it is your wedding as much as it is mine."

I wasn't sure whether I should be thrilled, frightened, or booked on the next boat back to Europe. In other words I was in love, and it scared me to death. After the phone call I wrote Sy another letter, asking him yet another question: *So what am I supposed to do? I am slowly getting out of the habit of doing things my way.*

As good a friend as he was, Sy didn't have any answers for me either. I was on my own. I had a few dollars in my pocket and less than a month until I had a young American wife to take care of. I suspected that she would take exception to living in debt in a room at the Roger Williams Hotel, even if it did have hot and cold running water.

Monday, June 26, ten days after my arrival, Radio Free Europe finally came up with a thousand dollars, half of what they owed me, and I immediately set about that morning on the hard work of spending it.

I paid off my hotel bill, plus another week in advance, then went over to Macy's to buy a jacket and tie so I could return those on loan from Irving Hoffman. It was good to wear clothes that fit me for a change. What was not so good was how quickly I was running through the cash.

I decided to do what I thought every proper American did with his money—put it in a bank and save it for a rainy day. But this turned out to be another gimmick. I opened an account, deposited what was left of my thousand dollars, and the bank handed me a book of blank checks. I quickly discovered that it was as easy to write a check as it was to pay cash.

Early that evening an unexpected visitor came up to my hotel room: Ladislas Faragó. He apologized for not being here to greet me upon my arrival, said he had had important business to take care of in Washington, invited me to a meeting of the Hungarian Self-Defense Committee scheduled for later that evening, and asked me to loan him a hundred dollars.

A man who always had his ears to the ground, Ladislas had it on good authority that I had recently come into some money. With all his chubby Hungarian charm and self-confidence, Laci had a way of making you feel like he was doing you a favor borrowing money from you. I wrote him a check. A couple of hours later, sitting with Laci and half a dozen other Hungarians around a couple of tables pushed together in a small dark pub over on First Avenue, I was elected action commander of the Hungarian Self-Defense Committee. The only action required of me was to pay for the round of drinks. It was a nonsalaried position.

I needed to set myself up, find work, and put money in my pocket. America had emerged from the war as the greatest power on earth, and Manhattan was the hustling, bustling heart of it, buzzing with possibility and promise. I just had to go out and find them and seize them. In America one has the right to the pursuit of happiness, not necessarily the possession of it. You have to work at it, and I was perfectly willing to do so. I also had plenty of friends, most of whom I'd met in Austria, to help me along the way.

Irving Hoffman sent me over to the William Morris Agency, where I met with Helen Strauss, who had established the agency's literary department. She listened to my story of arrest, incarceration, torture, and escape and could hardly contain herself. She talked to me about book deals, lecture tours, television appearances, and a technical advisor position on a movie being made at Columbia Pictures. I also spoke to Manny Reiner, a personal representative of producer David Selznick, had dinner with the writer Frank Gibney, and of course, there was Ladislas, who never stopped talking about the big deals and big money the two of us were going to make. Hand over fist, he kept saying, hand over fist. I'd believe it when I saw it. He still owed me a hundred dollars.

For all the talk—all the prospects and promises—I still had no money coming in, and I was just weeks from marriage. Desperate, I turned to the *New York Times* classifieds and landed my first job in America. I went to work for a diaper service. The deal was, "Buy our diapers, get a free baby portrait." What with the baby boom, there was plenty of work, and I made my way around Manhattan, Brooklyn, and Queens taking pictures of babies in their natural habitat. I made about fifty dollars a week. It was a start.

Radio Free Europe had pledged to give me a job, but their promises to me were about as good as their promises to Hungary. Empty. Like so many other fiefdoms that had emerged out of the Cold War, it had deteriorated into a black hole, sucking the light and life out of whatever came near it. The RFE office in New York was a dark corner of Eastern European intrigue, betrayal, and backstabbing. It was a nest of vipers run by political whores—American opportunists joined at the hip with former Hungarian Nazis—and they saw me as an enemy, someone to purge from the ranks. All I wanted was the rest of the money they owed me, nothing more. I was better off taking pictures of babies for a living.

There were a couple of other matters that I had to resolve before July 15. First was the question of Erzsi, the woman I had married amid the postwar ruins of Budapest. It occurred to me now, the reality of my upcoming wedding settling in with increasing urgency, that I had never actually unmarried Erzsi. Although it was never likely to drop, I didn't want the sword of polygamy hanging over my new life. Erasing my past turned out to be easier than I had imagined. My marriage to Erzsi had never been officially entered into the city's records, so officially I had never been married at all. In a nice ironic twist, Communist Hungary declared that I was a free man.

Once my first marriage was off the books, I had to start planning in earnest for my second first marriage. A big question was, where in New York were we going to stay? Frank Gibney answered it. A correspondent for *Time* and *Life*, and later an editor of *Newsweek* as well as several Asian editions of the *Encyclopedia Britannica*, Frank was not only one of the smartest men I've ever known but also one of the nicest. He and his wife lived in a large, lovely apartment in a white stone town house over on Sutton Place. He had invited me to join them for dinner several times, and when I mentioned my housing dilemma to him, he offered me his place. They were going to be out of the city on vacation from the second week of July through the end of August—why didn't we stay here? We'd have a good month to find a place of our own. The pieces were all falling into place. It was perfect. Almost too perfect.

A week before heading west to California, I checked out of the Roger Williams and moved uptown to Sutton Place. Wandering through the Gibneys' spacious apartment, I experienced a whole range of contradictory emotions and desires: gratitude, envy, anticipation, uncertainty, longing, and loneliness. I was walking around in somebody else's American dream, knowing that at fifty dollars a week I would never realize mine. I had to get out of diapers and move on to something bigger.

In my last letter to Sy before I left for San Diego, written at Frank Gibney's desk in Frank Gibney's library, I begged him to ship me a trunk full of pictures and negatives I had left behind in Salzburg. *It is almost impossible*, I wrote, *for me to find a job and start to work without all those.* I couldn't wait to put my portfolio together and show New York what I could do. I ended the letter with a kind of yearning. *I secretly have to admit, when I have the time for it, I feel lonesome. This town has no heart.* And I signed it *Your American friend, Bobby.*

I wanted what Frank Gibney had—a successful career, domestic peace of mind, material comfort—but I knew that wasn't enough. I wanted more. To me there is no such thing as contentment. I need to take risks, push myself to the limit. Life without adventure is not a life to me. I wanted a nice home—I just didn't want to lock myself into it.

In the early 1950s New York was alive with possibility, opportunity, and temptation. Put them together and you were bound to find adventure. Before I left for San Diego, Irving Hoffman treated me to one last night on the town. After all, I wasn't married yet. New York was full of "sexy dames," as I called them, thinking it made me sound more American, and, new to the city, I took it upon myself to flirt with every waitress and hatcheck girl I met. Unfortunately for me, most were immune to my charms, and I took it as a reflection of the excess of morality in American girls. Which was why Irving brought me that night to the bar in the Latin Quarter. He wanted to give me a proper send-off on my odyssey, and knew just the way to do it: introduce me to some immoral girls.

———

Marilyn walking down the aisle toward me, her shimmering white wedding dress accentuating her perfect California tan, was a dream come true—the beautiful young girl I remembered from Austria turning into a woman before my eyes. I wished I had my camera. Petite, pretty, a girl-next-door with pin-up good looks, Marilyn could have been a poster bride for postwar America. But she was mine, and I beamed as she came up beside me. She gave me a small, secret smile, and I knew that Salzburg hadn't been a fantasy or fairy tale. This was a good, true thing. I would take care of her and she would take care of me. All of my apprehension and uncertainty, my qualms about the future, evaporated in the warmth of her smile.

The dinner and reception that followed was a real blowout, a flashy oceanside hotel, three hundred guests, a Hungarian orchestra, a troupe of Gypsy dancers—Marilyn's father put on a show and spared no expense.

Marilyn and I had a quick two-day honeymoon. It was a chance to get reacquainted, but we were both anxious to get moving and see what the next chapter was going to be. My father-in-law drove me out to show me the family compound in the hills overlooking the bay and his yacht. He had built houses for himself, his mother, and his wife's mother and made it clear there was room for more. But as much as I enjoyed the climate, I didn't see that there was anything for me to do out there in California other than play golf or go fishing. This was a nice place to visit, but I belonged in New York. I wanted my own house and my own yacht.

The rest of my money had finally come through from Radio Free Europe, and I put it to good use. I went out and bought myself a sweet little MG TC sports car—with rakish styling, wire wheels, and a floor-shift gearbox—to get us back across the country. I just couldn't see myself in a Cadillac. Marilyn, however, had a hard time seeing herself in the MG and a harder one packing her things into it. There were just two seats and no luggage compartment—practicality not being my long suit—meaning we could bring just one suitcase tied onto the back of the car. The rest of her wardrobe, which was substantial, and all of our wedding gifts—one yard sale and I would have been set for a year—would have to be shipped to us when we had a place.

Four days married and four thousand miles to go, Marilyn and I climbed into our speedster and set out for New York—a hair-raising, knee-bumping, cross-country road trip toward a home we didn't yet have. Driving across miles of mountains, through endless acres of corn, dining on stacks of pancakes and hamburgers, and sleeping on rusty-spring mattresses in rustic roadside inns, Marilyn was a real sport. The drive had been my idea, and she gamely agreed but would have preferred a first-class seat on Pan Am.

We were both relieved to arrive on Sutton Place at Frank Gibney's place. I was overjoyed to discover that, thanks to Sy, my trunk full of photos and negatives had finally arrived from Vienna—pictures of my past that would help me piece together a future. I sat down and started putting together my portfolio. Marilyn had a headache. She took a three-hour bath.

The next day, first thing, Marilyn went to work looking for a place for us to live. She was thorough, quick, and organized, a grown-up little girl who had dreamed of this moment, imagined and prepared for it, her whole life—the wedding dress, the reception, and the building of her first nest. That the reality would ultimately fall short of the dream didn't occur to either of us. Why should it? We didn't know it was a dream. Within a week she'd found our nest—a newly furnished, two-room apartment with big windows out in Great Neck, only a few blocks from the bay and a half hour from the city. It wasn't Sutton Place, but it was ours for $115 a month.

When I wasn't running around New York taking pictures of babies, I was meeting with friends, friends of friends, agents, editors, radio and television executives—anyone who would listen to the many plans and projects I had. They were full of promises, but there was little in the way of fulfillment. At the same time, as much as I wanted nothing to do with them, I couldn't cut loose from the predators and parasites at Radio Free Europe. It was like a bad cold I couldn't shake.

I'd heard that my friend Louis Szathmary, with whom I'd gone through hell back in Salzburg, was now going through a hell of his own—persecuted and blackballed by the Nazis now running RFE in Austria. I went to see Andor Gellert, the man running the Hungarian desk in New York, to see what I could do for Louis. But Gellert turned out to be a prize idiot—which is one of the nicest things I've ever called him.

A pale, sickly man, Gellert had somehow convinced the Americans that he had a line on the Hungarian soul. He had told them what they wanted to hear: that he could help Hungary break free of the Soviets. Within several years, from behind his desk in New York, he would lead Hungary to disaster—and if he'd had his way, would have led the rest of us into World War III. When I went to see him, Gellert called me a Communist, and I walked out, knowing that if I stayed any longer I would have to throw him out the window. Louis Szathmary made it to America before the year was out and went on to find great success in Chicago, but neither he nor I ever again set foot in the offices of Radio Free Europe.

Leaving RFE was the right thing to do, but it meant abandoning another part of myself. I still looked back fondly, with a kind of nostalgia, on my adventures in Salzburg, and now I was breaking away from them—burning bridges behind me with no clear path to the future. I had a million projects running around my brain—writing books, giving lectures—but photography was my bread and butter. As for the diaper company, at the end of the week, there was very little bread to put the butter on. It was time for me to step up and take a chance. Five weeks after taking the diaper job, I quit and turned to the telephone book.

I copied down the name and address of every magazine, newspaper, and photo editor in the book and started the legwork. For three weeks I did nothing but pound the pavement and put my face and my portfolio in front of the people with the power to pay me to take pictures. I dialed up the European charm and dished out the bull. I was the best photographer they'd never heard of. Out of the hundred I saw, I convinced three to give me a shot. It was more than enough.

As an outsider, I had begun to make certain observations and judgments about the American way of life—at least as it played out in New York City. Everything, it seemed to me, was temporary—gadgets, cars, marriages, entertainment, and jobs—and everyone was restless, in a hurry to get to the next thing. At the same time, while always on the move, nobody was willing to go too far, to step outside the bounds of their safe little worlds. Everybody was in a mad rush to go nowhere.

Professional photographers were no different. They preferred the comfort of studio work, of controlled environments, spotlights, and still lives. Consequently there was a shortage of photographers willing to work on the fly, to drop everything at a moment's notice, grab a camera and a couple of lenses, and head into the hinterlands. That was the way I had been working—and living—since my mother sent me to live with my father when I was ten. I set no boundaries, adapted to circumstances quickly, and all a client had to do was point me in a direction and tell me where to go.

Detroit, Indianapolis, Pittsburgh, Toledo, Providence, Saint Louis, Seattle, Syracuse—I was all over the map. American industry was in its glory and on the make, and every industrial giant had a marketing team and publishing arm printing slick brochures for their customers and monthly in-house magazines for their employees. One cold call that paid off was a visit I made to a printer on 20th Street in Chelsea. The man running the shop said he didn't have work for a photographer, but that he subcontracted work for several bigger companies, printing their brochures and magazines. I agreed to buy the guy lunch in exchange for the phone numbers and names of his contacts. That meal was one of the most profitable investments I've ever made.

I ended up working for Western Electric, US Steel, US Rubber, and Standard Oil, riding the titans of American capitalism to a better payday. They sent me on six-thousand-mile, all-expenses-paid car trips, crisscrossing the country, taking pictures of molten steel being poured, turbines turning water into power, Fords rolling off the assembly line, and happy employees dining in company cafeterias.

These excursions not only paid the rent, they got me out of New York—a city of millions that can be strangely isolating and narrow. I've always needed room to stretch. The Metropolitan Newspaper Group, which provided content and filler to Sunday supplements, also sent me out into the country to take pictures. They wanted local flavor, the odder the better—assigning me to cover circus sideshows, thousand-pound pumpkins, and two-headed cows. The experience opened my eyes. For the first time I was not using the camera as an instrument of journalism or publicity, but as a conveyor of shock, amusement, and surprise—in short, of entertainment. I felt as though I was coming into my own, learning something new every day about how to frame a shot and create an image that people would pay to see.

For the first time I had enough money to set up a studio in Manhattan, sharing a space with Curt Gunther, then a struggling German immigrant freelancer. He was a good photographer and an even better self-promoter, ultimately making his mark in the 1960s, when, in London, he took some pictures of a new rock-and-roll band—the Beatles—and arranged to join them on their first tour in America. We leased the space from Jackie Cooper, the former child actor and future editor of the *Daily Planet*, who had a side business renting spotlights for opening nights on Broadway.

The studio was in a basement on 52nd Street between Fifth and Sixth Avenues—the block known as Swing Street, where a swarm of shoebox-size former speakeasies served up hot jazz, watered-down drinks, and a nonstop party. I set up shop just steps away from 3 Deuces, Club Carousel, Jimmy Ryan's—all the basement clubs and cabarets that lit up the night on that block. Working late in the darkroom, the vibrations seeped into my developing work—the sounds of Charlie Parker, Louis Prima, Dizzy Gillespie, or whoever happened to be headlining that night.

Jazz filled the air, and I was growing a business breathing it in. My father wouldn't have liked the music or my work—but sadly he wasn't there to disapprove of either. He was stuck in Budapest, in poor health, working as a clerk in a nationalized photography shop. I hoped one day to find a way to get him out of Hungary and bring him to America. For now I did all I could, sending him money every month to keep him from starving.

I looked forward to making my way back to Marilyn, whether from my studio in the city or from one of my frequent cross-country assignments. She was my sanctuary, my partner, the warm fire that kept me going . . . and kept me coming home. I have always seen myself as a puzzle and a paradox, which is to say a man like most other men. I wanted to achieve something on my own, but I never wanted to go it alone. Ever since I was a young man, whether sitting in a taxi with my mother, falling in love with Klâri, or making love to a stranger in bombed-out Budapest, I have felt that there was a missing piece to the puzzle, and I have looked to women to fill that empty space.

After my long absences Marilyn and I would take long walks down to Little Neck Bay, or she'd meet me in the city and we'd wander around until we found some restaurant—French, German, or Italian—that we'd never heard of before. She seemed as happy as I was at first, but over time appearances proved deceiving. We talked for the most part about the past, our time in Salzburg and the great romance we had. But the strain of disappointment and disillusion had begun to wear Marilyn down.

It turned out that she had married a memory—a charming, impetuous Hungarian freedom fighter, a character out of a novel who had swept her off her girlish American feet. She had ended up with a hustling young immigrant who made a living photographing factories, freak shows, and deformed farm animals. She had a difficult time flicking the switch from romance to reality. I was making more money now, but not nearly enough to compensate for the loneliness she felt when I went off to make it—leaving her to fend for herself in Great Neck. Marilyn was used to living in big houses on the Southern California coast with parties around the pool with her friends. Here she had settled for a two-room flat on Long Island with occasional nights out on the Lower East Side.

Always prone to headaches, soon Marilyn was taking ten or twelve aspirin a day, disappearing into a dark bedroom for hours on end. Just as I looked to her to fill the missing part of me, she turned to me to do the same for her. And what she decided was missing was a child. Again, there was only disappointment. It was not to be. As much as we tried, we could not conceive. The repeated failures drove Marilyn back into the dark bedroom.

Early in the summer of 1953, Marilyn's father came to New York to pay us a visit—and see how his little girl was doing. What he found didn't make him happy. He told me that the marriage was making Marilyn sick and that I had to get serious about making things right.

I thought if I showed my father-in-law what I could do, how creative I was in my work and how serious I was about my career, he would take some solace in that. I had been thinking for a while about a particular photograph I wanted to take, and now was as good a time as any, with my father-in-law at my side. I brought him down to my studio, where a belly dancer I had hired from one of the nearby clubs was waiting. I fitted her with a pinpoint light in her belly button, turned out all the lights, and told her to dance in a small space I had measured out in front of my camera, which I had rigged to snap off a shot every half second—a single frame of film, multiple exposures. I repeated the process a dozen times, dismissed the dancer, and took the film—and my father-in-law—into the darkroom.

The dance of light emerged from the chemicals. It was exactly what I had envisioned—a reflection of the dancer's performance, of her movement and energy, reflected in a constellation of stars suspended in the darkness. I was quite impressed with myself. My father-in-law was not. This was how I spent my time? He said he was going to talk to some friends of his about getting me a job on Wall Street. I decided not to tell him how much I had hated studying economics at the University of Budapest. All fathers, and particularly fathers-in-law, are very hard to please.

I had hoped his visit would bring some comfort to Marilyn, but the plan backfired. She read his concern about her and his questions about me as disapproval of the choices she had made and the life she lived. It only made her more anxious and angry. Adding salt to the wounds, I had just landed a new assignment that would take me four thousand miles away for four weeks, maybe more.

I was relieved to get away from it all. Where I was going, there would be no headlines, no propaganda, no news at all. Just me, my camera, and a vast uncharted expanse of ice and rock. I left early in the morning. I let Marilyn sleep. I didn't want to get caught up in another fight.

A twin-engine amphibious flying boat, an Albatross, under the command of the Air Force 10th Arctic Rescue Squadron, skimmed over the rim of jagged, rock-strewn peaks and made a quick, steep descent—my stomach trying desperately to catch up. The pilot fired a flare down into the plateau, dyeing the snow red to mark out a landing point in the ocean of white. He circled once and let the plane drop, its belly plowing into the ice cap at eighty miles per hour, leaving a deep v-cut in the snow behind. I tossed my things out of the plane, a tent, a backpack, a crate of scientific equipment, some skis, and a five-day supply of food. The pilot smiled, gave me a thumbs-up, and said, "No guts, no glory."

The plan over the next twenty days was for him to return four times, the first three to drop off another five-day food supply, and the last to pick me up and take me back to Juneau. A twenty-minute flight out of the Alaskan capital—thirty miles away from civilization—had transported me a million miles back in time.

Taku, nearly a mile thick, is the deepest tidewater glacier in the world, as well as one of the fastest moving, advancing some fifty-six feet every year. The native Tlingit called it *Kluuma Klutt*—"Spirits Home." Unpredictable ice floes in the frigid nearby rivers, streams, and ponds frequently capsize canoes, drowning all aboard. The Tlingit shamans, skilled at curing diseases, influencing weather, predicting the future, and protecting people from witchcraft, had always been powerless in the face of the Taku ice—as they later would be in treating Old World diseases like smallpox.

I had been dropped at the threshold of this Spirits Home at the behest of the American Geographical Society in New York—a league of extraordinary gentlemen dedicated to the expansion of geographical knowledge. They hired swashbuckling idiots like me to travel to the four corners and gather what knowledge we could, dispatching us to the most remote and forbidding landscapes in the Western Hemisphere. Places like Taku Glacier. My job was to drive metal stakes into the glacier at intervals along its thirty-four-mile length and to measure and record their movement. I had been hired to live on the ice for twenty days and take pictures of sticks. But that wasn't enough for me. I intended to do more, and I had an angle.

The American Geographical Society assignment in hand, I had spent a day in Manhattan visiting various men's adventure magazines pitching the true story, in words and pictures, of a "Journey into Fear: An Incredible Arctic Adventure." *Male* magazine bought it. One journey, two paydays, and I earned every penny.

The Albatross vanished into the dome of crystal-clear blue sky, and I got moving—across the sea of moving ice, a land of blazing sun and deadly cold, toward a distant line of peaks. I had been warned never to make camp in the snow, as I might wake up—or not wake up at all—at the bottom of a crevasse. Every night I'd climb hundreds of feet up a mountainside to pitch my tent on the exposed rocks.

By day the sun beat down mercilessly, a dazzling white, so bright that the needle on my light meter couldn't register it. I wore dark goggles and a ski mask to prevent the rays from burning and blistering my face. By night, still bright under the eerie arctic sky, the icy wind was just as relentless as the sun, infiltrating tent, sleeping bag, and socks. But my exhaustion at the end of the day was more powerful than the cold.

I woke up each morning, breakfasted on tea and powdered eggs, and prepared my pack for the day—all eighty pounds of it. Tent, sleeping bag, food, fuel, metal stakes and measuring devices, ice ax, gun holster, climbing rope, and first-aid kit. And my film along with three cameras—one or two of them invariably freezing up, like those old rifles the Hungarian soldiers carried along the Don River. Then I'd set out on skis, stopping to rest every twenty minutes, driving a stake into the ice, moving on, and making camp on the mountainside.

I mapped out a series of landmarks—mountain peaks and passes—visual cues to ensure that I could always retrace my steps. But at times, without warning, a fog would roll down through the valleys, growing so thick on the ground that I was virtually blind. I'd be forced to inch forward, scraping my foot ahead of me, making sure that I had ground to stand and walk on. Weighted down by the heavy pack and tent, I scuffed along exhausted and unthinking, driven only by the necessity to keep moving. In the middle of the night, the fog would sometimes dissolve into a downpour, a raw soaking rain that penetrated my tent, ice water running down my neck into my bedding and clothes and making my pack that much more heavy for the next day's expedition.

So it went. Sleep, pack, ski, slip, stagger, regain my balance and slip again, step by step, stake by stake, photograph by photograph—a twenty-day journey into the wild. There were hours of misery interrupted by moments of unexpected bliss: the taste of a can of peaches; and scenes of unimaginable beauty: the gorgeous colors of the snowcap revealed in the ever-changing light. As the man had said, *no guts, no glory.*

My experiences during the war had tempered my body, proved to me how far it could go and how much it could take. Cold, hunger, pain, and exposure to the elements were all familiar demons. Taku, however, introduced me to a different devil: a loneliness as howling and frigid as the glacier itself. My task complete, my pack full of exposed film, I returned to the rendezvous point for the last time, giddy with anticipation. My love of adventure had its limits. I wanted to go home, sleep in my own bed.

As I hiked down onto the plateau where the plane would land, I descended into a thickening blanket of fog, separating me from the sky. Late that morning I heard the Albatross approach, descend, and skim down the plateau between the mountain peaks. It circled, made a second pass, then a third. After twenty minutes the plane retreated, the sound distant, then gone. He had been unable to land, had only so much fuel, and couldn't be sure I'd be there to meet him anyway. My radio, a casualty of one of the rainstorms, had stopped working days ago. I had left it in the mountains, deadweight.

I knew that the pictures I had taken out here would be a boost to my career, but halfway around the world my father lived in poverty and my marriage to Marilyn had turned as slippery and creviced as the ice under my feet. It was the middle of July, 1953. I had been married exactly two years and had been in America just a little longer. My life was coming together and falling apart all at once.

Deep in a fog, fingers numb, stomach empty, I had two choices. Make camp and wait another day, hoping the fog would lift and the Albatross would find its way here. Or move on and make my own way. I really had no choice. I couldn't wait. Some twenty-five miles to the west, rising out of the mist, stood the mountain called Observation Peak—a two-day walk and a four-thousand-foot climb away. Other than my gun holster, ice ax, sleeping bag, cameras and film, and the little food I had left, I shed all my excess baggage in the snow.

I started walking to Juneau.

CHAPTER SIX

Going Stag. Going Rogue. Going Fishing.

A submarine has risen from the frigid waters, crashing through the arctic ice. A man stands on deck, rifle raised and poised to fire. His target: a massive, ferocious polar bear, its fangs bared, eager to maul and make a meal of this intruder into his icy world.

Such is the artwork on the cover of the January 1954 issue of *Male* magazine—a cover featuring two headlines. One—"NUDISM EXPOSED (America's STRANGEST Cult)"—teases to a story inside. But it's the account of my exploits on the Alaskan glacier that takes the lead, my very first cover story: "JOURNEY INTO TERROR (An Incredible ARCTIC Adventure)."

That there were no rifles, bears, or submarines in my story was beside the point. All of us—publishers, artists, editors, writers, and photographers—were in the business of selling men's adventure, the more lurid and provocative the magazines, the better. Playing fast and loose with the truth was our stock in trade. It wasn't about what was real. It was about what it took to be a real man—the promise of blood, sweat, sex, and violence. We were going after ex-GIs, guys who'd gone from cutting down Nazis to mowing lawns. The war vets wanted blood, and we gave it to them. It only cost them a quarter.

Ex-soldiers and expatriates, we were all in the same boat—I know I was—struggling to hold on to the past and bury it at the same time, creating new identities on the fly. We all had our cover stories.

I had emerged from the darkroom of the war focused and in fighting shape, and its aftershocks were proving a boon to my career. The men's magazine business was booming, and the gold rush was on. In editors' offices reeking of cigar smoke and bourbon, writers, artists, and photographers pitched stories from the hip. Writers like Mario Puzo, Elmore Leonard, and Ray Bradbury—guys who might otherwise have had to get a real job—found a home here.

But in the mid-1950s, in and around New York, photographers were a dime a dozen—and unless you could find some way to separate yourself from the herd, come up with a unique product, a dime was about how much you'd get paid. I had found my calling—the call of the wild—in the white wilderness of Alaska, carving my signature in the ice. I was the guy who would go anywhere, do anything, pull off any stunt to get a story and a shot. That was *my* cover story and I was sticking to it.

Want action, adventure, danger? Someone with harebrained schemes, a head full of steam, and the willingness to leap before he looks? *Get that Bob Halmi guy . . . he'll do it! He'll walk through fire and ice. He's crazy.*

———

The New Haven fire department had turned the condemned five-room dwelling into a pyromaniac's paradise. They punched holes in the wall studs and stuffed them with rags and papers that had been sloshed with highly combustible solvent; the floors, walls, and furniture got the same treatment. Packing crates had been smashed, the loose wood spread strategically around the house to intensify the fire's speed and heat. It was a perfect firetrap, and I stood in the middle of it, clad in a silver suit composed of asbestos cloth, fiberglass insulation, aluminum foil, and an inner lining of vinyl-treated glass cloth. The suit was guaranteed to withstand eighteen hundred degrees Fahrenheit—but if it failed, I doubt I would have been around to get my money back.

The place went up in a flash, not so much with a roar as with a gentle, deadly hiss—a bomb-burst that you see before you hear. From inside my bulky breathing mask, I could see the firemen back away from the searing heat. A window shattered. Tar paper melted. Thick, black, blinding smoke roiled overhead. It was a training exercise, and outside the firemen rolled out their hoses and axes and attacked the house, streams of water hissing in the flames. I started shooting pictures, gesturing to the firefighters where to direct their hoses for more dramatic effect. The breathing mask started to slip, and whenever I turned my head, the suit's glass faceplate touched my skin, raising a blister.

The walls of the house had begun to shiver and the floor to weaken. Four men with grappling hooks pulled the sagging wall into the street to keep it from collapsing on top of me. Without warning, two of them in oxygen equipment raced in and carried me out into the street. Ripping off my fire hood, the fire chief saw that my mask had completely fallen off. Angry, he asked why the hell I didn't come out. Shrugging, I said I wasn't finished shooting. My story—what a fire looks like to those trapped inside it—ran in *Argosy*.

Bill Austin loved caves. I didn't. I'd been sent on assignment several times to photograph the caves of western Kentucky, and if you wanted to know the ins and outs of the mammoth subterranean labyrinth buried beneath the knobby blue hills and forests of that region, Bill was your man. After several underground excursions into Bill's backyard—including one unforgettable expedition, seven straight days in the hole with the National Speleological Society—I figured I'd taken enough pictures of stalactites, stalagmites, and black bottomless pits to last a lifetime.

There was something deeply disturbing about the clammy chill and slimy, slippery, knifelike rocks one can only find in a cave—it's like shaking hands with Death. I vowed never again to go underground—a vow I kept until Bill Austin gave me a call. He told me to come on down to Kentucky—there was something I *had* to see. *Cavalier* magazine paid me to go see whatever it was and bring back pictures.

Austin told me to bring boats, the collapsible kind that we could squeeze into a small, dark hole in the ground. I also brought along a friend of mine, another man named Bill—Bill Homan, an amateur photographer, amateur adventurer, amateur everything. The two of us were a lot alike—both of us idiots, willing to try most anything once. The only difference between us was that Bill Homan had all the money in the world and I had none. He had inherited a fortune in tobacco money, which was why he was an amateur—he had no need to choose a profession, making him a bigger idiot than I was. I risked my life in order to make a living. He did it for fun.

There were four of us, Bill Homan and I, and Bill Austin and Jack Lehrberger, a math major at the University of Louisville and Austin's fellow caver. Austin and Lehrberger were legends in these parts, having descended deep into the Kentucky limestone and mapped miles of uncharted passageways and connections. All told, there are more than 390 miles of known passageways in the Mammoth Cave system. We were only interested in one small part of it.

Austin had discovered a new tunnel—with a black, swift-moving stream running right through it. Our idea—I should say, Austin's idea, the rest of us just went along for the ride—was to drop our boats into the subterranean rapids and see where they took us. Bill had no idea where the water came from or where it went.

I put on some strong coveralls, knee and elbow pads, my good mountain boots, and a hardhat with a flickering carbide lamp in it, then tied my two Leicas—wrapped in plastic—to my ankles, and, pushing one of the collapsible boats ahead of me, shimmied into the hole. It was seven in the morning. A chill ran up and down my spine as I entered.

We were headed through the Floyd Collins Crystal Cave—named for the young man who had explored the region thirty years before. On one excursion a rock fall had pinned Collins by the ankle, trapping him in a narrow tunnel. For days furious efforts were made to dig him out. On the ninth day, he died. Not much had changed over the last three decades. If any of us were injured or incapacitated down below, the chances of getting back out alive through the ten-inch-high "keyholes" and twisting crawlways were slim to none. We'd spend eternity in the company of bats, rats, salamanders, and blindfish . . . and the ghost of Floyd Collins.

For me it was just another day at the office, crawling or bear-walking hundreds of yards through damp sand, muck, and rocks and leaping across pits that it took three seconds for loose stones to reach the bottom of. Crossing canyons like a gymnast on a balance beam. Every step, slip, and slither, I had the same broken record turning in my head—*what the hell am I doing here in this bleak, black, hopeless hole in the ground?*

The geography of the place spoke for itself as we negotiated our way past Fishhook Crawl, Black Onyx Pit, Bogus Bogardus Waterfall, Mud Avenue, the Storm Sewer, and Castration Point. I occasionally stopped to take pictures, telling the others to keep moving, I'd catch up with them. I've been alone and on my own many times, but there is nothing like the isolation you feel deep below ground, crouching beneath tons of earth and rock. It closes in on you, and within a few minutes you begin to hear strange noises you can't identify, noises which, before long, you could swear are voices echoing through the darkness. You get a feeling for what insanity is—a cave in which the mind loses itself.

After several hours we came to the "chimney"—a hole in the rock about a foot and a half wide leading to Bill Austin's underground rapids. It was the only way down. I braced myself against the sides and let gravity do the rest, sliding straight toward the center of the earth—a forty-foot vertical drop.

We reached the banks of the stream and made an immediate discovery. Boats, easy to assemble on dry ground in daylight, require torturous groping and fumbling on a rough, slippery stream bank. At last we were ready. Two boats, four men, one hell of a crazy ride. These canvas boats were not made to withstand the jagged rocks emerging from the cave walls—and neither is human flesh.

With only the flickering carbide in our hats to guide us, we maneuvered past chunks of rock in the fast-moving stream. And it soon became clear we were on a ride to nowhere, the water siphoning off into black holes, which were no place for man or boat. Discretion being the better part of valor, we decided that the best course was to paddle back upstream and head home. But not before I spotted a thin cascade of water clinging to the black rock face, casting an unworldly sheen when the light hit it—a striking image the likes of which I'd never seen before and would likely never see again. I had to get the shot . . . and made the mistake of trying to get it. Somehow, attempting to lift myself up out of my seat to get a better angle on the shot, I ended up in the drink—floundering wildly, as blind as one of those eyeless fish.

I went completely under, over my head, submerged in cold water, suspended in total darkness. My coveralls and boots weighing me down, I knew that the current would carry me away if I didn't get out of there. Unable to breathe, I started to panic. There was nothing for my hands or feet to get a purchase on. In my desperation I rose too quickly, banging my head on an underwater ledge. The blow either knocked some sense into me or triggered a furious shot of adrenaline into my system. Whatever it was, I pushed my way to the surface, gasping for air. I saw the light—Bill Austin's helmet—and swam toward it like a man possessed, fighting not to be swept away. I got hold of his paddle, and he guided me back to the bank.

I lost one of my cameras. I didn't get the shot. But I did get a story. The journey back was an arduous one. My clothes and gear were sopping wet, and it wasn't going to dry out, the temperature down here hovering around fifty degrees, the humidity set at an eternal 90 percent. But I moved like a horse returning to its stable at full gallop—crawling, climbing, and slithering back to the surface with all my strength. We'd been down in the hole a good twenty hours, and breaking back onto the topside of the soil—the side we are meant to walk on—I looked up at the starry sky and vowed never to let it out of my sight. I'd collect my hazard pay from *Cavalier* magazine and would refuse to go underground ever again.

Until the next time Bill Austin gave me a call.

Martin Goodman had built a business empire on the fears, fantasies, and fertile imaginations of red-blooded American men. One of the original publishers of pulp magazines, he moved out of pulp and into superheroes with his line of Marvel Comics, and then, in the '50s, put his money into men's adventure magazines. He treated his publications—and most of the people who worked for them—like children. Two of his favorites were *Male* and *Stag*—and the two magazines maintained a heated sibling rivalry.

Male had published my first cover story, "Journey into Terror," with its artfully rendered exaggeration depicting a man with a rifle versus a bear with big teeth. One of the editors over at *Stag* spotted the cover and had a brainstorm—a way to stick it to *Male*. Instead of an artist's rendering, what if *Stag* got real photos? What if they sent someone up to the Arctic

Circle with a rifle and camera to bag a real polar bear? The only question was, *was there anyone crazy enough to do it?* My name came up.

It was twenty degrees below zero in the middle of the afternoon, under a bright arctic sun. I had my cameras. Bob Savaria, the bush pilot who flew me out here, had my back, a .375 Magnum rifle in his hands. What I didn't have was much of a prayer. A twelve-hundred-pound polar bear was charging across the snow toward me, and luckily for him, Bob's rifle had chosen that very moment to jam. I was literally about to become dead meat. What made that bear, three feet away from having me for lunch, suddenly put on the brakes, I'll never know. Maybe he thought I was pulling some kind of trick. Or maybe he thought I was just too dumb to eat. Whatever gave that bear pause, Savaria took the opportunity to swing the butt of his rifle, delivering a swift uppercut to the bear's chin. The blow stunned the bear—he wheeled and strolled away—but very nearly killed Savaria. The collision with the bear's chin had somehow unjammed the rifle, discharging a .375 Magnum bullet into the snow at his feet.

I had flown into Barrow, Alaska, the day before, landing at the Wiley Post–Will Rogers Memorial Airport—the only public airport I know of that's named for victims of an airplane crash. The entire peninsula, accessible year-round only by air, has an aura of mortality about it. The community itself is traditionally known as *Ukpeagvik*—"place where snowy owls are hunted." The only reason to come to Barrow was to hunt, whether your prey were owls, beluga whales, or Soviet ICBMs—the US Air Force maintains a long-range radar and early warning site on the peninsula. I had come for the great white bears. But in order to reach them, I would have to walk on water.

I was headed a good one hundred miles to the north of this northernmost point in US territory. Savaria, who flew mail and supplies in and out of Point Barrow, did a side business in delivering hunters to the fleet of massive ice floes that churned and shifted across the arctic waters—a region known as America's Polar Bear Seas. Now here we were, the bear turning once again to face us—no more than fifty yards away—deciding what his next move would be. I knew I had to make my decision before he made his.

The polar bear lives on the top of the world, master of his icy, white, watery kingdom—until we humans get in on the act, knocking him off the top of the food chain. I don't know what it's like to be a polar bear, but it must baffle him. This beast that has never felt fear, that has always had his way and has always taken his time, lounging on his throne of snow, to suddenly face an animal with the power to take his life. He doesn't know to run away; it's not in his makeup. All the animals he's ever seen have run away from *him*.

As a photographer, I was a hunter, stalking my target, getting in close, feeling his pulse—and feeling my own fear. Then, my heart racing, moving in for the shot. If I wasn't afraid, then I knew it wasn't worth the effort. I may not have known what it was like to be a polar bear, but I could at least look into his eyes. Which is why, as a hunter, I never understood the concept of going after the great bears, or any big game, from the seat of a low-flying airplane. You might as well shoot chickens with a machine gun. It's not hunting. It's slaughter.

I made my decision. I handed my camera to Savaria and took the rifle. I told him to follow close behind and just keep snapping pictures. I started walking toward the bear, raising the rifle. He rested on all fours, watching me approach. When I came within twenty yards, he rose up on his hind feet to his full height, making a better target of himself. Was he confused, startled, angry, insulted, excited . . . I don't know; that was the beast in me. The bear's thick white fur rippled in the wind. I took aim and shot him once through the upper chest. He staggered, seemed finally to understand that he ought to be moving away from me rather than toward me, then fell dead.

I traded the rifle for my camera. I had loaded up some color film for this assignment. The readers would want shots of blood on the snow against a backdrop of bright-blue, pristine sky.

—◆—

In terms of the work I've done over the years, all other things aside—things like money, family, and a future—this was the best time of my life. I reveled in the pure visceral experience of it—the freedom and excitement, the thrills, chills, and spills that came from running off at the drop of a hat to some wild new frontier in pursuit of another story. It was just me, my camera, and some crazy idea in my head—an idea that I'd tame, frame, and ultimately bring to life in my darkroom.

Hanging from the rigging of a hot air balloon, at the mercy of the wind, floating silently across the sky. Hunting alligators in Jamaica by day and unlocking the secrets of the young Jamaicans who breathe fire by night. Running with the wolves, rallying with the race cars, riding with the rodeo cowboys, and catching up to the cardsharps in Reno. Every week I was off on another adventure, and I loved every minute of it. I knew that the mischief and madness couldn't go on forever. Sooner or later I'd have to grow up. But it was fun while it lasted.

My main accomplices in the fun and games were the Fawcett family—the publishers of *True*—and Ken Purdy, its editor. *True* was the big bad boy of men's adventure magazines, the one all the others aspired to be. The one with the biggest circulation, the biggest budget—and the biggest balls.

Gordon Fawcett, the third of the founder's four sons, acted as general manager of the magazine division. As lurid and lusty and lewd as *True* was, Gordon's personality was the antithesis of everything the magazine represented. Buttoned up and buttoned down, Gordon was a square and proud of it, shocked, SHOCKED, that anyone would even think of knocking back a cocktail before five or would contemplate hitting on one of the secretaries in his office. We struck up a lifelong friendship—proof that opposites do indeed attract.

Whereas the publisher, Gordon Fawcett, moved at his own glacial pace, taking his time, *True*'s editor, Ken Purdy, moved at the speed of sound, in a race against time. Ken wrote about automobiles, and no one did it better. The two of us shared an interest in cars, the faster the better. As far as Ken was concerned, if you were going under a hundred miles an hour, there was no point in going anywhere at all. We often put that philosophy to the test on the roads of Westchester County and southern Connecticut.

Ken moved on from *True* after a couple of years; he never stayed anywhere very long, but we stayed in touch until 1972, when he put a gun to his head. It came as a shock to everyone who knew him, but he was about to turn sixty, and I suspect he just didn't have it in him to slow down. That's the problem with living life like you're in a race against time. You can't win. Time eventually catches up with you.

I went on doing stories for *True* well into the next decade, the 1960s, but even back in the '50s, I began to sense that the men's adventure magazines had hit a wall. There were only so many mountains to climb, animals to rip your flesh, or Gestapo sex dens to revisit. In 1953 Martin Goodman, the publisher of *Stag*, had sued a young man in Chicago who had started a magazine called *Stag Party*. Goodman won the suit but lost the war. The young man in Chicago went ahead and published his magazine under a different name, *Playboy*, and before long the men's adventure magazines were losing market share to bunnies and bare-naked ladies.

The adventure magazines soldiered on for another decade or so, but as sure as Eisenhower would inevitably give way to Kennedy, the idea of man in the rough would give way to a slicker, sharper package. Advertisements for foot itch powder, hair grease, and Kentucky bourbon could no longer sustain the business. We were real men facing a new reality. Real women.

I had to make another move, branch out, give my identity and my career a little kick. Back in Chicago, that rising young publisher—Hugh Hefner—had exercised his First Amendment rights, selecting a meteoric young movie star to be his first "Sweetheart of the Month." It was time for me to embrace *my* First Amendment rights.

━━◆━━

I love women. But I know that sometimes I make it hard for them to love me back. It's just that I require that they love me on my schedule. I'm always going somewhere. I'm a moving target. Even when I'm sitting still, my mind wanders. It's a character flaw, originating, I suspect, in my childhood—all those hours left to my own devices, dreaming of all those places I would go. And I've been pursuing those dreams ever since. I see something shiny, I reach for it. I'm off in pursuit of my next job, my next picture, my next story. I can't wait. I don't have the time. I'm not a patient man.

I dabbled in fashion photography—pictures of pretty young women in smart new dresses—and failed miserably. I found it easier to photograph a black rhino charging toward me through the underbrush than I did a demure young lady, recently arrived in New York from Iowa or Idaho or someplace, wearing the latest black evening gown. I could yell all I wanted at a rhino; he wasn't going to cry, he was going to charge. I suppose that's one of the reasons I later had so much success in the movies. Filming a good actor—male or female—is much more like pointing a camera at a rhinoceros than at a fashion model. No movie actor on earth is afraid of any camera on earth.

In 1954 Henry Luce—already in command of *Life* and *Time*, which begat a *Fortune*—had another brainchild, *Sports Illustrated*. In the early days the magazine suffered growing pains, floundering around looking for a receptive audience. It began by appealing to the polo and yachting crowd, which meant you could fit its entire potential readership into the Harvard Club dining room without breaking any fire laws. The big ad agencies weren't buying and ultimately pushed the magazine out of the polo business and into less snooty, more lucrative arenas—baseball diamonds, basketball courts, race car tracks, football fields, and fishing holes. Right in my wheelhouse.

Within a few months of its appearance, I was on assignment for *Sports Illustrated*. The sport they asked me to illustrate: spelunking. My favorite. But I needed a new angle, because like *Life* and *Time*, Luce wanted a magazine that appealed to both sexes.

I gave my friend Bill Austin a call down in Kentucky, and within few minutes we hit on it. The American middle class was growing; it had more money and more time than it knew what to do with and was looking for interesting new ways to spend it. We'd do a story about a family vacation, Bill and I on a double date, taking our wives into the hole for a tour of Crystal Cave. Because every middle-class caveman needs a middle-class cavewoman at his side.

My marriage to Marilyn was on the rocks, her insistence that I give her more of my time growing as acute as her headaches. So here, I imagined, was a chance to kill two birds with one story—go on assignment *and* give my wife what she was asking for. If I couldn't bring the mountain to Marilyn, I'd bring Marilyn to the mountain—all on my schedule, of course. I had to hand it to her, though, Marilyn jumped in with both feet.

She marched up and down the aisles at the local sporting goods store shopping for boots and a helmet with the same military precision and authority she brought to the business of buying a new hat and heels at Bergdorf's.

But if I'd gotten it into my head that crawling hour after hour in the cold, humid darkness, climbing over massive boulders and sliding down twenty-foot muddy inclines, descending into the bowels of the earth was going to save my marriage, I was sadly mistaken. It was at best a delaying tactic. We felt our way along the walls of the cave, the beams of light from our tungsten lamps crossing in the darkness, and we felt closer than we had in a long time—moving, at least, in the same direction. Then we reached our destination.

There's a full-page photograph that ran with the piece in *Sports Illustrated*. A huge onyx stalagmite rises like a miniature Matterhorn from the cave floor, the centerpiece of a great dome of hollowed rock. Behind the stalagmite, but out of sight, is a bright explosion of light, outlining each cut and ridge on the face of the walls, while casting the foreground in deep shadows. You can almost see in the contrast of light and dark the thousands of years and millions of drops it has taken this spectacle of mineral and stone to form. On the right, Bill Austin has raised one foot and one hand onto the stalagmite, as if he's preparing to scale it. Off to the left, nearly out of the frame, her face aglow with reflected light, stands Marilyn, dominated and subdued by the surroundings, her hands buried in the pockets of her coveralls. The shot sums up the state of our marriage at the time.

Back in New York I found a bigger studio for my growing business a block further west of my current studio on 52nd. I had branched out from my first love, outdoor adventure photography, and added a second love— indoor adventure photography. Taking pictures of women. Not fashion models—I couldn't handle the mascara—but young actresses looking for exposure. They were not hard to find in New York.

Fly fisherman Arnold Gingrich invented the modern American magazine, and *Esquire* was his electric neon light in a field of flickering candles and dim bulbs. Publishing writers like Hemingway, Faulkner, Fitzgerald, and later Updike, Mailer, and Baldwin, Gingrich's mission for the magazine was to teach men what to eat, what to drink, what to wear, how to play, and what to read—with a few pictures of pretty girls along the way to keep the pages turning. By the mid-1950s the magazine had moved from Chicago to New York, its growing audience of young men in dark suits filling Manhattan's office buildings.

By the winter of 1955, I had already done a couple of spreads for *Esquire*—seminude, semisuggestive shots of various young women lounging about on beds and in bubble baths. "Cheese-pie" poses, as one of the girls called them—a striking young Hungarian actress who had better command of the poses than she did of the English language. The spreads were nice, dramatic in their way, but nothing new. I wanted to do something unique and unusual and pitched my idea to *Esquire*. I would be Pygmalion in reverse, transforming beautiful women—the objects of American male desire—into true objects, Greek statues. I would turn earthly flesh into heavenly alabaster and bronze. A gallery for Galatea.

The editors flipped over it. They could see the competition—*Playboy*—in the rearview mirror, and it was gaining on them. Here was a chance to move from seminude to totally nude, and to do it artfully and tastefully—a touch of the erotic under a classical cover. Who, the editors wanted to know, did I have in mind for the spread? The most beautiful women in New York, I promised. But whom, exactly, I couldn't say—because I had no idea.

First thing I did was call Irving Hoffman. By the next day I had two aspiring Aphrodites, a blond and a redhead, lined up for the piece, ready to climb out of their skirts and into the pages of *Esquire* in the name of art and their careers. But two wasn't enough. I wanted someone else—someone, preferably, with a recognizable name or face who would put the spread on the map. I couldn't stop thinking—*Eva Gabor*. She might have been more Titian painting than Greek sculpture, but getting her to come down to my studio and climb onto my pedestal would have been a real coup.

I had met her several times, first at The Stork Club in my early years in New York, then later at various other nightclubs. She couldn't have been nicer to me, drawing me into quick two-minute conspiracies of conversation in which we'd exchange pleasantries in Hungarian, leaving all around us to wonder what we were up to. Not much—it was just a little game she liked to play, creating a sense of mystery where there was none. Once she had said to me, if there was anything she could ever do for me, to get in touch—the kind of thing any Hungarian in America would say to another, never expecting to hear anything about it again. But that didn't stop me. I intended to find out if *anything* included posing nude for me.

Miraculously, she took my call. Of course she remembered me, the photographer from Budapest—I was never prouder to be Hungarian than at the moment—and of course the answer was no. She was flattered, but no, she wouldn't pose nude for me in a million years. I said I would wait. She laughed but was adamant. She only took her clothes off for her husbands and lovers. If you don't leave something to the imagination, she said, then there's not much left at all. Apparently being Hungarian would only get me so far.

But she didn't want me to leave the phone call empty-handed. She knew someone who not only happened to be in New York, but who might take an interest in the project. She asked for my phone number and said she'd call right back. I thought, what the hell, never expecting to hear from her, but within a half hour the phone rang, and Eva Gabor was asking for the address of my studio. She said to be there the next day, a Saturday, at one, and be ready to shoot. She had just the girl for me.

I wasn't thrilled about committing my time and money to some unknown, but I wasn't going to say no to Eva Gabor either. Worst that would happen, I'd waste a few dollars on overtime for my assistant and a few hours of my time taking pictures—and then move on. I'd do it for Hungary.

The next day, one o'clock, two o'clock—nothing—and I was getting more steamed by the minute. Who was this woman to make me wait? Unless it was Eva Gabor herself, I was primed to make her mascara run. Finally, three o'clock, me bouncing off the walls, there came a knock—more like a mousy tap—at the door. I pulled it open and stepped back.

She was pretty, but in a simple, unassuming way—not the sort of knockout who stops a crowd or even attracts much attention. In fact, in a gray sweatshirt and blue jeans, she seemed determined to deflect attention. But of course I recognized her.

"Hi," she said shyly, lowering her eyes and putting out her hand, "I'm Marilyn. So sorry I'm late."

Marilyn Monroe.

I told her there was nothing to apologize for and invited her in. She took a few steps and stopped, a small case in one hand, the other buried in the back pocket of her jeans. She glanced around the studio, not quite sure what to do next. I asked her if there was anything I could get her, and she just wondered if there was a place she could get ready. I pointed out a mirror in the corner with a curtain she could draw around it—my poor excuse for a dressing room—and she said that it would be fine.

She didn't bother drawing the curtain, and as I moved around the studio moving lights and tripods around, I watched her prepare. It struck me how long she stood in front of the mirror, a good five minutes staring at herself, as if searching for something or wondering who this person was staring back at her. Then she opened a little case and went to work. Her mastery of makeup was remarkable: oils, creams, powders, color bases, and lip color. It was like magic, except it wasn't a rabbit she pulled out of her hat; it was a legend. She went into the dressing room a simple, attractive, unassuming girl named Marilyn and came out Marilyn Monroe, movie star.

"Hi," she said again, as if knowing she had to reintroduce herself—that by changing her face she had changed who she was.

I explained I wanted to take a few shots to get the light right, and she nodded. She knew the drill, and I asked if she understood I would be shooting her nude. She said she did but had one condition: body paint. They did it all the time in the movies, she said, changing skin color, and she wanted to be a dark bronze. She handed me two jars of color she had brought along with her. It puzzled me that she had gone to the trouble to apply all that makeup before, only to cover it up now, but I gathered it was all part of her process: putting on her face, shape-shifting, assuming a role. That was something I could understand. And if that's what she wanted, I wasn't going to say no.

Without another word she took off her shirt and dropped her dungarees, nothing underneath, and kicked them out of the way, shedding her shyness as easily as she shed her clothes. She explained that I should begin by applying a translucent cream to her skin—a kind of primer—followed by the bronze, smoothing and evening it out with my fingers as I went. She couldn't do it herself because if she moved too much, the stuff wouldn't take. I rolled up my sleeves and went to work. My assistant, recognizing that this was a moment I might want to put in my scrapbook, took up a camera and started clicking.

It took a half hour to apply the stuff and another half hour for the stuff to set. While we waited, I tried to draw her out, but she always turned the conversation back to me—listening to my answers intently. She took a particular interest in my cameras—the lenses, the lighting, and the angles—saying she loved still photography so much more than movies. Still photography, she said, got to the essence of a person. Movies barely scratched the surface. At last we were ready.

I didn't have to give her a single direction, her movements graceful and precise, her expressions spot-on, her relationship with the lens giving and intimate. Marilyn danced, teased, flirted, and conspired with the camera. She wasn't posing, she was performing. For a moment, she reminded me of my mother—a thought I had to scrub out of my head with soap and water.

This was the first time I had ever worked with a great actress—and the first time I saw how an actor can take charge of a camera without touching it. I've worked with many actors since, but none whom the camera loved so much.

The preliminary shooting to get the light right out of the way, now I needed her to become a Greek statue, and it was as if she had the figure inside her and all she had to do was summon it to the surface. She climbed onto the pedestal, putting all her weight on her right hip, her right leg and foot extended straight out, her left leg rising up at a ninety-degree angle from her midsection and bent at the knee to form an imperfect triangle with the bottom leg. Her left arm extended out from her shoulder, bent at the elbow nearly touching her left knee, her index finger pointing out over her head, her right hand resting on the pedestal, fingers spread. Her mouth was slightly open, as if words were about to form, and her eyes were nearly shut as she looked down at something out of the frame that only she saw. The image I had of her on film was not of some extraordinary feminine goddess—she was less Aphrodite and more Eros, the mischievous and playful god of love.

An hour later, makeup washed off, back in her jeans and sweatshirt, Marilyn went on her way, saying she hoped that she hadn't disappointed me. I told her that my only disappointment was that the shoot was over so quickly. She smiled and nodded on her way out, as if to agree with me, leaving me with the feeling that she had let me in on one of her secrets—a feeling, I suspected, that she gave a great many people.

Two days later, Monday, I received another unexpected visitor. He introduced himself as Milton Greene. He said he was Marilyn Monroe's business partner—my guess was that there was something more than business between them—and she had not consulted him about the photo shoot. Marilyn had told him she hadn't signed a release, she'd been hurt before by unauthorized photos, and she had had a change of heart about the photos I had taken. He was polite and professional, even sympathetic to my position, offering to pay me for my time and the negatives.

But I refused payment. If Marilyn was uncomfortable with the shoot, I wouldn't go against her wishes. I handed over the negatives without protest. I didn't really believe she was uncomfortable with it—I think *he* was—but that was a mess I wanted no part of. And anyway, when I gave him the pictures, my fingers were discreetly crossed behind my back. I kept one of the negatives, and the photo ran six months later as part of the spread in the September 1955 back-to-college issue of *Esquire*. Marilyn Monroe—nude, noir, and anonymous—welcoming the university boys back to school. Coming to me in the first place had been an act of defiance on her part, and this photo of her—hiding in plain sight—must have made her smile.

There was also the roll of film in my assistant's camera, with the photos of me applying the paint to her skin. One in particular showed me rubbing makeup on Marilyn's breasts, both of us clearly getting a kick out of it, laughing at some joke one of us had just made. The boys over at *Esquire* had some fun with it, mocking up a press pass for me with that shot. But not everyone saw the humor.

One night when I was working late at my studio, Marilyn—my wife Marilyn—happened upon the press pass lying around our apartment. I don't know what went through her mind—aside from the image of me rubbing the movie star's breasts—but it seemed to trigger all the resentment and feelings of betrayal seething inside her. An absentee husband, a childless marriage, a two-room apartment in Great Neck—it was all there, in my hands, in that damning photo.

Marilyn caught a train into the city and a cab to my studio. I survived. Several hundred dollars' worth of my equipment did not. She smashed whatever she could get a hold of, and I waited for the storm to pass, making no move to stop her. I knew the marriage was over, and it scared the hell out of me.

Her headaches were growing more and more severe, darkening and intensifying her moods, and I don't know if one of them had contributed to her rage. But I do know that I had become just another headache in her life. My work had become my hobby, and my hobby had become my work. There just wasn't enough room left for Marilyn—even if I did love her. I couldn't have been happier than during our fairy tale romance in Salzburg, our wedding bash in San Diego, and our adventures together in New York. Yet here we were, as broken as the lights on my studio floor.

I've had the good fortune to enjoy the best education possible. I've survived a hot war and a cold one. I came to America with few dollars in my pocket and made a fortune. But for all the things I've seen, learned, and known, what happens between a man and a woman remains a deep, dark mystery to me. Love is crazy. Love is a cave. The problem is, I can't live without it.

Although it would make a nice headline, I can't say that Marilyn Monroe broke up my marriage. I could as easily and accurately say that a polar bear or hot air balloon came between us.

In April 1955, Marilyn went to Reno to get a divorce. I went to Africa to live with the Pygmies.

—◆—

My marriage to Marilyn had degenerated, but my marriage to America was going strong. I had applied for citizenship and had regular assignments from *Esquire*, *True*, *Sports Illustrated*, and a dozen other magazines; I watched TV when I had the time and always paid my bills and income taxes. I loved the country and the opportunities it gave me. But even in a happy marriage, a man might sometimes take a mistress. Mine was Africa—and, as one would expect of a mistress, she was wild, unpredictable, dangerous, and a source of surprising revelations and pleasures.

Africa was a world apart then, different from any other place I'd been, with the capacity to bring out the best—and worst—in those who took it on. I've seen famously courageous men, writers who portrayed themselves as the next Hemingway, cowering in a tent and refusing to come out, frozen with a fear so paralyzing it never made an appearance in any of their books or columns. But I've also seen Hollywood actors, movie stars who had never faced anything more frightening than a bad script or angry producer, stand up to a charging two-ton rhino without blinking an eye. Africa defied all expectations. Every journey there was an adventure, and every adventure was a story, and I never knew how it would end.

My introduction to the continent had come by chance a couple of years earlier, by way of Chicago. A dozen of the city's richest restaurateurs had cooked up an idea to get away from it all and go someplace off the beaten track—and they wanted a professional photographer to tag along and record the trip. They'd seen my magazine work and figured I'd be perfect for the job. I had no idea where they were going, what they were going to do there, or what they expected of me, and I said sure, why not? I've been called a lot of things in my life, but never indecisive. I packed a few shirts and cameras and met them at the airport.

Our destination was Chad, then a territory of France, and as soon as we rolled out into the broad grasslands to the south—me snapping pictures of hippos, rhinos, elephants, and giraffes, unfettered and in their element, I was hooked. That accidental journey was the beginning of my love affair with Africa—an affair that led me, in the spring of 1955, to the Pygmies. I was on the trail of Henry Morton Stanley.

Born in Wales, Stanley came to America in 1859 to seek his fortune but failed to find it—landing instead in the middle of a civil war. An adventurer and opportunist, at war's end he found a position that suited him well—journalist. And it was on assignment in Africa, capitalizing on such exploits as his expedition in search of Dr. Livingstone, that Stanley finally found his elusive fortune. There, too, in the jungles along the

Congo River, he earned the name *Bulu Matari*—"Breaker of Rocks"—a name he wore proudly. He went to his death, inscribing the name on his gravestone, unaware that the Congolese who gave it to him were laughing at his expense—the white man who had rocks in his head.

Hero, conman, or fool, Stanley was an extraordinary character who fueled my fascination with Africa, the place where he built his own legend out of the mud. Somehow I got it into my head to retrace portions of his Emin Pasha Relief Expedition into the northeast corner of what was then the Belgian Congo—a journey into the Ituri rain forest that Joseph Conrad drew on for his novel *Heart of Darkness*. I wasn't sure where the journey would take me, but I knew I'd come out of it with some pictures and a piece I could sell in New York.

Naturally I found no trace of Stanley. I didn't expect to. The rain forest had washed away any hint of him. Following Stanley was just a story, a pitch—a path into the jungle. Once there, the story became my own. What I did find on the banks of the Ituri River was a way to put Marilyn and my failed marriage out of my mind.

There is no other light in the world like that which falls through the canopy of a rain forest, dappling the undergrowth and ground underfoot. Shafts of the white-hot light cut through the humid air, deepening the darkness of the surrounding shadows—the shadows from which the Mbuti forest people emerged. Four feet tall, with perfectly muscled limbs, small potbellies, and glistening eyes, they had us surrounded—*us* being me and Momoti, my guide and translator. The Mbuti were neither hostile nor threatening, but simply guiding us, as their guests, into their camp. They were the silent herdsmen, and we were the noisy stumbling herd of two.

Arriving at their camp, the Mbuti made me feel right at home. Although a little bashful at first, they were as curious about me as I was about them. I offered a gift of some slabs of salted fish and enjoyed some roasted antelope in return. After dinner—the light draining quickly out of the jungle—I put on a magic show with my cigarette lighter, some water, and a Bromo-Seltzer tablet. They were quite amused—whether by the fire and bubbles or by the big white man playing with his toys, I'm not sure—but the performance won them over. In less than an hour, they built a hut for me to sleep in, a kind of prefab crib made of vines and saplings and a waterproof siding of giant shiny leaves of the Mongongo tree.

In the morning I joined them on a hunt—a six-mile walk to a narrow ravine. The men stretched nets of vine—about the size and shape of the nets at Wimbledon's center court—across a narrow ravine, anchoring them to trees. The women went off to the far side of the ravine to beat the animals out of their hiding places. Suddenly the women began to call out, signaling to the men that animals were headed their way. A gray boloki antelope slammed into the net, and two of the Mbuti charged at it with their spears, the antelope dead in less than a minute. A squealing wild pig followed and met the same fate, the hunt over as quickly as it started.

We headed back to camp, several of the hunters pointing at me and nodding their heads. Apparently the success of the day's hunt had endeared me to them. I was their good-luck charm, and while they had me, they'd put me to good use. I slept in the next day, exhausted by the hunt, and I awoke to find they were waiting for me. First thing I had to do was smear elephant dung on my legs, arms, chest, and cheeks. Today they were going after a real prize—an elephant—and they didn't want the herd to get wind of us.

After several hours of tracking, we spotted a small family of elephants, and after a short conference, they settled on one cow in particular for attack. She was distracted by an amorous bull's advances toward her, and thus would make easier prey. The price of love can be high in any jungle. The Mbuti moved with the patience of commandos, inch by inch through the mud, until they were close enough for a rush. Five of them broke from their cover and hurled themselves under the elephant's belly, springing upright with their spears extended. The cow let out an anguished scream, and after a moment's indecision, stumbled off into the brush.

All that afternoon into the evening, the relentless—and tireless— Mbuti Pygmies stalked her. Again, darkness came quickly, and we settled for the night in the middle of nowhere. At dawn we picked up the elephant's spoor, coming on a trail of congealed blood covered with flies. One of the hunters yelled something, and we all ran up to him. He had found a spear, which the animal had evidently removed from her belly. Apparently a good sign, and indeed, a few hundred yards ahead, there she was, fallen on her side, dead.

The Mbuti, in a collective ecstasy, butchered the cow, hacking out the prime cuts. Elephant meat was a great delicacy, and once smoked would feed the entire tribe royally for more than a month. That night, they served it with jugs of palm wine and treated me—as their lucky piece—to an unusual gift. They allowed me to bear witness to their celebratory dance—a feverish, erotic, graceful, and undulating ballet between the men and women who had participated in the elephant killing. A celebration of death that was a celebration of life. And then they ordered me back to my hut. Apparently I had seen enough. It was time for me to go home—to an empty apartment in Great Neck.

Marilyn had gone from Reno directly to San Diego to restart her life, and I would never see her again. Nor would I ever see the Mbuti again. But I would return to Africa again and again. I sold the story, "I Lived with the Pygmies," to *Male*, and it ran in their November 1955 issue—seven months after my divorce from Marilyn and two months after my spread with Marilyn Monroe appeared in *Esquire*.

Then it was 1956.

February. In Moscow, in the early morning hours of February 25, 1956, Nikita Khrushchev summoned the delegates of the Twentieth Party Congress of the Communist Party to a closed session in the Great Hall of the Kremlin. There, to a stunned audience, he delivered what came to be known as the "secret" speech—"On the Cult of Personality and Its Consequences." The consequences of the speech would ultimately lead to 2,500 dead in the streets of Budapest.

The contents of the "secret" speech remained secret for little more than two weeks. In the middle of March, Radio Free Europe broadcast the details of the speech into Hungary. They reported, with a tone of breathless opportunity and optimism, that Khrushchev had denounced Joseph Stalin, his regime, and his purges as, in essence, criminal.

It was not easy to communicate with Budapest. I often exchanged postcards with my father, but if they contained anything remotely political, they invariably disappeared en route. The news I did get came from Sy Bourgin and other correspondents who covered the region. They told me that the RFE broadcast had changed the conversation in the cafes and universities. Mátyás Rákosi, who ran Hungary, was long considered to be Stalin's puppet. And now the Kremlin had cut the strings. The feeling was that not only had the conversation changed, but everything had. There was a growing sense of anticipation. Possibility was in the air. The fuse had been lit.

Freedom is a tricky thing—seductive, slippery, unpredictable, and at times a pain in the ass. Something like Marilyn Monroe, I suppose. Because once you've had a taste of freedom, you never want to give it up, and you're never quite satisfied. You always want more of it. The divorce final, I was a free man in more ways than one—but not an entirely happy man. As bad a husband as I had been to Marilyn, I missed her company. I believe in sharing life with a woman. In other words, I'm the marrying kind.

Marilyn left me behind, and I did the same to our home in Great Neck, taking an apartment on 62nd Street near Madison Avenue in Manhattan. Coincidentally, I was also making a move professionally to Madison Avenue. I made a good living taking pictures for stories in magazines but knew I could make a better one taking pictures for the advertisements that ran alongside them. I wasn't giving up on the magazine work, just branching out . . . restless.

The war had been good for business; ad agencies were throwing money around like it was confetti, and I wanted to catch some of it. At first I worked with the smaller agencies, establishing my credentials and building my portfolio. Down the road I'd join the fun at J. Walter Thompson and at some of the other monsters of Madison Avenue, but for now I just wanted to get my foot in the door. One of my first campaigns was for a local furniture store—a campaign that would feature the client's sofas and chairs comfortably nestling a father, a mother, and a couple of kids with a dog curled up at their feet. I had to put together a family.

The hardest part was the kids. That's always the hardest part. A modeling agency sent a mob of them over, but the auditions didn't go well. My furniture family would have to wait. But I did get a start on a different family that day. Mine. Five-year-old Kevin and his three-year-old sister Kim both struck poses for me, but neither got a callback from me. Their mother, however, did, and within a few months Kevin and Kim would be squirming around on my sofa and chairs. My father had first met my mother in his studio. It was fitting that I would first meet Eleanor in mine.

July. Convinced that the time was up for Stalin's best pupil in Budapest, the Kremlin suggested to Rákosi that he travel to Moscow for his health. He didn't return to Hungary until 1971, when his ashes were smuggled back to the country to be buried.

The political atmosphere in Budapest that summer was electric. Sy Bourgin told me that the situation was uncanny. The secret police had vanished, he said, and the waiters in the cafes didn't listen to you, because no one in Hungary took orders from anyone anymore. Dozens of political prisoners being released every day, the government had begun to hold press conferences, unheard of under Rákosi, and there was open talk in the public squares and clubs of bringing change to the system—talk that would've landed you in a prison cell six months earlier. The fear Hungarians had been living with for the last decade was replaced with anger.

Bourgin told me he had contacted several of his friends in the CIA and American Army intelligence to see if they were aware of the volatility in Budapest. He said they just shook their heads: "Hungarians? They're all talk and no action." It was just a bunch of poets and professors, they said, eggheads agitating, and nothing would ever come of it.

Apparently, except for the "nothing would ever come of it" part, Khrushchev agreed. As he would later reflect: "If ten or so Hungarian writers had been shot at the right moment, the revolution would never have occurred."

Meanwhile, in the United States, 1956 was an election year. Eisenhower, seeking reelection against the liberal Adlai Stevenson, tacked to the right, speaking like a good Cold Warrior, promising to bring freedom and democracy to *all* of Europe. Some Hungarians may have been guilty of taking him at his word. As Vice President Richard Nixon put it, behind closed doors, "It wouldn't be an unmixed evil, from the point of view of the US interest, if the Soviet fist were to come down hard again on the Soviet bloc."

Something else Bourgin told me: Hungary's borders were opening up, the government issuing more passports. It was time for me to work some angles—and find a way to get my father out of Dodge. Sy wrote me that the country most likely to issue a visa was Colombia, in South America. I began a correspondence with the Colombian authorities, but the more I heard from them, the less I liked the idea—to free my father from one dictatorship, then ship him off to another.

August. The morning of August 10, I achieved a lifelong dream. Irving Hoffman and Frank Gibney agreed to perjure themselves before a federal judge, swearing that I was a decent guy. I took a test, pledged my allegiance, and became an American citizen. In Hungary, the natives were restless, but officially I was no longer one of them. Not to say that I wasn't restless.

<hr />

If I had gone out into the world in search of a mate who was the polar opposite of Marilyn, I might well have found Eleanor. Part Irish and part Polish but as American as fireworks on the Fourth of July, Eleanor was raised in Troy in upstate New York, a working-class brick-and-smokestack town on the Hudson River. Nothing had ever been handed to her—and she never expected it to be. Her father worked hard; her mother counted the pennies and put food on the table. Life was tough but worth the struggle.

Eleanor didn't harbor resentment. Anger, happiness, sadness—the moment she felt it, you knew about it, her temper as quick as her laugh. In her heart, though, nothing was more important than family, and she put all her energy into building a nest for those she loved. But she also liked to spread her wings, never shying away from a challenge. She agreed to take me on, after all.

The divorced mother of two, she lived with her kids in a small apartment on the Upper East Side. Whenever I was in town that summer, we spent time together—dinners in the city, drives into the country—and discovered we had a lot in common. A love of good food and fast cars, for instance.

Doug Kennedy, who in 1955 had replaced Ken Purdy as editor of *True*, had introduced me to one of his passions—rally racing, a motorsport that takes place on public roads. He had also introduced me to some of his friends at the New York headquarters of Triumph Motor Cars. Triumph was looking for ways to increase its visibility and thus its market share. They hired me as an in-house photographer for their advertising— a small account, but one that came with perks. They were also looking for someone to drive one of their cars in several upcoming American rallies; they wanted the free publicity. I raised my hand. I had plenty of experience breaking speed limits. Not only that, I could do some stories on the rallies and get them published. I was in.

When I told Eleanor about this fast new hobby of mine, she said she'd love if she could go along for the ride sometime. I said, let's get married, promising her it would be one hell of a ride.

In the middle of the summer, Eleanor and I tied the knot. Her family was in no position to give us a big wedding, and neither of us wanted one anyway. My friend Bill Homan, the amateur photographer, said we could say our vows at his bachelor pad on 75th Street. Letting her fingers do the walking, the ever-resourceful Eleanor found someone in the Yellow Pages to officiate over the proceedings, and in the blink of an eye we were husband and wife with two kids. My life was moving as fast as one of those race cars, and that fall it would pick up even more speed.

October. Eleanor was pregnant. The news took my breath away, replacing it with joy, excitement, anxiety, uncertainty—a range of emotions I hadn't felt since first stepping off the ship into the streets of New York. I had been many things in my life, but never a father. I was entering a whole new country.

Meanwhile, halfway around the world, in Budapest, something else was born: a revolution. On October 22, five thousand students crammed into a university lecture hall and created a sixteen-point manifesto demanding free elections, a free press, the reintroduction of Hungarian national holidays and symbols, the removal of the statue of Stalin from Heroes' Square, and the evacuation of all Soviet troops from Hungary.

To many in Budapest, the sixteen points were a call to action, a vision of Hungary's future. To the Kremlin, they were a poke in the eye with a sharp stick.

The next day, hundreds of thousands of people took to the streets, gathering at the Parliament building and laying siege to the radio station. In Heroes' Square, factory workers finally succeeded in toppling the bronze statue of Stalin, breaking off pieces to take home as souvenirs. At the radio station, members of the state security service (AVO) shot into the crowd, killing several students. A unit of the Hungarian army arrived, but the commander refused to fire on the demonstrators. Some of the soldiers joined the protesters; others handed their rifles off to the students and returned to their barracks. By midnight, the radio station was in flames, the protest had turned into a riot, and then there was an armed insurrection. The streets were on fire.

There were no leaders, no plans, no organization, no command structure at all to the uprising. Fighters materialized out of nowhere, attacked the Soviet troops and tanks, then evaporated back into the alleyways and courtyards. In the first few days, there was only enthusiasm and excitement—which quickly turned to blood, anger, and a desire for revenge.

Over the next week chaos took hold of Budapest, street fights interrupted by short-lived ceasefires, slaughters, and atrocities on both sides. Soviet tanks and AVO men fired indiscriminately into crowds, massacring women and children. Mobs attacked anyone they suspected of working with the AVO, lynching them or hanging them by their ankles from trees and beating them to death. The torturers had become the tortured, bodies swinging from every lamppost.

Radio Free Europe, meanwhile, continued to broadcast its encouragement, urging the freedom fighters to stiffen resistance, reporting massive defections of Soviet soldiers to the Hungarian side. At best it was wishful thinking. At worst it was a deception designed to raise false hope and induce more fifteen-year-olds to risk their lives hurling Molotov cocktails at Soviet tanks.

Hungary's leaders were no longer in charge of anything but a complete state of confusion. They desperately tried forming one new government after another—hoping to placate both the Kremlin and the people in the street—but their actions were empty. They didn't matter anymore. The decisions that would decide the fate of Hungary and the uprising would be made in Moscow and Washington.

The Kremlin didn't know what to do, changing its tune by the hour. They'd withdraw all their troops from Budapest. They'd send more in. Or they'd just wait and see what happened next. In the White House, Eisenhower's team looked forward to Election Day. Confident of victory, they eyed Eastern Europe anxiously, hoping nothing would happen to tarnish the president and alter the electoral math.

A week in, the rebellion had all come to nothing. A stalemate.

Then, on October 29, a battalion of Israeli paratroopers were airdropped onto the Sinai Peninsula—an attack on Egypt soon joined by the British and the French in response to Gamal Abdel Nasser's decision to nationalize the Suez Canal. The eyes of the West turned to the Middle East, and the uprising in Hungary had become a sideshow—yesterday's news.

On October 31, while kids in America were dressing up like cowboys and Indians and heading out for candy, Nikita Khrushchev reached a verdict. After screening newsreels of the fighting in Hungary, including the lynching of AVO officers, he ordered an all-out invasion, to be conducted ruthlessly and without mercy. "Budapest," he said, "was like a nail in my head."

At his morning briefing to President Eisenhower, CIA Director Allen Dulles said, "There's some good news." The Soviets, he went on, appeared to be pulling all their forces out of Budapest. And in that city, Hungarians were dancing in the streets, toasting their victory.

November. It was a Sunday, and I was at my studio developing some film and sorting through some pictures I had taken on another recent assignment to Africa, Kenya this time. The idea of the piece was that you could hunt and shoot big game, and even bring back trophies, without killing them or even carrying a gun. The story was titled "Camera Safari." I had the radio on, listening to music, and late in the afternoon, the news. I put down my work.

There were reports coming out of Vienna of fighter jets flying over Budapest, of the ground shaking inside the city, and of the sky lighting up on the horizon. I had known all along that sooner or later it would come, and now I knew it had started. I also knew that it would soon be over. I worried about my father. Locking up my studio, I headed home to Eleanor and the kids. They'd moved into my apartment—it was cozy, but we made do. I made some phone calls, but it would be days before I'd get any news about my father.

The headline of Monday's morning paper announced the British and French invasion of Egypt. The subheadline said "Russians Crush Hungarian Rebels." It was over and done. Khrushchev sent 150,000 troops, 2,500 of the Soviet army's newest tanks, along with plenty of air support, into Hungary. Eisenhower promised twenty million dollars in food and medical aid and sent a message: "At this moment, the heart of America goes out to the people of Hungary."

The following day, Tuesday, November 6, I cast my first vote in an American presidential election. I voted for Eisenhower. I knew who he was. He had liberated Western Europe. All I knew about Adlai Stevenson was that he had a hole in his shoe and that some of his fellow Democrats—particularly those from the south like Strom Thurmond—didn't seem to believe in democracy at all.

I didn't blame Eisenhower for what had just happened in Hungary. I saw how things worked. I had been inside Radio Free Europe, and Eisenhower couldn't be held responsible for what had been said in his name. It was the people in the dark shadows and secret rooms, the provocateurs and public relations men, who drove the Hungarians to slaughter.

Although I, too, like so many others, was crushed by the failure of the uprising, I draw a line from 1956 to 1989. The Hungarian revolution was the beginning of the end of the Soviet Empire, the first real crack in the Iron Curtain. From then on, the writing was on the Berlin Wall. For a few days in 1956, the Hungarians danced in the streets, believing that they had beaten back the Soviets. In the Congo the Mbuti Pygmies danced around the fire when they brought the elephant to earth—a celebration of life in death.

December. Finally some good news out of Budapest. With Sy Bourgin's help and influence, my father had applied for a visitor's visa to Austria. Although there was a backlog and the machinery was slow, my father, according to Sy, could be out of Hungary within a few months. I could grease the wheels on this end, run around to the various churches, charities, and government agencies that facilitated the movement of refugees out from behind the Iron Curtain, and if all went well, he should be here by spring.

My elation was tempered by a tiny voice in the back of my head: *What have I gotten myself into?* A wife, two kids, as well as another kid—*and* my father—on the way. In addition—multiplication is more like it—my father over the last decade had grown a brood of his own, composed of a wife and two children. I was losing count, my circle expanding and closing in all at the same time. What kind of freedom was this?

With two kids and a third on the way, Eleanor and I had recently purchased a house in Connecticut. I couldn't afford much, but I found a deal in Weston. The house was set on a lot at the edge of an empty field next to a cemetery—not prime real estate, but it served my purpose. Most buyers shied away from the proximity of ghosts and skeletons. I jumped at the twenty-thousand-dollar asking price. I didn't mind if a few goblins were thrown in.

I spent Christmas in Connecticut, surrounded by the ghosts of the past, present, and future. 1956 had been a hell of a year. I had gone from free agent to family man—husband, father, son, citizen, ad man, madman, breadwinner, suburbanite, king of my castle. Truly an American home-owner with a mortgage on my future. But for now, the only neighbors I could afford were dead people. Under the snow I might as well have had all of Hungary buried in my backyard.

Three generations: Robert with his grandfather, a farmer, and father, a photographer for the Hungarian royal family.

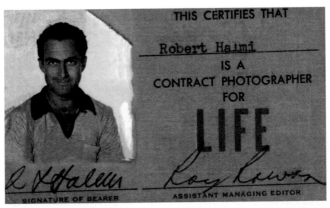

Becoming a *Life* photographer.

Alaskan glacier on assignment.

Photographing New York from a helicopter.

Hunting in Kenya.

Robert lived with Pygmies for three months in the Ituri rain forest in what is now the Democratic Republic of the Congo.

Kirk Douglas and Robert in Palm Springs.

Robert with a pet cheetah on the family's Kenyan game ranch.

On the set of *The Race to the Pole* with Richard Chamberlain.

Candice Bergen on the set of *Mayflower Madam*.

With Raquel Welch in Australia.

Jodie Foster and Peter O'Toole on the set of *Svengali*.

With Vanessa Williams on the set of *The Odyssey*.

With Paul Newman talking about race cars.

Accepting the Genesis Award with Isabella Rossellini.

Whoopi Goldberg as the Cheshire Cat in *Alice in Wonderland*.

With Kelsey Grammer.

John Lithgow as Don Quixote in Spain.

Robert accepting the Genesis Award for *The Last Elephant* (later changed to *Ivory Hunters*) with Jimmy Stewart.

With Patrick Stewart during the making of *Moby Dick*.

CHAPTER SEVEN

From the Bottom of My Heart by the Seat of My Pants

In the mid-1960s I worked on an advertising campaign for Canadian Club whiskey. The idea was to position Canadian Club as the world's favorite alcoholic beverage—with an adventure in every bottle. That's where I came in, circling the globe and uncorking the adventure. I trekked from one exotic locale to another, young North American men and women in tow—models playing tourist, soaking up the local culture and color, accompanied by a small shot of them soaking up a whiskey on the rocks at the local cantina. One assignment took me down to South America to photograph a young fellow in an oxford shirt and purple sweater waving a red cape in front of an angry bull. The ad's headline read:

"They told me it wasn't a real bullfight. But they forgot to tell the bull."

From the late '50s into the '60s, that could also stand as the headline of my life. I was always messing with bulls who didn't know the rules. *My only rule was to make sure I was running with the bulls rather than away from them.* I wanted to see what I was up against. But for years I didn't stop moving, going off to god knows where to get into god knows what.

The first week in March 1957, I went fishing. But instead of bringing along a rod and reel and a bucket of worms, I packed an ice ax, wet suit, scuba tank, harpoon, underwater flashlight, and camera. I had no intention of luring the fish to come to me; I was going to go in after them. Together with my two-man team—this not the kind of fishing you want to do alone—we chopped a hole in the frozen surface of a glacier-fed lake at the northern edge of the Canadian Rockies, donned full-body sets of woolen underwear topped by quilted underwear and our rubber suits, and dived in.

I might as well have taken the plunge naked, the icy chill seeping through the layers of wool and rubber as wantonly as a ghost through a brick wall. But it would make a good story.

The piece ran several months later in *Sports Illustrated*, the money shot a picture of a hand poking up out of the ice like the Statue of Liberty clutching an eight-pound walleye pike—the hard-earned trophy of our frostbitten descent into the watery gloom. And that walleye took on a life of his own. The photograph ran in a nationally syndicated newspaper column, touting the adventures of Bob Halmi, the wild man of photography. In it the writer included my advice to budding photographers on how to seize the moment and capture nature in the raw. I didn't reveal all my secrets, though. What I left out of the story—neglected even to tell my editors at *Sports Illustrated*— was that we couldn't catch a fish that day to save our lives.

After an eerie half hour in the murky lake, we surfaced empty-handed. I told my team to hold tight and made a quick trip back into town, buying the biggest, fattest walleye I could lay my hands on. I took it back to our hole in the ice, handed it to one of the others, and told him to dive in and thrust that fat fish into the air. Sometimes reality just isn't good enough. You have to give it a nudge, add some props, and give some direction. But I got my shot.

The next morning I got something else: a telegram from home. *It's a boy*, it said, fatherhood beginning for me much in the way it played out over the next decade, with me missing out. Two days later, back in Weston in my house by the cemetery, I held Robert Halmi Jr.—Robi—in my arms. He was about the size of that walleye pike. A surge of joy mixing with a sense of adventure, I felt for a moment as helpless as the baby. It was like falling in love.

As I look back over the decades, in Robi I see a reflection of my fish story—improvising, turning obstacles into opportunities, running into town to get the fish so I could get the shot. To this day, when I need money to make a movie, I turn to Robi to go out and find the financing. Whether it's a suitcase full of cash or a hundred-million-dollar line of credit, I can always count on Robi to make something out of nothing. Just like his old man. But that was years away. My genius financier was still in diapers. For now and the foreseeable future, I had to go out and catch my own fish.

Sometime in the late 1940s, an American missionary whose name has been lost to history brought his love of God and of the water hyacinth to the Congo River basin. Put off by the dull brown water that flowed past his mission, he set out to redecorate, tossing several seedlings of the plant onto the riverbank. The water hyacinth produces a gorgeous flower, pink with a flame of yellow and blue at its heart. Each plant also produces thousands of seeds a year, its population doubling every two weeks. The hyacinth is a beautiful, seductive serial killer with the capacity to strangle entire river systems.

I learned all this from Captain Jacques. En route back to the States from an elephant hunt, I met the captain on the *Congolia 9*, a ferryboat plying the Congo River between Brazzaville and Leopoldville. He told me that great beds of the stuff floated randomly down the river, breeding swarms of blood-sucking insects, blocking out sunlight and killing the fish, clogging hydroelectric plants and the propellers of his ferry. "The missionary made his hyacinth bed," he said, "and now we have to lie in it." The French government, he concluded, would pay a lot of money to figure out a way to kill the weed.

Before leaving on this trip, back in New York, I had made a deal with the producers of an NBC radio program called *Monitor*. Hosted by Dave Garroway and Monty Hall among others, *Monitor* was a weekend-long program featuring news, music, comedy, sports, and remote live interviews. I had told the show's producers that I often came across colorful characters in my travels, and as they were always looking for five-minute spots to fill their air space, they agreed to give me a shot. To that end, I had brought along a shortwave radio.

I told Captain Jacques that his story was an important one, and I wanted to get it out to the world. I said I would talk to my friends in America and come back the next day, Saturday, early in the afternoon—early evening in New York—to interview him, live, on the radio. He enthusiastically endorsed the plan, as did *Monitor*'s producers when I reached them that evening. We'd go live, "from the Heart of Darkness," Saturday at 6:25 p.m., their time.

The next day, I showed up at the ferry dock a little after noon, giving myself a good hour to make sure I could set up the shortwave connection with New York. That turned out to be no problem. What did turn out to be a problem was that Captain Jacques was nowhere to be found. One of the crew members told me in French that the day before had been Captain Jacques's last day before going off on a two-week holiday. And there was nobody else on the boat who spoke a word of English. There was only one way out of this pickle. I would interview myself, act as interviewer and interviewee. I would have to be Captain Jacques.

I made the connection to New York at the appointed time, the quality of the sound less than stellar, which was just as well. Then we went on air. I introduced myself: "This is Robert Halmi, reporting from a ferryboat crossing the Congo River, between Leopoldville and Brazzaville, speaking with the boat's pilot and commander, Captain Jacques." And, putting on my best French accent, I related the story of the missionary and the water hyacinths and the dying fish and the clogged propellers just as he had told it to me. But I wanted to give Captain Jacques a big finish, announcing that the French government was offering a million-dollar reward to anyone who could rid the Congo of its hyacinths. At which point I signed off.

I was in a hurry to get out of Leopoldville, but I wasn't headed back to New York just yet. The night before my interview for *Monitor*, I had received a message at my hotel. It was from my father. Austria had granted him a visitor's visa, and Hungary had let him go. Finally, he was a free man. I caught the first plane to Vienna.

My father, his wife Kato, and their two daughters Julie and Györgyi ran out of the hotel lobby and into the street as my taxi pulled up to the curb in front. They surrounded me, the five of us one big mess of hugs and tears. A week ago I had held my newborn son in my arms. Now, for the first time in twelve years, my father held me in his. We had some catching up to do. But first I had to make a phone call.

My wife Eleanor had left a message at the front desk for me to phone her as soon as I arrived, which I did. She told me that one of *Monitor*'s producers had called, three times already, urgently needing to talk to me. The hotel connected me to New York's NBC offices, and they put me through to the producer. I thought he was going to have a heart attack.

Apparently the French embassy in Washington was being deluged with offers to help clear up the water hyacinth problem on the Congo River and questions on how to claim the million-dollar reward. The embassy had called NBC to find out what the hell was going on, NBC had called *Monitor* to ask *them* what the hell was going on, and now the producer was asking *me* what the hell was going on. I told them to ask Captain Jacques and hung up. My first story for *Monitor* turned out to be my last. If I'm not mistaken, NBC still owes me for the spot.

———◆———

The last time I had seen my father, as I climbed onto the bicycle to ride off to freedom, he had radiated strength and defiance—a man standing on his own two feet. But now he appeared unsteady, betrayed and beaten down by his own country. He had shrunk by several inches, stooped under the weight of it all.

I had brought him this far, out of that nest of vipers in Budapest. Now I had to find a way to bring him home to America. Austria was no place for him. I spent three days running around, knocking on doors and knocking my head against the wall at every religious and diplomatic agency in the city. The only way to get anything done was to get back to the States.

I told my father I'd wire him enough money so that he and his family could stay in the hotel and then made him promise that, once his visa came through, he'd leave all his stuff behind in Vienna, old clothes, bedding, and half-empty bottles of cologne spread around his hotel room. I made a particular point about his giving up his prized portfolio—a black leather box in which he carried his art collection. I explained to him that many Americans did not have a discerning eye for art, and that they might very well mistake his prints for pornography.

When not busy painting portraits of kings, queens, and Russian tsars, the nineteenth-century Hungarian artist Count Mihály Zichy took it upon himself to capture the history of the sexuality of man, from birth to death. Whether done in paint or pen and ink, they are exquisitely detailed and true to life, both physically and emotionally, and they appealed to my father's eye—both as an artist and as a man. I feared, however, that they would not appeal to the eyes of American customs agents.

My father raised an objection: America is a free country, isn't it? Yes, I said, up to a point. What's the problem, then? he wanted to know. They don't know what sex is in America? No, I answered, they don't. In America they make love and they make babies, but they don't have sex. Give the prints to a library, donate them to charity, but leave them to Europe. He grumbled but finally came around, willing to sacrifice erotica for freedom.

The American government's guilt over its disappearing act during the Hungarian uprising combined with a unique opportunity to gather intelligence and poke a stick in the eye of the Soviet bloc led to Operation Mercy. Between November 1956 and the following summer, more than thirty thousand Hungarian refugees were granted asylum in the United States, many of them flown into McGuire Air Force Base in New Jersey and bused to the US Army's Camp Kilmer for processing. My father and his family—now part of *my* family—were among them. They landed Easter Sunday, April 21, 1957, and I drove out to the camp to meet them.

When my father and his family made their way in, I saw that they hadn't left a single thing behind. Two trunks full of clothes, pots and pans, a featherbed—everything, it seemed, except the kitchen sink had made the crossing. And on cue, the customs agent rifling through the stuff stopped and shook his head. My father, who thirty years ago might have challenged the customs agent to a duel, stood up stiffly to his full height and started shaking his finger at the man. Here we go, I thought— my dad, the pornographer, turned away and shipped back behind the Iron Curtain. Who the hell am I going to call to get him out of this one?

In the end I didn't have to make any phone calls. This was Operation Mercy, after all, and they showed it to my father. After a short discussion the customs official let him and his family pass. First thing I said to him was:

"Didn't I tell you to leave your art collection behind?"

"They didn't care about that," he said. "They took away my salami!" The salami he had brought all the way from Budapest had been confiscated by the Americans. An outrage—the first of many.

The second came after I arranged to have his belongings stored at the camp until I could have them shipped to Connecticut. We headed out to the parking lot, to my gorgeous Jaguar saloon, a pearl among the swine of Fords, Chevys, and Plymouths. The look on my father's face reminded me of his expression back when I was on trial in Budapest. He whispered to me, as if to hide the family shame: "Are things so bad with you that you can't afford a big car like the other Americans?"

And then there were the tollbooths on the turnpike: "It is unsocial and undemocratic to collect tolls from the free American people."

My father's health might be failing, but his voice wasn't. He was a man of many opinions, and America brought them all out. How was it that stamps were only sold in the post office, and he could never find one? Why were advertisers allowed to interrupt the entertainment on the television? And who was responsible for the muddy water Americans called coffee? He refused to drink it and didn't trust frozen foods. Once, when after much debate and negotiation around the dinner table I convinced him to try a single corn niblet prepared from a package of Birds Eye, he turned to his wife Kato and said with the greatest surprise: "It tastes like corn."

My house, meanwhile, was bursting at the seams. If nothing else, the IRS would take notice—me taking no dependents one year and cooking up half a dozen the next. I tried to set my father up in business for himself, but his brand of photography was not for this world. There were no dukes and duchesses to pose in front of the camera here.

My father came with me into my studio every day, but there was nothing much for him to do there, except express amazement that I managed to make a living taking the kind of pictures I did. To his way of thinking, taking the camera out of the studio was akin to having a steering wheel without a car: pointless and a little ridiculous.

At lunch, to break up the day—and give my father something else to think about aside from my shortcomings as a photographer—I took him out to see the sights. He ogled at the Empire State Building and the Fifth Avenue office girls on their break. He liked to walk around Greenwich Village and the Italian neighborhood south of it. The small shops and cafes reminded him of Budapest when he first arrived there. He had mixed feelings about the city as a whole, however. He had been in America for over a year, and we were walking up Park Avenue, toward the brand-new Seagram Building. "New York is very proud of itself," he said. "Covering itself with glass and mirrors, all designed to reflect the city's wealth and power and business."

I rented an apartment for my father and his family on Long Island. It was also time for my family to move on. Between Eleanor, the kids Kim, Kevin, and Robi, and me, the house in Weston couldn't contain us anymore; we needed room to breathe. Leaving the cemetery behind, we headed to greener pastures—and a bigger house—across the New York state line in Rye. And in the nick of time.

Before the decade was out, a new member would be added to the cast. On February 26, 1959, Billy came into our world. Naturally I wasn't there to see it—I was off in Wyoming photographing clowns, bucking broncos, and rodeo riders—but Eleanor told me it was the strangest thing: Billy didn't cry at all at birth. He came out laughing. When I first saw him, he gave me a crooked smile, and I knew: *This one's trouble*. He had mischief written all over his face. Where he got that gene from, I have no idea.

The house in Rye was leafy and spacious, an American Dream house with lawns to mow, hedges to trim, and a mortgage to pay. But that's not the way my father saw it. A house made of wood? Peasants lived in wood houses, and he wanted to know why I couldn't afford one made of stone.

My family kept growing, but I didn't let them hold me down. If anything, my family life fueled my ambition and accelerated my passion for work. In other words, it was always good to get away.

❦

Going fast is fun, but speed is only one ingredient in a successful sports car rally. Without precision and perseverance you haven't got a chance. You're driving according to a very strict schedule with very little sleep from city to city, down back roads, through small towns, through endless expanses of desert, and across snow-covered mountain passes, taking very great care not to leave any civilian casualties in your wake. Rallying requires meticulous preparation, mechanical skill, endurance, resourcefulness, and a certain single-minded ruthlessness—much like making a movie or living a life. My life, at least. It's cross-country chess with a crash helmet.

January 1958, I took off for France with *True* editor Doug Kennedy, the sole American competitors in that year's Monte Carlo Rally. The fun began with champagne in Paris, a bottle of Cognac packed into our Triumph TR3 for the road. The first sixty-three hours of nonstop driving were uneventful, other than the many villagers along the way greeting us with bread, cheese, and wine and urging us to go faster. As we rose into the foothills, a light snow started to fall—nothing to worry about until we climbed a little higher into the mountains and deeper into the darkness of the night.

The light snow resolved into a winter wonderland, lovely in a postcard, but nowhere near as inviting when illuminated by the headlamps of a small sports car. Doug kept pestering me about my experience as a snow driver, and I assured him I had plenty. Hungary, I improvised, was the Vermont of central Europe. He was not assured. But I figured that if we survived, my driving skills would be vindicated, and if we didn't, what difference did it make?

The road turned as slick as an ice rink, cars stuck in ditches and snowbanks all along the way, me maintaining control of the Triumph with the tips of my fingers and toes, my sphincter clenched tight. It was a relief, finally, to leave the ice and drive into half a foot of snow. We came upon a Jaguar, inching through the snow, driven by a couple of British military types, and we had to pass them. I gave a little beep, and the car moved slightly to the right . . . and disappeared. I had beeped them straight into a two-hundred-foot gorge. We stopped and called down, "Are you all right?" "Yes," came the faint reply, "Did you pass okay?"

We didn't get far before taking a fall of our own. The visibility down to a few feet, I took a blind curve and spotted the flashing lights and three-car pileup too late for the brakes to do any good. I told Doug to hold on and yanked the Triumph into a snowbank. We bounced off the bank, and the car did a side flip, landing roof-side down. We slid slowly down the road until we came to a gentle stop in another pile of snow. We crawled out, and with the help of a couple of Frenchmen, turned the car over. We'd lost a few quarts of oil and some of my camera equipment, but none of our enthusiasm.

We got back into the race, with Kennedy at the reins. He pointed out that he couldn't do worse. Which was true. Several miles on, he found a snowbank to call his own, from which it took us a good two hours to disengage. In the end none of it—not a dent or a ding or a twisted fender or crushed roof—mattered. Pulling into Monte Carlo, we were disqualified for arriving fifteen minutes too late. Sometimes there's something to be said for just reaching the finish line.

Later that same year, at the Alpine Rally, I met a civilian Peugeot head-on. My steering wheel was broken, my windshield smashed—thanks to my helmeted head—and the Peugeot driver had come away from the collision and toward me with a rather nasty gash on his forehead. I fixed that problem with five thousand francs. But the gash in my radiator required a more creative solution. A bystander—a farmer—suggested I plug it with cement. I'm always open to suggestion, and the farmer graciously brought me out a sack. Miraculously, a few handfuls plugged the holes and held water. I stripped off the car's gnarled bumper, hood, and fenders, and off I went, arriving at the finish in Marseilles just in time to pick up entry forms for the next year's event.

As many cars as I cracked up—and tried to nurse across the finish line with chewing gum and chicken wire before they gave up the ghost—that's how many friendships I cemented on the rally circuit. I first met Walter Cronkite at the American Press Club in Vienna just after my escape from Hungary. It was a passing acquaintance, Walter on his way to cover the Nuremberg trials and then Moscow for United Press International. Our paths had crossed several times over the years since, but it was only now, in the late '50s, that our paths merged—at the first running of the American International Rally in October 1959.

Entries originated in eight North American cities. The Triumph team, four cars in all, gathered in front of Sardi's on West 44th Street at two in the morning. The drivers were *True*'s Doug Kennedy, me, Walter, and in the ladies' entry, the legendary Denise McCluggage, my wife Eleanor acting as her navigator. We took off at twenty-minute intervals, bound for Denver. Cronkite made it as far as Tennessee, where he drove into a fog, then into a lake, his car rolling over twice on its way into the water. Although he and his navigator walked out unscathed, their Triumph drowned.

I managed to keep my car on the road for another fourteen hundred miles or so, until, just outside of Albuquerque, I caught a deer in my headlights, swerved to avoid it, and rammed into a pine tree. No amount of cement could save this car. It died a quick death. My navigator didn't have a scratch, but the tree gave me a good beating. The whole right side of my head turned black and blue, and I could barely see out of my right eye. But I was going to make it to Denver come hell or high water—and I was going to do it in a Triumph. Disqualification was one thing, failure another. Somehow I convinced a local Triumph dealer to sell me one of his floor models on the spot, though I could only give him a check and asked him not to cash it for a week.

I reached Denver, drove across the finish line, then headed for the nearest hospital, where the doctors saved my eye. It still twitches when I try to read the fine print on a star's contract or when my driver swerves through Manhattan traffic.

The American International Rally wasn't a total loss. Eleanor's team brought home several awards, and I made a great friend. Back in New York I met Cronkite—again at Sardi's, but this time for dinner. We compared notes about the rally and didn't stop talking for the next forty years. He was one of the nicest, classiest men I've ever known—and one of the most fiercely competitive. But his rally days were numbered. After losing himself and his car in the Tennessee fog and water, CBS took him out of the game. He was too valuable a property to be driving around in a sports car crashing into lakes.

No one gave me any such advice, however. I could drive to the ends of the earth if I wanted to—and I did.

The more work I had and the more places I had to go, the happier I was. Between the rallies, my magazine assignments, and my increasing number of clients in advertising, I was an extremely happy man. So happy and so busy, in fact, I took on a couple of assistants to help around the studio and keep the place from going dark during my long and frequent absences.

Victor Sketa never found great success as a photographer, but he was outgoing, a good talker who liked to tell stories, and always entertaining. His primary responsibility around the studio was to play chess with me first thing in the morning—a job he held for the next twenty-five years and which earned him the title of assistant to the producer on several of my early movies. Thomas Veres, on the other hand, was quiet and shy but with a sly sense of humor, and one of the best film developers I've ever worked with. It was a skill he honed during the war as Raoul Wallenberg's personal photographer. I put Thomas in charge of my darkroom, but unlike Victor, he only stayed with me a short time, moving on to a bigger and better darkroom at J. Walter Thompson.

Both Victor and Thomas had joined the exodus out of Hungary after the failed uprising, and I was happy that I was in a position to give them work. I was even happier that they were in a position to take it—because their passage across the Atlantic had not been smooth sailing. Like my father before them, they raised eyebrows and red flags with the American customs officers. But it wasn't salami and erotic etchings that gummed up the works; it was a deal they had made in transit. Somewhere between the two landmasses, moved perhaps by the swell of the ocean, Victor and Thomas had swapped wives.

Everyone wanted out of Hungary now. Even Sy Bourgin, who loved Budapest as much as any man, had had enough. For the better part of a decade, he had reported out of Vienna for *Time*, *Life*, CBS, NBC, and various US government agencies. But whenever his work began to weigh him down, he'd head to Budapest for a breather. By the time of the failed uprising, though, the city had lost its spirit. The people were tired and hungry and afraid, and Sy couldn't abide it. Eastern Europe had worn him out. So when *Newsweek* offered him an escape, as their West Coast bureau chief, he packed up his books and went to Hollywood.

I've always valued my correspondence with Sy, but in the summer of 1959 I received a note from Sy that hit me like a punch to the stomach. He had always liked my former father-in-law Robert Thompson, and coming to California gave him a chance to renew their friendship. So it was through Sy that I learned of my ex-wife Marilyn's sudden death. A brain tumor had stopped her heart, and she was gone before the doctors could do anything.

I thought about her migraines and her temper and wondered how long the malignancy had been taking a toll. I remembered Salzburg and how young and beautiful and lively she had been—my own Miss America. Sooner or later, of course, we are all betrayed by our bodies. As I learned during the war, life is an arbitrary thing, and time is never on our side. We are helpless in the face of death; it always wins. The best we can do is make ourselves a moving target, seek out distractions, tell ourselves stories—though I'm sure no story in the world gave any comfort to Marilyn's father. A large piece of him must have died with her.

I did know that she had remarried and given birth to a son, which must have made her very happy. That was something. Or at least that was the story I told myself. I had to keep moving.

❦

September 1959, and I stood just miles from the Hungarian border clutching a rifle in my hands. But this time I wasn't hunting Nazis or Communists.

The stags were so close we could hear them grunting, followed by the sound of their antlers clashing and crashing—like steel on steel, swordsmen pressing for an advantage. It was rutting season for the European red deer, and the woods around us were full of bulls, half a dozen of the wandering, lustful stags announcing their presence with a deep bellow before butting heads, fighting for control of the harem.

Yugoslavia's President for Life Marshal Josip Broz Tito stood quietly, rifle ready, staring into the dawn mist and the tall reeds only a few yards away. But the deer must have gotten wind of us. They suddenly went quiet and bolted, unseen. Tito—a short, solid man with a commanding presence—lowered his rifle, turned to me with a big grin, and shrugged. He was in no hurry. He had all the time in the world.

We were in the fabulous, marshy forests of Belje, in what is now Croatia, but which for centuries had been the haunt of European royalty, hunting grounds reserved for kings and crowned princes and Presidents for Life. But Roger Fawcett had had a brainstorm, conceiving a series for his magazine, *True Goes Hunting with Famous Men*, and Tito would be the first. As luck would have it, the savvy Yugoslavian president had decided to open the forest to foreign hunters and saw the *True* piece as an opportunity to attract American dollars to his country.

I traveled with Ralph Daigh, Fawcett's swashbuckling editorial director. We were private citizens who had no official portfolio. What we did have were loaded guns. Tito's entourage, his bodyguards and several members of his cabinet, were stern-faced and edgy. They all knew firsthand about the many agents that Stalin had sent to Belgrade to eliminate their leader and had no doubt heard about the American CIA's attempts in Africa and Cuba. As we were introduced to him in the large main room of the lodge, the only person who seemed unconcerned was the smiling Tito himself.

This man—who had fought in the October Revolution in Russia, in the Spanish Civil War, and then as a leader of the partisans in Yugoslavia against the Nazis—was not fazed by a writer and a photographer. He had not come as far as he did without being a shrewd judge of character, and he saw us as fellow sportsmen. He was especially pleased by the gift we brought him.

Roger Fawcett had commissioned the design of a custom-made .300 Weatherby Magnum rifle inlaid with abalone and gold, fitted with a sophisticated fold-aside four-power scope. The moment Tito got his hands on it, he sighted the chandelier and tested the trigger, then insisted on loading it and taking it outside. As we all headed out of the lodge, I warned him to be careful of the scope. As one of the most powerful hunting rifles around, the Weatherby delivered a sharp recoil. He waved me off. He knew what he was doing and took aim at a tree some two hundred yards across the clearing. He pulled the trigger and fell down flat on the ground, blood pouring from his eyebrow. Sonny Liston couldn't have hit him harder.

Half his bodyguards swarmed around Tito, the other half around me. "You shot Tito," they were shouting. "No, no, no," I said in Hungarian (as none of them spoke English, this was the best I could do), "Tito shot himself." No one understood much of anything for the next thirty seconds, until Tito managed to get back to his feet and told his men to let me go. "The Hungarian is innocent," he said. "Let's not start World War III." Nonetheless, for the remainder of our stay, Tito referred to me as "the assassin."

After a couple of stitches to stanch the bleeding, dinner was served: a clear soup with a raw egg floating in each bowl, and cold cuts, including an entire suckling pig sliced like a loaf of bread. Sitting next to me, the vice president, Aleksandar Ranković, touched my shoulder and pointed out a shoulder cut. It proved to be delicious. A row of wine bottles awaiting Tito's command stood at attention down the length of the table. We drank the wine and shared hunting stories—a sometimes baffling back-and-forth of English, Serbo-Croatian, and Hungarian. Later in the den, under the mellow influence of slivovitz, a pale-yellow plum brandy, Tito shared the secret of how he honed his skill as a hunter: shooting Nazis during the war.

The next day, after a few hours' sleep and a big breakfast, we climbed into a row of jeeps waiting outside in the morning twilight. Belje was alive with lovelorn stags. The jeeps came to a shallow river and a scow-like ferry connected by pulleys to a rope. The drivers jumped out and pulled us across into a deeper, darker, thicker forest—a setting for a Grimm's fairy tale. After several stops and starts, following the trail of bellowing stags, we came to an open glade. On the far edge a string of ghostlike figures, female deer, moved through the mist.

Weatherby in hand, Tito climbed down from his jeep. He would have the first shot. The celebrated guerrilla fighter moved off the road into the camouflage of the forest and crouched beneath some branches, waiting for the stag that was certain to accompany the deer. Then came a flash of antlers, the stag moving cautiously at first, but then breaking into a run. From 150 yards away, Tito took his shot, one shot, and the stag ran on another thirty yards and dropped to the ground. The deer lifted his head once to see who had done this to him, and then he died, a bullet in his heart. Tito said that every animal deserved a clean kill, adding that a fine would be levied on any hunter who shot a stag that got away. He didn't like the idea of his deer slowly bleeding to death in the forest.

A little further on, we switched from the jeeps into several horse-drawn surreys, which took us to a small chalet in the forest. As we approached, we saw men carrying chairs and cushions to a long, cloth-covered table that had been set out under a large oak tree. There was a fire, with a yearling pig and a lamb on two spits turned by a couple of the men. Tito pulled a transistor radio out of his pocket and tuned it to some popular music, then strolled over to the fire. He cut himself a willow switch, stuck a piece of bread on it, and getting down on his haunches, held it under the spitted pig to catch the drippings.

Our hosts brought out more wine and slivovitz, but I decided I needed more pictures for the piece. I climbed into one of the surreys with my jaeger—my hunting attendant—my cameras, and a rifle. Within an hour I had photographed four or five stags, but when I reached for the rifle the jaeger shook his head, held his nose, stuck out his tongue, or simply sneered with contempt. These were all apparently too young or too small, and a sin worse than wounding an adult stag was killing a boy. The pantomime lasted well into the afternoon, the forest shadows growing longer. But a hunter must not only be a good shot, he must have the patience to get one. And I did.

The jaeger heard the bellow and put up his hands, eyes wide. He looked at his watch, waited ten minutes, then led me on foot through the woods, to within a hundred yards of the stag. I dropped to one knee, carefully took aim at his neck and pulled the trigger, severing the animal's spine. "*Kaput*," the jaeger said. We cut off the stag's head and loaded it onto the surrey. I asked what would happen to the meat. He told me that they would come back later, pick up the carcass, and freeze it. Most of the stag meat was shipped to the English at Christmastime.

Back at the chalet, Tito nodded his head and congratulated me on my kill. While I shared with him the details of the hunt, two chairs had been brought forward onto the lawn, and the stag head leaned against them. The jaeger approached, swishing a fresh-cut limber stick about the length and diameter of a golf-club shaft. I was then instructed to bend over the chairs with my head and shoulders hanging between the antlers, and my bottom in the air. With obvious relish, Tito's avid encouragement, and three hard whacks to the backside, the jaeger initiated me into the ranks of Yugoslavian stag hunters. Inscribed in ink on the stick were the words *Belje, September 14, 1959.*

Not long after my initiation, the festivities at Belje were interrupted by a distant and far-different kind of hunt. An aide carrying a dispatch case came hurrying over to Tito and handed him a sheaf of pink sheets. Studying the papers intently, Tito motioned to one of his generals, and the two of them withdrew into the chalet, the rest of us standing around sipping wine and waiting for the other shoe to drop. Minutes later, Tito emerged onto a second-floor balcony to say he had an announcement:

"Early this morning," he said, "the Russians hit the moon."

It took a moment to sort out exactly what happened, but it soon became clear that a rocket carrying the flag of the Soviet Union had successfully crash-landed on the moon. His aide asked him if he wanted to release a statement. Tito nodded thoughtfully and lit a cigarette: "It is a truly extraordinary day, and President Tito would like to extend his congratulations—on behalf of all the Yugoslavian people—to my American friend Robert Halmi who today killed a stag—and got a good spanking for it."

Tito then looked down at me and spread his hands out apologetically. "But I'm afraid the news will not be the headline tomorrow."

—◦—

I loved America and loved democracy but was befuddled by those who professed to lead it. After 1956 I had no tolerance for American politicians. With a few exceptions, they came across as poor actors reading from a bad script auditioning for a part. They were shadows without substance.

The difference between my life in Hungary and my life in America was that here I could express my distaste for the country's leadership without fear of persecution or prosecution. I was free to sound off at one of Cronkite's parties, in a room filled with the William Paleys and Henry Kissingers of the world, and not have to worry about being rousted out of my bed later that night and hauled off to prison. Speak my mind, go home to my family, and go back to work the next morning—that, to me, is the essence of freedom.

At the end of the '50s and start of the '60s, the craziest assortment of jugglers, clowns, and lion tamers performed under the advertising tent. On Madison Avenue there was only one rule—and that was, *there are no rules*. History didn't exist, and where you came from didn't matter. You could graduate from Harvard or drop out of high school; as long as you had the goods and could do the work, you'd get the job. It was a pure meritocracy.

Lennon and Newell, the first big agency I worked for, was right in the thick of it, their office on Madison Avenue in the upper forties. Its account executives went the extra mile to serve, entertain, and provide for their clients. They acted as best buddy, bartender, tour guide, accomplice, and dating service, billing for every minute, martini, and hot-sheet hotel room. The agency even went so far on behalf of one client—the sponsor of a *Playhouse 90* episode dealing with the Nuremberg trials—to demand that all references to gas chambers be removed from the script. The client was the American Gas Association.

I knew to schedule my meetings for the morning. After that the clients took over. The lunches were liquid, and the afternoons a wash.

Wherever You Go, You Look Better in an Arrow Shirt. And I set out to prove it, joining art director, account guy, and former Olympic track star turned male model Bill Albans—a cross between Robert Mitchum and Jean-Paul Belmondo—as we rode a wave of Arrow Shirt cash on a round-the-world trip to fourteen countries in twenty-eight days. And Arrow Shirts do look great on former Olympic track stars posing with beautiful female models under an umbrella in a Paris rain shower, riding a painted elephant in New Delhi, reading a book at Oxford, mounting a windmill in Holland, taking in the sun on the Lido in Venice, or sharing a moment at the Parthenon, Pyramids, or Taj Mahal.

Considering the logistics of the campaign—connections we had to make, shoots we had to set up, languages we had to speak, regulations we had to skirt, palms we had to grease, and shirts we had to press—the Arrow job was one of the most challenging I've ever taken on. Until, that is, I started making movies.

Advertisers flocked to the *Wherever You Go* idea, looking for ways to showcase their products in far-flung locales. Consequently, I was all over the map. Newport Cigarettes wanted blue sky and blue water—the bluest of the blue—sending me to Sicily and Acapulco. For Canadian Club, who sought to pack the world into every bottle, I flew off not only to Ecuador for the bullfight, but to Austria for the skiing and Australia for the surf.

I was going places—for Lennon and Newell, J. Walter Thompson, and BBDO. I had steady work and more money coming in than ever before. I'd gotten my father out of Hungary and settled comfortably on Long Island. I had a growing family sitting pretty in a nice—even if it was made of wood—house in Westchester. The world, it seemed, had become my oyster, and I ate it up. Not that I had seen any of it coming. I never had a five-year plan. I never had a five-*day* plan. I just followed my nose and followed my camera, making it up as I went along. All I did was take pictures. Maybe *I* was that bull who didn't know the rules.

Even cosmetics companies were getting in on the act. Dubarry planned an ad campaign with a storyline—*Beauty and the Beast*—and the next thing I knew I was making camp in Kenya with a professional hunter and four models from New York. The idea was to photograph the beauties—blond, brunette, red-, and raven-haired—as closely as possible to the beasts—lion, elephant, water buffalo, and whatever else we could scare up. We tracked the animals by day, but the nights were a different story. The hunter and I had our eyes on bigger game. We had pitched two tents, one for us and, a shout away, another for the women. But how often does one find oneself out on the savannah, miles from civilization, in the company of four stunning models? It seemed natural to us that we mix up the sleeping arrangements. But the women didn't see it that way.

Our advances deflected, we decided to take more desperate measures. We'd scare them into our tent. We told them all about the wild animals surrounding our camp and suggested that, if they ever felt themselves in danger, we'd be there to protect them. All they had to do was give us a yell. Then, late that night, the hunter and I grabbed some raw steaks out of our meat locker, crept into the darkness, tied the meat to the ropes of the women's tent, and hurried back to ours. Within minutes hyenas were howling around the camp and scratching at the canvas. But these weren't just beautiful models. These were beautiful *New York* models. They had chased away far more dangerous predators than we could conjure up. All of us—both hunters and hyenas—slept alone that night.

The world wasn't quite the oyster I had thought it was. As rewarding as the advertising business was—a nice house in Westchester and a growing bank account—I knew it wasn't the final answer. I took satisfaction in every job I did, but I never found fulfillment. Advertising was a nice place to visit . . . but I'd keep hunting.

Of all the men I've photographed, His Imperial Majesty, King of Kings, Light of the Aryans, and Head of the Warriors Mohammad Reza Shah Pahlavi not only had the most impressive title, he was also the most impressive shot. I watched him pick off an ibex at four hundred yards on his Royal Hunting Preserve outside of Tehran. Back then, October 1960, everything seemed to be breaking the Shah's way. *True* writer Peter Barrett and I happened to arrive on the same day that the Shah's wife, the queen, gave birth to his son and heir—and with that heir in place, he could finally begin to plan the celebration of 2,500 years of uninterrupted Persian monarchy. Instead of handing out cigars, the Shah gave us Persian rugs to take home. He was on top of the world.

Royalty isn't what it used to be. It's a small, shrinking club of kings and queens and sons holding on to their palaces and hunting grounds, their titles and entitlements, and not much else. Whether hunting three-hundred-pound boars with Prince Bernhard of the Netherlands and the young Prince Juan Carlos of Spain, or shooting pheasant with His Majesty King Paul of Greece, I found them all to be relaxed, gracious, good with a gun, and at ease with their role in the world—which was to put on a good show.

King Paul invited Gordon Fawcett and me to join him for a hunt on shipping magnate Stavros Niarchos's private island of Spetsopoula. After several rounds of good Turkish coffee, followed by several more rounds of good martinis, we headed out with our shotguns to the blinds carved into the island's cliff walls. Down below, fifty beaters chased the pheasants— imported to the island along with wild sheep, goats, and stags—out of the grass and into the sea air, at which point the shooting would commence.

Speedboats circled in the choppy blue water to gather up the kill. It was a hunting ground built on imagination and money—like a movie set.

Gordon Fawcett prided himself on his ability with a shotgun—he had even competed for a spot on America's Olympic team—and was eager to show his stuff to the king. A bit *too* eager. The moment the birds leaped out of their hiding place, Gordon unloaded, winging one of the beaters, who fell back into the grass. As a couple of the other beaters hauled the poor fellow off to have the pellets removed from his arm and shoulder, His Majesty waved his hand and said, "Don't worry, it happens all the time."

The most charismatic and intriguing leader I ever had the good fortune to photograph refused at first to let me take his picture. He feared that once the shutter was snapped, his warrior soul would be sucked out of his body and imprisoned in the little black box forever. To show my good faith, I handed over my Nikon and offered up my own soul as guinea pig. I figured I had lost mine to the camera years ago, so had nothing to lose. Surrounded by fellow warriors and advisors nervously shaking their heads, he carefully wrapped his large fingers around the camera, aimed, and shot. He nodded his approval. I was in. The Masai chief had conquered the little black box.

I had come here for my stepson Kevin. I had told him stories about the Masai tribes, legendary warriors living out in the bush among the wild animals, and he couldn't stop talking about them. As a gift on his tenth birthday, I offered to take him on safari.

I had made a promise to all my kids and to myself. I might not be around much, and I wasn't going to be their butler or chauffeur. But if they'd find their way around the neighborhood, I'd show them the way around the world. I wanted my kids to be self-reliant, and I wanted them to know that there was more to life than Rye, New York. So if I couldn't bring Kilimanjaro to Kevin, I'd bring Kevin to Kilimanjaro.

As much as Kevin looked forward to the safari, seeing some animals in the wild wasn't going to cut it. He wanted to meet the Masai themselves. I told him I couldn't promise anything. They were a fiercely independent people and distrustful of strangers. Kevin wouldn't take no for an answer. He didn't want to take anything away from them. He just wanted to meet them.

In Nairobi I hired Edgar, a driver and guide who had experience with the Masai tribes. He suggested we bring them a gift of several sacks of powdered milk. Kevin thought we could do better than that. The car was packed with stuff like hunting rifles, radios, and binoculars—why not give them some of that? But as Edgar pointed out, in their parched, drought-stricken country, nothing was more valuable to the Masai than milk. Other, that is, than cattle, which would not only be an impractical gift, but an empty gesture as well. The Masai, Edgar told us, believed that in the beginning of time, God gave them all the cattle on earth, so if we did figure out a way to bring them a cow, we would have simply been returning something that was already theirs.

The powdered milk did the trick. The chief, distinguished from his warriors by the old British army coat he wore—no matter the blistering heat—was persuaded by the gift of milk to let us make camp on Masai land. And after my trick with the camera, he even allowed me to record our visit with it. At first the chief kept his distance, a wary host—waiting for us to live down to his expectations. But after a few days he began to warm to us—thanks to our boys.

Kevin, the ten-year-old kid from Westchester, hit it off with the chief's son, Dionni. They became instant best buddies. Kevin taught Dionni how to play baseball, and Dionni gave Kevin a lesson in hunting lion with a spear. Dionni took Kevin out in the bush to catch a glimpse of elephants, water buffalo, and a family of dik-dik—antelope that are not much larger than rabbits. Kevin, eager to show off his prowess with a rifle, joined Dionni as they stalked zebras. Kevin shot one and immediately regretted it. Seeing what he had done, he started to cry and vowed never to kill another animal. Dionni's take on it all was that, as he saw it, live animals were more interesting than dead ones—and maybe this zebra had to die to save all the other animals that Kevin would now refrain from killing. The boy was going to make a great chief.

In the end, Dionni painted Kevin's face with the blood drained from a living cow's jugular, and then Kevin drank, or pretended to drink, some of that same blood mixed with milk. He had come to Kenya a curious kid and had come away a blood brother. I never imagined that my birthday gift to him would be to make him into a Masai. It did make perfect sense to me, though. Life is all about blood mixed with milk. I drank mine when I chose to become an American. Why couldn't Kevin choose to become a Masai?

One of the first places I had gone when I came to New York was to 9 Rockefeller Plaza—the offices of *Life* magazine. *Life* had already published a couple of my pictures—including the one of the Krupp cremation—and with Sy Bourgin's recommendation, I had thought it a good place to kick-start my American career. An editor said that I could be a stringer, which would mean a lot of spec work and wasted time and very little money. He suggested that it would be to the magazine's advantage and mine if I came back when I had a story to tell . . . and sell. It took me twelve years, but I finally had it—and *Life* ate it up. They promised me the cover.

But the same week that "I Go Visit a Chief's Son" ran in the magazine, another story broke on the set of *Cleopatra* in Rome, and *Life* had pictures: a demure Elizabeth Taylor in Eddie Fisher's lap alongside a shot of sexy Cleo all wrapped up in Richard Burton's arms. Kevin and Dionni didn't stand a chance against Liz and Dick. I couldn't blame *Life*. I would have made the same choice. An African queen with a new love in hand will beat out an African prince with a baseball bat in hand every time. But I can still hang my hat on the knowledge that "I Go Visit a Chief's Son" was the issue's featured story and that it got equal billing alongside the two movie stars on the cover.

April 13, 1962, a candid shot of Richard Burton and Elizabeth Taylor, in costume and in conversation but not in character, appeared on the cover of *Life* magazine. I doubt they worried about the camera stealing their souls—although, looking back at how their romance played out, maybe they should have.

—◦—

Being a photographer for *Life* changed the whole picture, and I could write my own ticket. All I had to do was flash my credentials and the seas parted. But in removing the challenge, some of the joy drained away as well. Half the fun in being a photographer was beating the game—facing a closed door and having to pick the lock or go through the window. So I went out in search of my own challenges. For my next assignment, I talked the editors at *Life* into sending me on "The Wildest Ride on Earth."

The East African Safari Rally was the most grueling and perversely designed rally of them all, knocking out nearly 90 percent of the driving teams reckless enough to take it on. Starting out and ending in Nairobi, the rally took in the most inhospitable parts of Kenya, Uganda, and Tanganyika. It had originally been run in 1953 as the Coronation Rally, named in honor of Queen Elizabeth, but in 1960 had changed to the East African Safari Rally—the sun setting on this corner of the British Empire. It was just as well for the queen. All this race did was drag her name through the mud.

I convinced *Life* sports editor Marshall Smith to be my navigator— a decision he regretted the first bump we hit. We knew going into the race that it was the rainy season and that we were at the mercy of the weather—blinding dust storms turning into rivers of mud in the blink of a sleep-deprived eye. We had been warned about the flash floods and washed-out roads and fender-bending collisions with the wildlife. We were fully informed about Mount Kenya—or the 10,000 feet of it we would climb, including ninety-eight hairpin turns in ninety-nine miles. We knew all about this race . . . or thought we did.

But no one bothered to tell us about the potential for ambush—about the machete-wielding locals en route who made it their business to dig hidden trenches, strew the road with boulders and tree trunks, and hurl rocks at white men in numbered sports cars tearing through the land that had been appropriated from them by other white men. Our ignorance was far from blissful, as we drove into the heart of a simmering insurgency.

The Mau Mau Uprising had been crushed in 1956, but the spirit of it lived on in the rocks smashing into our windshield. It was late in the evening when we spotted the silhouettes of our attackers moving around bonfires set back from the road. Seeing a set of headlights, they'd go into their windup and let the missiles fly.

Both of us were cursing, Smith saying all he wanted to do was get the hell out of there and drive to the nearest airport. But I just pressed the gas pedal to the floor. My solution to everything: Damn the torpedoes, move forward, drive faster. If Hannibal could get his elephants across the Alps, I could get this Triumph through this rain of rocks.

Fortunately for us, the rocks were thrown with much more anger than accuracy, and aside from our frayed nerves, we escaped the onslaught unscathed. If they had wanted to kill us, they could have and would have. They simply wanted to make a point. To me, running that gauntlet represented the essence of driving in a rally. The pure thrill of movement combined with the ever-present and unpredictable potential for disaster—the sense that you are most in control when you are on the edge of being out of control. To Marshall Smith it represented the essence of insanity. But we'd come this far, and he was just crazy enough to want to see how far we would go.

Three days in and we were badly behind schedule. On our way up Mount Kenya, at one of those ninety-eight hairpin turns, we experienced an unfortunate but unavoidable mash-up with a vertical rock ledge. As we were going up the mountain, we met a bus coming down, and there wasn't enough room for both of us. We had either to hit the rock or the bus. I chose the rock. It took several hours to straighten out the car's front end. Early morning of the next day, on the other side of the mountain, we rolled into a deep, unfathomable fog. Determined not to lose points, I plowed ahead into the mist and mud.

Within minutes I lost the road and found an elephant. His rear end, to be precise. I don't know which of us was more shocked and unnerved—me or the elephant. But I do know that it was the elephant who sat down on the Triumph and emptied his bowels. We had scared the shit out of the poor guy.

We should have seen the writing on the wall—or on the great beast's backside. Driving your car into an elephant is like breaking a mirror or spilling salt. Bad luck. The next day, the fifth and last of the rally, with no other excuse than that I was groggy from lack of sleep, I went straight where the road turned and slammed the car into a ditch, smashing the steering mechanism. And all the king's horses and all the king's men couldn't put it together again. And neither could I. We were finished. And I was done.

The East African Safari Rally would be my last. After three thousand miles of flash floods, impassable mud, incoming rocks, and elephant poop, I had gone as far as any rally could take me. I hitched a ride back to Nairobi, where word was waiting for me. My father was dead, a massive heart attack. The flight back to New York was the longest, hardest journey I've ever taken in my life.

I wasn't there to see my sons born or to see my father die. I missed all the crying. But as far as my father goes, there was nothing I could have done to save him—as he had saved me from a Hungarian prison. Knowing him, though, I'm sure he didn't go quietly. It must have been a duel to the end.

I was determined to hold on to my father's ashes until I could figure a way to get him back to Budapest. For years the urn sat under the desk in my studio, right next to where I played chess every morning with Victor. "Think ahead," my father used to tell me during our games in the courtyard, "always think six moves ahead." It's one lesson that never took. Moving on, moving forward—it's the only direction I know. A bull who doesn't know the rules.

Planning ahead is a good way not to get anywhere. If I'd thought about what I was getting into, I doubt I ever would have picked up a movie camera—especially one attached to a firearm.

———

I've never met anyone who was more *American* than Fred Bear. He was a man who killed what he ate, a throwback, a frontiersman, a kind of Davy Crockett, or Don Quixote, tilting at the windmills of the modern world with his bow and arrow. *American*, too, in the sense that he was as adept at creating his own legend as he was in promoting and profiting from it. Having seen my work—photos from my various hunts and safaris—Bear reached out to me, wondering if I would join him on his quest. He was arranging to hunt Bengal tigers in India with the maharaja of Bundi and wondered if I'd tag along to record his adventures—play Sancho Panza to his Quixote.

Bear told me he had custom designed a camera for the event, taking an Éclair NPR—a favorite of documentary filmmakers, as it took just seconds to change magazines—and attached it to a shotgun stock. All you had to do, he said, was point and pull the trigger. I liked the sound of it. But Bear had one question for me. He wanted to make sure I had the right résumé for the job. Had I ever used a movie camera before?

Sure, I said, many times.

The truth, of course, was that I didn't have a clue. But if Bear could hunt Bengal tiger with a bow and arrow, I could point, pull the trigger, and follow the action.

How hard could it be to make a movie?

CHAPTER EIGHT

Will the Real Robert Halmi
Please Stand Up?

Tyrannosaurus rex, the bloodthirstiest killer that ever lived, bares his six-inch teeth. That was the caption under one of my photos in a short piece in the back pages of *Life*. The headline proclaimed "THE DINOSAURS INVADE."

That week's *Life*—December 6, 1963—was one of the most widely circulated issues of the magazine ever. But it wasn't the rise of the dinosaurs that made news; it was the death of a young man, President Kennedy. *Life* was there to reassure America that life went on ... that even as the country absorbed this violent blow, the giant plastic brontosaurus sailing up the Hudson River would still reach its intended destination—the Sinclair Oil exhibit in the upcoming New York World's Fair at Flushing Meadows.

I, too, had gone to the funeral—not to take pictures, but to be with my son Kevin, who had just turned twelve. We were living in Pelham at the time, and when the news of the Kennedy shooting broke on Friday, Kevin's school, Prospect Hill Elementary, closed early. Coming home, he was heartbroken—confused and inconsolable. He didn't understand what had happened ... or how it *could* happen.

The next day, Saturday the 23rd, I took Kevin to LaGuardia and bought two tickets to Washington. I could see that this was a rite of passage for him, and I wanted him to understand that he didn't have to go through it alone—that like his friend in Kenya, the son of the chief, he too had a tribe. He had to see with his own eyes what I already knew:

As terrible as these days were, this wasn't the end of the world. Leaders assassinated, assassins murdered, conspiracies and secret handshakes in the shadows . . . I had been there before. The events of the last few days had a distinctly Eastern European flavor.

I admired and respected President Kennedy—the right man in the right place at the right time, the embodiment of what postwar America aspired to be. Of all the American presidents in my experience—from Truman to Obama—there have been, to my mind, two great ones: Kennedy and Reagan. Both stood their ground against the Soviet Union, and both were extraordinary performers and entertainers. They were accomplished actors on the world stage, and they took command of it, exuding wit, charm, or gravitas—whatever the moment required. They were both perfectly cast for the role. Unfortunately, Kennedy's Camelot, which had begun as a romance, ended in tragedy.

Kevin and I landed in Washington late in the evening and took a taxi to the Capitol building. Kennedy's casket was still lying in repose in the White House, but it was to be brought to the Capitol rotunda the next day, Sunday, to lie in state. We took our place in the line that had already started to form. After several hours standing in a chilly drizzle, I proposed that we get a hotel room and come back in the morning. He seconded the motion. The city, of course, was packed, but I'd traveled enough to know that if you carry enough cash you can get a room anywhere anytime.

We returned bright and early Sunday to find that the line, now ten people wide, had grown overnight, stretching from the Capitol some ten miles into the city streets. The drizzle was gone, the skies cleared, but the cold was even more biting than before.

We didn't stay to view the casket. Kevin had seen enough. He made the journey, he stood in the rain, he shared his grief. And he knew that the show would go on, even if everything—the plot, the players, and the expectations of the audience—had changed.

We went back to Pelham. The funeral would be televised. Kevin was so touched by the sight of John Kennedy Jr.—John-John, as everyone knew him—saluting the casket, he asked me if he could send him a copy of his book, *Visit to a Chief's Son*—based on the article in *Life* magazine—as a Christmas present. I mailed it from my studio, and within a week he received a letter from the White House. In lieu of a postage stamp, the envelope had Jacqueline Kennedy's signature on it. The note was written and signed by Nancy Tuckerman, Mrs. Kennedy's secretary: *Dear Friend, Mrs. Kennedy appreciates your thoughtfulness in remembering her and her family at this time. She is extremely sorry that the tremendous volume of letters and gifts prevents her from thanking you personally, but we hope that you will understand.*

Kevin understood. The framed note and envelope still hangs on his living room wall.

The world was changing, and it was time for me to change too. If I kept taking pictures of plastic dinosaurs floating down the river, I might turn into one.

—⁓—

As much as I loved—and continue to love—still photography, by the early '60s my brand of picture taking had begun to feel outdated. The world was shrinking, as were the opportunities for an adventure photographer like me. I was facing the same slide into professional obsolescence and extinction my father, the studio portraitist, suffered after the war in Hungary.

One of my first experiences with television, aside from sitting down in front of one and watching it, was to declare, "My name is Robert Halmi," after two other gentlemen had just made the exact same claim. And once I had made the statement, my job was to convince a panel of judges that I was, in fact, lying and was not myself after all. The whole business—a contest of artifice and deflection in which the better bullshitter wins—appealed to the Hungarian in me. . . .

In the spring of 1962, following the success of my two Kenya stories for *Life*—"I Go Visit a Chief's Son" and "Wildest Auto Ride on Earth"—the magazine's publicity department arranged interviews for me on several morning radio and television talk shows. I continued the blitz, appearing as a guest on the panel game shows then based in Manhattan—*What's My Line?*, *Play Your Hunch*, and in June, on the evening edition of *To Tell the Truth*.

Like many of CBS's game shows, *To Tell the Truth* was filmed at the network's Studio 52 on 54th Street, which would later stake a claim to fame—and infamy—as the Studio 54 nightclub. I arrived on stage wearing my race car jumpsuit, a crash helmet, and a devilish grin. My plan was to make the panel think that I *wanted* them to think that I was this Robert Halmi character—and thus must not be him at all. One of the other fellows took a similar tack, wearing a safari hat on his head and a Leica around his neck.

The host, Bud Collyer, read the introduction. I, Robert Halmi, am an adventure photographer. Within the past three weeks, I have photographed a hunt with King Hussein in the Jordanian desert, a tiger hunt with the maharaja of Bundi in India, and the world's most punishing automobile race, in which I also drove one of the cars . . . and so on. The three of us, myself and the two impostors, then walked down a short, curving staircase and took our seats opposite our panel of inquisitors—Ralph Bellamy, Kitty Carlisle, singer Richard Hayes, and actress Peggy Cass—which proceeded, over the next five minutes, to test our knowledge of East African history, Middle Eastern geography, and royal Indian protocol.

In the end my plan didn't work. Richard Hayes voted for me (#3) because, in his words, "It didn't appear as though number three has spent much time outdoors"—the logic of which still escapes me. Peggy Cass chose me, in fact, because I had such a terrific tan. And Kitty Carlisle wrote a 3 on her card because she thought that I gave the best answers. Only Ralph Bellamy was fooled, claiming that all the answers I gave were wrong. At the end of the day, though, the real question I had to answer was this: Was I fooling myself?

In that same month, June 1962, in addition to me, *To Tell the Truth* featured a champion lady lock-picker, a baldness researcher, and a plowing champion. Had adventure photography become a curiosity, a sideshow? Did I belong with the fire-breathers and sword-swallowers? In the '50s, I had been on the front lines, pushing boundaries, at the tip of the spear. A few years later and I was beginning to wonder if I was just tilting at windmills with my camera. There were several different paths I could take. I decided to take them all.

One of my earliest films was a short. It didn't win any awards, wasn't screened at Cannes, was never released, and didn't even have a title. It was, however, a classic. The movie was two minutes long—in a story conceived by, and starring, Kirk Douglas. Kirk had already won a Golden Globe, had been nominated three times for an Oscar, and had taken on such roles as Spartacus, Vincent van Gogh, and Doc Holliday. But in this two-minute film, he shows a side of himself never seen before or since. It's the story of a man, stark naked and clutching a roll of toilet paper, desperately searching for a proper spot to use it. The film was shot on location in what was then Tanganyika (now Tanzania).

One night over dinner with Gordon Fawcett, I found a new angle I could work. I pointed out that pictures of nature in the raw—polar bears on glaciers and tigers in jungles—didn't sell magazines like they used to. You were better off stalking celebrities. So why not put the two together—celebrities on safari. Gordon's eyes lit up . . . and the next thing I knew I was on a Pan Am flight to Rome, shaking hands with Kirk Douglas. We made a connection through Athens to Nairobi, where we were met by a couple of professional hunters, Don Bousfield and John Fletcher, and several thousand fans who were hunting down the movie star for his autograph.

A safari, Swahili for "journey," is always hard work. You have to be prepared to walk as much as twenty miles a day, climb mountains, ford rivers, and shimmy up and down trees. Kirk was all for it. He's played plenty of tough guys in the movies, and it's no act. The toughest part he ever played was growing up, surviving a rough childhood in an American ghetto.

But as tough and plainspoken as he was, he was still Kirk Douglas, Hollywood star. And when you go on safari with a Hollywood star, you don't rough it. This was a luxury hunt with warm meals and hot baths. After several nights at the five-star New Stanley Hotel in Nairobi, we set out for northern Kenya, a safari at forty miles per hour in two Land Rovers and two four-wheel-drive, five-ton Bedford trucks loaded down with supplies and twenty-two locals—skinners, trackers, cooks, and assorted other camp personnel. We weren't leaving civilization behind; we were taking it along with us. Kirk was, after all, a valuable property. Three weeks from now he was due on a movie set. He had also just bought the rights from Ken Kesey to his novel *One Flew Over the Cuckoo's Nest* and was set to star in a theatrical adaptation on Broadway. We were obligated to bring him back in one piece.

The cars and trucks kicking up dust en route to the savannah, Kirk was like a kid going to camp for the first time—excited, anxious, a little bit nervous. Staring out the window at the green and yellow grasslands stretching out beneath a hot blue sky, he told me that he was tired of traveling to Europe, but Africa, he said, "is new and vital." I knew what he meant. It's a continent that brings you back to life.

We made camp alongside a giant acacia tree, some fifty yards from a watering hole—the center of life in any wilderness and a point of departure in the morning in our bid to track wildlife. We then set about to build our own watering hole: a thirty-foot-long mess tent with an assortment of bottles—Irish whiskey, Kentucky bourbon, Polish vodka (Kirk's drink of choice)—standing at attention on a table in the corner. That evening we cracked open the bottles for what hunter John Fletcher called "a smash before dinner."

Over cocktails John gave Kirk a rundown of the firepower that would be at his disposal on the trip: two .264 Winchesters, a .375 Winchester, a .300 Magnum, and a couple of double-barrel English .500s. Kirk listened, nodded his head, and explained that for all the guns he had handled in the movies, he knew very little about them and had never fired one with actual ammunition in it. The hunters were pleased. They preferred, as they put it, to work with virgins. They'd teach Kirk how to do the thing right and not have to break him of any bad habits. It was at this point that I chimed in.

I was done with guns. I had fired my last bullet. The only weapon I took on safari was a camera, and I was always on the hunt for a good shot. I threw down the gauntlet—and Kirk had drunk just enough vodka by that point to pick it up. I suggested that because he was a novice hunter, Kirk should think big . . . and start the hunt off by going after an elephant. And not just any elephant, but a one-hundred-pounder—meaning that that's how much each of its tusks would weigh. "What a good idea," I said, agreeing with myself. "And what a picture!"

"I'd like that," Kirk said. "Might as well start at the top."

The next day Bousfield and Fletcher gave Kirk a crash course in shooting. He turned out to be a natural, breathing easy, lowering the gun, squeezing the trigger, and blasting clay pots at fifty yards to smithereens. The following morning at five, after tea and toast, we were on our way. We headed for the water hole, in search of fresh tracks and elephant dung. We spotted our first elephant within a few hours, but our expert hunters dismissed the animal as a mere eighty-pounder—not good enough for our story—and we kept moving. We scoured the area without success, returning to the camp late in the afternoon, disappointed but undeterred.

For several days we followed the same routine. We had tracked and spotted a total of nine bull elephants, but none of them came close to the one-hundred-pound bar we had set for Kirk. Finally, determined to get a shot at our Holy Grail, we picked up stakes and moved our camp north, to a village on the edge of the Gof Redo crater near the Ethiopian border. This was Borana territory—a people renowned for their elephant tracking abilities. We hired several as guides.

What struck me about our Borana guides was their strict discipline. They were Muslim, and it was Ramadan, meaning they could not eat or drink between sunup and sundown. Leading us out into the sweltering heat, they would stop every hour to give us a chance to drink. While we were gulping down our water, Cokes, and beers, they sat to the side, waiting patiently, refusing to drink a drop, their lips sealed by the Koran.

Our discipline, meanwhile, was facing a different kind of test. For two weeks we had been getting up at the crack of dawn, walking our asses off, sitting in trees for hours on end, but even with the Borana guides pointing the way, Kirk not only didn't have his trophy—he hadn't even taken a single shot.

"Just between us," Kirk asked the two hunters over dinner, "how many hundred-pound elephants have you men taken?"

The two of them looked at each and shook their heads. "None."

Kirk's eyes widened, and he turned to me. "How many pictures do you have of hundred-pounders?"

My answer, unfortunately, was the same. "None."

I thought the vein in Kirk's neck was going to burst. He slammed his fist down on the table, rattling the silverware and us. "And you expect me, some Hollywood actor," he yelled, "this Yiddish kid from upstate New York to suddenly turn into the Great White Hunter?"

Bousfield took command of the situation. He leaped out of his chair, bear-hugged me from behind, and pulled me out of my seat. "The game's up," he said. He told Fletcher to go grab the double-barrel English .500 and said to Kirk: "Here's the one who suggested a hundred-pounder. It's open season on Hungarians."

"I'd love to," Kirk said, "but I can't shoot any Hungarians . . . I'd never work in Hollywood again."

"I'd make a lousy trophy, anyway," I shrugged. "Who'd be crazy enough to want a Hungarian hanging around in his house forever?"

Kirk decided that if he couldn't have a hundred-pound elephant, he didn't want any. He'd seen so many elephants over the past couple of weeks that I think he began to grow fond of them and didn't like the idea of killing one. So I came up with another idea—and for some reason they still listened to me.

"Let's go to Tanganyika," I suggested. "There are all kinds of game there." It was only four hundred miles away.

I used our shortwave radio and made arrangements to bring in an Aero Commander to fly Kirk and me to our new hunting ground. Bousfield and Fletcher packed up the camp and made the long drive south, meeting us at the Hotel Safari in Arusha, Tanganyika. After a luncheon of Dover sole at the hotel, with a nice view of Mount Kilimanjaro, we drove sixty miles south and made camp at the foot of a three-thousand-foot rock cone aptly nicknamed Mount Baboon—for all the old-world monkeys staring down curiously at us from their perches above.

We only had five days left with Kirk, but we kept him busy. In that time he managed to rope a zebra, skin an oryx, shoot a leopard, and make a lifelong friend of the Hungarian-born photographer who had led him on a wild elephant chase. And, discovering that I had in my possession a small, unused handheld eight-millimeter movie camera, Kirk suggested we make a movie, giving me the opportunity to produce the two-minute film project of a man in search of a place to relieve himself—a universal theme.

Later, in his memoirs, Kirk expressed regret about our hunt. He wrote that he had come to realize that killing animals for sport is a sin. But as far as I know, he has never expressed any second thoughts about making that short film.

As a photographer and later a moviemaker, I find I am often invisible. In the process of making a picture, I sometimes disappear behind the camera, and all that's left is the image I've captured or the story I've told. But there's another reason why I occasionally melt into the background. It's the company I've kept. Stars are called stars for a reason—they enter a room and all eyes fall on them, drawn like moths to a light. Those around them, in the stars' orbit, fade from view. And I've never been more invisible than when I traveled with the King of the Cowboys.

In the early '60s, Roy Rogers was at the height of his popularity, the extent of which was beyond anything I have experienced before or since. I might as well have been on the road with the Beatles. We were on our way to Mozambique for another *True* hunt, and from the largest cities to the smallest villages in the African bush, everyone recognized and revered Roy. They asked after Trigger, his horse; Bullet, his German shepherd; and Dale, his wife—in that order. Women got down on their hands and knees to get a better look at his gilded double-eagle cowboy boots.

At the airport in Salisbury, Rhodesia (now Harare in Zimbabwe), a huge, shrieking crowd waving autograph books broke through a wire fence and surged into the terminal, pinning Roy against the wall for an hour. Later when he finally broke free, disheveled and perspiring, they rushed after him down the hall into the men's room. It got even worse on our layover in Beira, Mozambique. We pushed our way through the crowd to get to the safety of our hotel rooms, only to have his fans pound up and down the corridors, banging on doors and shouting "Roy! Where are you, Roy?"

Our last night before heading out on safari, Roy, the *True* editor Peter Barrett, and I were determined to slip out of the hotel and enjoy a quiet evening to ourselves at a nearby beach resort. Our plan was foiled. By the time we pulled up to the place, we couldn't even get out of the car. We were surrounded, the car shaking. We were in the middle of a riot—a frenzy created not by anger, but by proximity to a celebrity. But how did they catch on to us? I'm convinced that someone had called ahead—and that that someone was Roy himself.

He relished every moment, every autograph and adoring scream, smiling and shaking his head even as the car was nearly lifted off the ground. He didn't have to wear the fancy boots and cowboy hat, but he did everywhere he went. He said he didn't want to disappoint his fans. Some stars will tell you that they wish they could live a normal life, walk down the street unrecognized. But the instant they do, they begin to look around anxiously, wondering where their audience has gone.

When the car had finally inched its way out of harm's way and we were headed back toward the hotel, Roy glanced back at the crowd and muttered, "It must be TV." Yes. Television. It had become a global force, a Pandora's box, and in time I, too, would reach into it and see what kind of tricks I could pull out.

Roy was far more than a singing cowboy, though. His skills in the saddle and as a sharpshooter were not just made for TV. Growing up poor in a place called Duck Run, Ohio, Roy had to shoot squirrels and rabbits for food, and, as he said, "had to make every bullet count." That proved true on safari, as well, Roy bagging a buffalo, a bushbuck, a kudu, and a spiral-horned nyala with his rifle, then, for good measure, shooting a red forest hog with the .357 Magnum revolver he carried at his hip. He even knocked off several game birds, which we had for our supper, with the slingshot he had brought along with him. Then after dinner Roy would go out to a river near the camp and fish until after midnight. He was a real cowboy.

He was also a true romantic. One morning, stopping by his tent to let him know we were gathering for breakfast, I caught him with his pants down. Fully aroused, he was capturing the moment with his Polaroid camera. He smiled and explained that he took the same picture every morning, writing on the back of it *thinking of you*, then sent it off to his wife back home. It meant more to Dale, he said, than a dozen roses. That was Roy Rogers, making every bullet count.

True Hunts with Famous Men, as the series came to be called, was not always true to the facts on the ground.

Legendary golfer Sam Snead had agreed to join publisher Gordon Fawcett, writer Doug Kennedy, and I in Tanganyika on one condition: He wanted to "bag a big tusker" and bring the ivory home. Bagging Snead—one of the most famous golfers in the world, known for his down-home country-boy personality—Fawcett readily agreed, figuring the story would write itself. But after several days on safari, the story started to fall apart.

Snead was no match for the blistered feet, the blistering heat, and the swarming tse-tse flies. His enthusiasm for the hunt waned, and he ducked back into his tent, which was where he and Gordon spent most of the remainder of the safari. Both were degenerate gin rummy players. But that didn't mean that Gordon had given up on the story . . . or that Snead had given up on getting his elephant. Every morning the trackers would head out into the bush, and whenever they spotted a herd, one would rush back to camp and yell, "Elephant!" Snead would grab his hat and his rifle, jump in the safari car, and speed out to the appointed spot. The first few times he arrived too late, the herds catching wind of us and beating a retreat, Snead going back to his cards. The way I felt about the whole business, I almost felt like warning the elephants myself.

Snead did finally get his elephant, and according to the *True* piece, it was his bullet that killed it. He did take a shot, but so, too, did the two professional hunters accompanying us. The three of them triangulated and assassinated the big bull. That part didn't get into the magazine. And though the article ended with the death of the elephant, the story wasn't over.

At the end of every day, after dinner, I'd get in touch via shortwave radio with the manager of the New Stanley Hotel in Nairobi, who'd pass along any messages that had come in. One evening toward the end of the safari, he asked if he could have a word with Snead. The hotel was sponsoring a charity golf tournament, and they'd be honored if he would participate. Snead said sure, how much would he get paid? After a pause the manager politely reiterated that it was for *charity*. Snead thought for a moment, and responded, okay, he'd do it . . . in exchange for seven leopard skins.

We weren't on a closed radio frequency, and a number of people back in Kenya overheard the comment. The sale and import of leopard skins was prohibited and a very sensitive subject in Nairobi, touching on issues of poaching, exploitation, and imperialism. Snead's request created a real goddamn mess, and I had to clean it up. I convinced him to play in the tournament, for nothing, and went back on the radio and said it had all been a joke; he'd be happy to give of his time. I later learned that Snead had somehow managed to get his hands on the seven skins after all. He came away from Africa with a couple of tusks for his trophy room and a leopard-skin coat for his wife.

I came away feeling that my days doing this kind of work were numbered. This latest safari didn't sit right with me. I, too, needed a new skin.

In April 1963 I received a long-awaited cable from the maharaja of Bundi. It said: *Lots of tigers. Bring aspirin and Alka-Seltzer. I'll supply the hangovers.* I had met and befriended the maharaja the year before when I was on another assignment in India. He had invited me back to join him on a tiger hunt and to bring a guest. My hunting days were over, but I wasn't going to pass up the opportunity to photograph it. I asked archer Fred Bear to come along. We left for New Delhi, Fred with his bow and arrow, me with my camera, on assignment for *Life.* But at the same time, I was also working for Fred. He made a practice of filming his hunts, using the footage to promote his business, Bear Archery. He had rigged up a special movie camera on a shotgun stock just for me. His tiger hunt in India would be my first chance to pull the trigger.

The train ride from New Delhi to Bundi lasted just short of eight hours, covered some three hundred miles, and took us back in time across several centuries.

The maharaja of Bundi—aka Colonel HH Maharao Raja Shri Bahadur Singhji Bahadur—was a direct descendant of the sun, his earliest ancestor a four-armed prince born of fire in the presence of the god Vishnu. But the present maharaja remained a maharaja in name only.

Although his family's reign over Bundi had lasted over six hundred years, it had recently come to an abrupt end. After winning independence from Great Britain in 1947, the Indian government officially deposed the country's five-hundred-odd hereditary princes, leaving them only their titles and enough money to keep their domains from going broke.

His Highness was a handsome, affable, graceful man with a pencil-thin mustache, two palaces, and fifty thousand acres of forest and farm-land. The older palace was over five hundred years old, the newer less than twenty. It had been designed and built toward the end of World War II. There had been a POW camp nearby, and among the prisoners were several Italians who claimed to have experience as painters and plaster-ers. The maharaja put them to work, their handiwork evident throughout the place—murals of nude women dancing in waterfalls and splashing around on the seashore adorning the walls in nearly every room. He lived in this newer palace, Phoolsagar, with his wife, his son Prince Peter, and his daughter Princess Kitten. His other wives lived in the older palace on the other side of Bundi. *Life* had authorized me to pay the maharaja five hundred dollars to photograph his harem, but he politely declined, fear-ing that they weren't pretty enough and thus would reflect badly on him.

When not off playing tennis or inspecting his grounds, the maharaja favored khaki shorts and short-sleeve bush shirts, urging us to follow his lead—to relax, put our feet up, and make ourselves at home. It took some getting used to, though. In a place where every meal is served by three or four footmen, you feel as though you should put on shoes for breakfast. But I adapted quickly, padding around the palace in shorts and bare feet, taking the maharaja's nearly one hundred servants, all dressed in bright white uniforms with brass buttons and orange turbans, and his private army of twenty-five soldiers in stride.

From midmorning to late in the afternoon, life at Phoolsagar came to a standstill. It was the dry season, the searing heat scorching the leaves off the mango and banana trees on the palace grounds. Nothing moved except for the servants and the large overhead fans stirring the hot air. Dinner was rarely served before midnight, in the relative cool, under the night sky, at a table next to a courtyard pool, which was fed by a lotus-lined lake. We ate from silver platters and drank beer from silver mugs, inscribed by those who had given them to the maharaja: *Queen Mary*, *Empress of India*, the *Prince of Wales*, and *Lord Mountbatten*. Peacocks wandered around lazily looking for bread scraps.

Everything in Bundi moved slowly, and the hunt was no different. It could take days, even weeks, for word to come and the hunt to begin. Before you can kill a tiger, you have to kill time. Because you can't stalk the cat. He has to come to you.

To amuse myself while we waited, I went out and played with my new movie camera. I drove into Bundi and filmed the vegetable markets, the goats and pigs and children in the street—anything that moved. I caught an outdoor wedding, the bride no older than twelve, the terrified groom looking as though he was the one about to face a tiger. Back at the palace, I recruited Fred to climb onto an elephant—we named her Rosie for the pinkish tinge of her upper trunk—and go bow-fishing for carp in the lake. The water was teeming with fish, and his first arrow hit the mark. But he had inadvertently wrapped his line around Rosie's tail, and when he yanked it free, the carp swung around and hit Rosie smack in the face. She reared up and threw Fred to the ground. The scene turned out a bit wobbly, I was laughing so hard.

Time was running out on us. We were heading back to the States on Monday, May 13, whether the hunt succeeded or not. Saturday morning, word finally came that a tiger had taken the bait ten miles from the palace. Fred and I were ready to go in five minutes, but the maharaja just smiled and said there was no need to hurry. Midday was too hot, the cat would be lounging out of sight somewhere in the shade. We wanted to wait, he said, until late in the afternoon and early evening when he'd start to move again. First, lunch would be served, while preparations were made. Slow down, he urged us.

A tiger hunt in Bundi was as integral to the life of the place as a Friday night high school football game was to a Texas town. Every soul had a stake in the hunt. The big cats ravaged the cattle and camels and livestock that the locals depended on to put food on their tables, and farmers and villagers were constantly on the lookout. When a tiger was sighted, bait would be set—a living water buffalo staked to the ground with a stone bowl full of water nearby. On a hillside above, attendants armed with binoculars would keep watch. After a tiger struck, he would kill the buffalo, gorge on it, then lie by the remains, guarding it through the night from hyenas, jackals, and buzzards. The bowl of water kept him from wandering off to slake his thirst.

That Saturday morning, one such tiger kill had been spotted—a bicyclist dispatched to the maharaja's palace to convey the news. Two in the afternoon, following a leisurely lunch, we were nearly set to go. There was just one last piece of business to see to. A servant brought out some black powder and drew a foot-long outline of a tiger on a white stone in the courtyard. He ignited the powder and stood aside. Fred studied it for a minute, then carefully stomped out the embers just as he would soon snuff out the life of the tiger.

The maharaja's jeep had an orange and yellow flag affixed to the radiator, alerting locals along the way to step off the road and bow down until the car had passed and was out of sight. Fred and I went with the maharaja, a motorcade of jeeps close behind us. We drove for about twenty minutes, the maharaja driving as fast as the curving road would allow, through the village from which the kill had been reported and on to within a quarter mile of where the tiger was believed to be. About fifty beaters had assembled there under the maharaja's chief hunter. A few had ancient, muzzle-loaded muskets, but most were armed only with sticks and crude, hand-forged axes. Rosie was on hand as well, elephants an integral part of tiger hunts in India for centuries.

The maharaja spent nearly an hour going over strategy with his chief hunter, who then meticulously arranged the beaters along the hillside. The bait had been staked out in a deep ravine with brush-grown hills rising steeply on either side. Only now did we learn that there was not one, but three tigers, a large male and two cubs. They were lying not far from what was left of the buffalo. We climbed to a spot three hundred yards from them, and Fred got into a machan—a hunting blind—some ten feet off the ground in a thorn tree. I joined the maharaja in a second machan thirty yards further back. He was armed with a double-barrel rifle; I had both my still camera and my new motion picture camera.

If Fred missed with his bow and arrow, the maharaja would be there to back him up, and if the maharaja missed, there was a firing squad of a dozen other men with rifles deployed along the ravine to finish the job. Two of them sat in the howdah on Rosie's back. A few minutes passed as all the beaters and riflemen took their positions. The chief hunter nodded to the maharaja, who nodded back. Then there was a sharp yell, and the beat began.

They moved slowly down the hill, shouting as loud as they could, whacking axes into trees, firing muskets, rolling rocks into the brush. The monkeys were the first to emerge, beating a retreat down the hill and scurrying past us—the lower animals on the food chain getting out of harm's way. A good twenty minutes passed, the beaters in no hurry. It would not go well for them if they came too close to the tigers' lair.

Suddenly, fifty yards to the right, I caught sight of the stripes. I fixed my camera on the spot, following the tiger's slow, cautious, graceful movements through the thickets. I could see that Fred had spotted it as well, an arrow strung, the bow stretched, and the line tense. But then the cat was gone, evaporating into the brush, his stripes blending perfectly with interplay of light and shadow. It was like filming a dream. The beaters, however, were relentless, and the tiger reappeared, zigzagging along the hillside. Moving slowly, he didn't seem to be making much of an effort to get away—perhaps out of concern for the two cubs still hidden somewhere down below.

Fred let the arrow go. It fell harmlessly behind the tiger, who glanced back at the missile and kept moving. Fred quickly reloaded and got off a second shot just before the cat once again melted away into the bush. A few seconds passed, followed by a terrible, blood-curdling roar. Every beater immediately jumped into the nearest tree and climbed into the highest branches. Snarling and raging, the tiger spun around three or four times, then came barreling down the hill into the thickest brush, not thirty yards away from us. We could hear him whipping around, roaring, growling, tearing things apart. He was fighting his last fight, the only one in his life he couldn't and wouldn't win.

After five excruciating minutes, the roar was gone, leaving behind a throttled groan, the sound of surrender—of the tiger's heart stopping. It was over, the silence absolute.

We went in to look at the cat. The arrow had caught the tiger square under the rib cage, the trees and rocks around him splashed with blood as if it had been thrown from a bucket. All of our waiting had come down to this—a few furious, terrible, violent moments. The two cubs had vanished into the brush.

The tiger's body was brought out and laid on the open ground. He was a magnificent, beautiful creature, a gold and white coat with narrow black stripes, a fierce, defiant face even in death. Rosie didn't think him so magnificent, though. She plodded over, trumpeted in triumph, and gave the carcass a kick. She would have crushed it where it lay if her mahout hadn't led her away.

On the way back to the palace, we stopped in several villages where the big tiger was laid out in an open space, and veiled women danced around him to the dull throb of drums. Later in his courtyard, the maharaja staged a more elaborate ceremony with cocktails, a roast saddle of boar served on an immense silver tray, musicians, and two younger dancers who didn't wear veils. I asked the maharaja why these two women were allowed to show their faces.

"Because they have agreed never to take husbands. But they are free to be with any man they want. It's one of our traditions . . ." he said with a little shrug, as if it didn't make sense to him. It struck me that the maharaja was not enjoying the celebration. Withdrawn and distracted, he was just going through the motions. Perhaps he was mourning the tiger, or mourning the loss of his domain. He knew that he had been reduced to a figurehead and that he was playing a role for us. The only power he had left was all bound up with tradition—tiger hunts and dancing girls—and as soon the traditions died away, so would he. He retired early that night.

If not for Fred Bear, I might never have made *Lonesome Dove*, *Merlin*, *Moby Dick*, or any motion pictures at all. He put the first movie camera into my hands and, as such, was my native guide to this undiscovered country of making motion pictures. It was, of course, an education into the most fundamental elements of the craft, but you have to learn how to turn on the stove and boil water before you can make a five-course meal.

Fred was well suited to the role, as he was a fundamental kind of guy—a rough-hewn character who had patterned his life after the Native

Americans of the western plains. As I discovered in his company, when you hunt with a bow and arrow, you can't shoot from two hundred yards away. You have to get up close and personal with your prey—know the animal as well as you know yourself. And although you are always teetering on the edge of chaos, you can never lose control of yourself; otherwise you risk missing the best shot. All that goes for a movie camera as well. I found my time with Fred to be a learning experience unlike any other.

I learned from Fred how to move in near total silence through a forest, river, or scrubland. I say "near total" because there was one sound that came with the territory—the whir of the movie camera. That alone was enough to spook some animals—and, as I later discovered, a few actors as well. A movie camera is not a passive instrument. The moment it starts to roll, it alters the environment, inducing flight, fright, and overacting.

Still, back in the woods with Fred, I became adept at reading and taking command of my surroundings—at making myself, and my camera, as unobtrusive as possible. I gained new appreciation for the value of stillness, the importance of silence, and the power of preparation, patience, and persistence. I saw how effective a slow, tense, uncertain buildup could be when leading to a sudden, often violent, resolution.

I was making movies.

My pictures were moving now. I had to give flow to the movement, make connections between shots and scenes, and between the images and the sounds. And as I soon realized, I wasn't documenting reality; I was creating it, choosing what the viewers would see and in what order they would see it. If a scene didn't work, I'd go back and reshoot it or fix it in the editing room. I could film a fallen grizzly, then get a shot of Fred firing an arrow, and re-create his tracking of the animal the next day. I'd put it all in proper order later. I could speed time up or slow it down, build suspense or break it down. Making a movie—whether a documentary or otherwise—I realized that there were an infinite number of possible moves with just one endgame . . . finding a way to capture the audience's attention.

The films I shot for Fred did attract the attention of one significant viewer: a producer of sports programming at the American Broadcasting Company. At the time, the early to mid-1960s, ABC had firmly established its place in the television ratings—and that place was dead last, a distant third to the two giants, CBS and NBC.

Roone Arledge, an up-and-coming producer, took full advantage of the network's history of failure. Working at ABC gave him the opportunity to experiment and invent new ways to cover athletics. From the Olympics to the *Wide World of Sports* to *Monday Night Football*, he turned every game into an event, and every event into entertainment. Arledge had the freedom to come at sports from a different angle.

I had met Arledge, and Fred Bear had appeared on his program *The American Sportsman*. Arledge had produced most of the first season, but as a vice president in charge of ABC's new sports division, he needed someone to take over. He had seen my footage of the tiger hunt and asked if I would do it again, this time for *The American Sportsman*, with actor Craig Stevens, who was best known for his starring role as *Peter Gunn*.

There were any number of reasons to say no: The money Arledge was offering me to spend two grueling weeks in the Bundi heat left me cold, I had plenty of other work, and I had grown wary of working with celebrity hunters. But I said yes. How could I say no to television? It was the biggest circus in town—even if it was ABC.

Life at the maharaja's palace had changed dramatically in the three years since I'd been there. The paint was peeling, the pool was murky, and most of the servants had moved on. All the silver had either been sold or locked away. The maharaja was still the same good-natured fellow with a smart mustache, but India's democracy had clearly taken a toll on his realm. He welcomed Craig Stevens into his home and promised him a ferocious tiger and a good show.

Stevens was a terrific actor. He must have been. He played a cool, tough, suave private detective on television and turned out to be anything but that sitting in a machan staring down the sights of his rifle at a charging two-hundred-and-fifty-pound striped cat.

This hunt was far smaller and far less organized than the one with Fred Bear. There were maybe a dozen beaters, only the maharaja and one other man with a rifle to back Stevens up, and no Rosie the elephant. The tiger had taken the water buffalo bait very near to the palace, and rather than wait until the late afternoon, we impatiently headed out into the brutal one-hundred-degree high-noon inferno. This was for television—I had a budget, I was on a schedule, and I couldn't afford to let the tiger slip away.

Stevens climbed into his blind and I into mine, about twenty yards to his right, where I could get an angle on him and on the cat. The maharaja and the other shooter were set up some thirty yards behind us. The beaters began their work in the bushes, and for well over a half hour the sun beat down on us. The sweat dripping rivers down my arms, I struggled to maintain a grip on my camera. I gripped even tighter when the cat, ferocious as promised, emerged one hundred yards away, racing out of the brush and directly toward my blind. The machans were some ten feet off the ground, but a determined tiger would have little trouble ripping it—and me—to shreds. My eye glued to the camera, I whispered "Shoot. Shoot. Shit. Shoot!"

Within seconds, the tiger closed the gap, and suddenly he stopped short ten yards away, crouching, hissing, and eyeing me as I eyed him back through the lens. I believe it was the sound of the camera—the whir of the film inside—that gave him pause. Finally there was a shot—the maharaja pulling the trigger. The bullet kicked up some dust, missing the cat, but it spooked him, sending him racing back for cover. Stevens said his rifle had jammed, which was possible in the heat, but he didn't seem too keen on staying put and taking another shot. I agreed, saying we'd try again tomorrow, knowing all along that we were done. That tiger didn't have to worry about Craig Stevens coming back for him, and I didn't have to worry about getting out of India in one piece.

I had gotten some good footage of the cat's charge and the next day, when the light matched, I filmed Stevens—a fierce, determined expression on his face—firing several shots from the blind into the trees. Later I'd take some of the old footage of downed tigers from the Fred Bear hunt, patch it all together in the editing room, and deliver it to Arledge at ABC. The Craig Stevens hunt was the featured story on *The American Sportsman*'s second season premiere, airing Sunday afternoon, January 23, 1966. Doing publicity for the show, Stevens told a reporter: "When I saw him . . . my heart skipped a beat. I drew a bead, waited till he was close enough, and then squeezed the trigger. It was like a Warner Brothers movie . . ."

My first made-for-television movie was not the only thing I brought home from Bundi on that trip. The maharaja was quietly trying to sell off everything in the palace that wasn't nailed down. There was one thing he wasn't sure what to do with, and he wondered if I might help him find a buyer. He took me out to the garage where he kept his cars. In the back was one covered with a tarp. He carefully pulled it off. It was the sexiest goddamned thing I ever saw: a red Rolls-Royce Phantom convertible, fitted with an elephant gun, commissioned in 1925 by the maharaja's father and custom-built for hunting. It hadn't been used in years but had been kept in pristine shape—a pearl-white steering wheel, black leather interior, two powerful searchlights, and a hidden safe to protect your valuables. And under the hood a six-cylinder engine you could eat off of. I was in love. I paid five hundred dollars for it on the spot, a steal.

On my way out of the country, I stopped by the American Express office in New Delhi to arrange for the Rolls to be shipped from Bundi to New York. It ended up costing me more than the car itself, and thanks to the leisurely way of doing things in India, it took some three months for the car to actually get to the docks in Mumbai. But when I got word of the freighter's imminent arrival, I gathered up the kids and headed for the west side of Manhattan. I wanted to watch my ship—and my beautiful car—come in.

I couldn't wait for them to unload the Rolls, so I slipped one of the crew a twenty and hustled Kevin, Robi, and Billy onto the ship. The sight of the car broke my heart. It had been loaded onto the deck and left there, without so much as a canvas to cover it. My beloved Rolls had rusted all to hell. The Phantom was dead. The crossing had killed it. I paid a scrap-yard to come haul the junk away and took the kids home.

Presidents, tigers, gorgeous 1925 Rolls-Royces . . . nothing is meant to last. Even *Life* was dying a slow death. Circulation was plummeting, and the writing was on the wall: It said *television*. Why bother to flip through a magazine to see last week's news when you could see it right now, beamed into a box in your living room? *Life* didn't stand a chance. The audience was vanishing, and the advertisers went with them. And so did I.

And just like that, my still photography—the creative engine that had propelled me from postwar Budapest and Salzburg to midtown

Manhattan and the heart of American media—had become little more than a hobby. My future was now in moving images. I knew I could produce the documentaries—I had done it; the question was, how could I get them into that box in people's living rooms without answering to the Roone Arledges of the world? I had no intention of working for ABC or any of the networks. I had always called the shots and followed my camera where it led me. I hadn't drawn a regular paycheck since Radio Free Europe, and that had soured me for life on working on other people's dreams. I was independent, taking orders from no one but myself—and occasionally from my wife. I'd make my own movies.

All I needed was money and a plan.

CHAPTER NINE

Just Say Yes to Everything
(Except to Your Kids)

After wrapping up *The American Sportsman* episode with Craig Stevens and the maharaja, I came home to New York ready to make the leap into television.

Liberty Mutual sold insurance, and their target audience was husbands and fathers—the men of the house; the best way to reach them was through sports, action, and adventure. The company sponsored shows like *The American Sportsman* and paid a premium for the privilege. They also financed their own show—*Outdoors with Liberty Mutual*, which featured Gadabout Gaddis, otherwise known as the Flying Fisherman. But after several years Liberty Mutual was less than thrilled with the program.

There are not many people who will return week after week to watch a man fishing for a half hour, and the audience was shrinking fast. They wanted a show with more action and different challenges. That's where I came in. Robert Maddox, Liberty Mutual's director of advertising, called me and asked if I had any interest in producing a syndicated outdoors program for them. Yes, I said, I did. Did I have any ideas about content and cost? Yes, sure, of course. Could I come up to their Boston headquarters the next day to discuss with the company executives what I had in mind?

Absolutely, I could. I'd figure out what it was I had in mind on the train ride up. My strategy was simple: Whatever they would ask for—smaller budget, faster turnaround, the world on a string—just say yes . . . to every-thing. I'd work out the details later.

It was the easiest sale I've ever closed.

———

Joe Foss had a hell of a résumé: US Marine fighter pilot in World War II; America's "Ace of Aces," scoring twenty-six kills of enemy aircraft at Guadalcanal; Congressional Medal of Honor recipient; cover of *Life* magazine; brigadier general in the Air Force; two-term governor of his home state of South Dakota; first commissioner of the American Foot-ball League. And host of *The Outdoorsman*, presented by Liberty Mutual and produced by Robert Halmi. Joe Foss was John Wayne, only for real—a true American hero . . . and at times a truly difficult son of a bitch.

He was a soldier, a military man through and through, and he approached life—and the show—with a degree of discipline and defined goals and expectations that not all of us shared. When those expectations were not met—when some equipment broke down or a shot was missed or his coffee was too cold—he'd start barking out orders. But they gener-ally fell on deaf ears: neither I, nor the crew, nor the wild boar we were chasing had ever been members of the National Guard. Still, I developed a working relationship with Joe; he did teach me a few things. Later, when I started making movies with big casts and bigger budgets, I found that a certain amount of military discipline was useful. I, too, have barked out a few orders in my day, and I'd venture to say that there are times when I've been described as a "difficult son of a bitch."

Now that I had a host on board, a face to put in front of the camera, and an eye behind it—me—I needed a good set of ears, a soundman, to bring the documentaries to life. It would not be an easy job. The world is full of noise, but I needed someone who could sort it all out and give my twenty-minute slices of wildlife a soundtrack. He'd have to bring home every whisper and roar, the wind bending the trees, the water rushing through the riverbeds, the rifle shots that send the flocks of birds flying into the air.

The answer to my soundman prayers turned out to be right under my nose, in the same building as my studio, one floor down. Mark Dichter was born and raised in the business. His grandfather—another Hungarian who brought his dreams to America—had worked in the theater in Budapest, and after immigrating to New York in the 1920s, started producing and directing Yiddish silent movies. In the 1930s Mark's father joined *his* father and took charge of the fledgling new technology of sound production in the now talking pictures. A decade later he started his own company, Dichter Sound Studios, which later became Photo-Mag Sound Studios, focusing on television commercials.

Mark Dichter's whole world was sound. Barely out of college, he knew more about recording, editing, mixing, and designing it than anyone else in New York whose last name wasn't Dichter. And all I had to do to find him was walk down a flight of stairs. He was eager to spread his wings and get out on his own, and I didn't have to do much convincing to get him to sign on as my sound engineer. A producer is only as good as the talent he works with, and hiring Mark made me a genius. He was a Mozart with a microphone. What he wasn't, was an outdoorsman.

He was a native New Yorker, and before he met me, I doubt he had ever strayed much farther from the city than Long Island or maybe New Jersey. Now I was about to take this chubby, curly-haired kid from Brooklyn to places that were about as far from Park Slope as you can get. As I would discover over the next few months, Mark was like a cat, a very clumsy cat, because although he almost never landed on his feet, he did have nine lives and would need every single one of them.

Once I had contracted a film editor in New York, I was ready to go. All Liberty Mutual required was a half hour of programming, one twenty-three-minute segment a week. The rest—where we went, what we shot, and how we put it all together—was up to me. Nobody bothered me. I was in complete control. Except for the things over which I had no control—things like Joe Foss and Mark Dichter. Climbing mountains was in Joe's nature. Falling off them was in Mark's. But both were game for anything and would have followed me through the gates of hell if I thought we could get twenty-three minutes of reality television out of it.

Filming the first segment of *The Outdoorsman*, I managed to avoid going through those fiery gates, though we did have to navigate a course down the River Styx—otherwise known as the Florida Everglades. I've been to lot of places in the world, but I've never experienced anything quite like Florida. Breathtakingly beautiful, spectacularly ugly, it is a freak of nature, a great big accident. Florida is a thriving civilization built on top of a swamp, a place where neighborhoods are washed away by hurricanes, houses are swallowed up by sinkholes, and high-rise condos and swanky nightclubs are surrounded by waterways filled with cranky, prehistoric creatures waiting to snap up the occasional family pet. Death is a way of life down there. It seemed a good place to kick off the show.

The storyline of the first episode involved an airboat, a Florida wildlife officer, and an alligator—a big, bad old boy who had been emerging from the swamps to terrorize fishermen and tourists. Foss, Dichter, and I joined the officer, Ron Davis—formerly a football player for the University of Florida—whose job it was to track down, engage, and capture the animal, then transport it deeper into the Glades where it wouldn't scare off the tourist trade. Foss and Davis climbed into the airboat, while Dichter and I loaded our cameras and sound equipment into a small Boston whaler to follow close behind. Davis led us slowly forward into a labyrinth of intricate waterways, sawgrass marshes, stands of cypress and sweet gum trees, and tangled banks of mangrove.

Every hundred yards or so, Davis killed the engine and listened. I don't know what it was he heard, but he was on to something, adjusting the boat's direction until it slipped through a narrow opening and stopped. Our boat pulled up beside theirs in this nearly enclosed body of water some fifty yards wide. Dichter quickly set up the sound equipment, wiring up both Foss and Davis with microphones. I then slipped over the side into the water—it was cold, waist deep, and the walking was rough—careful to keep my camera dry, and started filming. Davis whispered a warning to me not to step into any holes. My feet sliding along the water bottom, I kept one eye on the viewer of my camera, while the second scanned the nearly half mile of shoreline surrounding us. My senses were fully engaged. Fear and alligators will do that.

Davis was pointing to a section along the water's edge where the tall grass was flattened as if a heavy body had been dragged over it. He eased into the water and waded toward the spot, beckoning me to draw closer. Peering into the vegetation, he raised his hand and gestured toward the path. He was staring at the alligator. Davis retreated to the airboat and pulled it closer to the shore, whispering to me:

"Stand back and close to the edge. When he comes out, he's going to make a rush for the deeper water. You don't want to be in his way." He then turned to Foss, still in the airboat, who was holding on to a gig—a handheld snare on a long cane pole with a locking mechanism.

"You get him gigged and hold on, and I'll get his jaws clamped shut, then we'll wrestle him aboard and . . ."

Foss's eyes widened. What the hell had I gotten him into? But he was on camera now, and there was no turning back. He was the guy who'd shot down Japanese Zeros over Guadalcanal; he had a Congressional Medal of Honor hanging in his den. He'd never backed down from a challenge, and he wasn't about to start here. He was going to be the first TV star to wrestle an alligator on film. Davis, however, must have sensed some hesitation on Foss's part.

"Quit worrying," he said. "We may even live through this." Then he climbed out of the water and bolted into the grass. He was herding the alligator back into the water.

And out it came, the grass parting before it. The gator paused for a moment at the water's edge and looked around, then slid in. I thought it must have been a good twenty-five feet long. It was actually just half that. I had to remind myself to breathe. I was sharing this tiny body of water with a primeval predator. I was in his house. I saw the water surface ripple in the animal's wake and warily inched forward to catch its movement on film. I glanced up at Dichter to see how he was doing. Lost in his world of sound—headphones clamped to his ears, microphone moving slowly back and forth in front of him like a metal detector—he was completely oblivious to the danger gliding around us in the marsh.

Davis, meanwhile, dashed out of the grass, splashed into the water, and climbed onto his boat, quickly maneuvering it toward the alligator.

"Get ready," Davis shouted.

The boat closed in and pulled alongside the fleeing gator, about a foot below the surface. Foss slammed the gig down on the animal's shoulders—and the pole broke. But somehow Davis had managed to get a nylon line around the beast and pull it tight. He handed the line to Foss and plunged overboard. Whatever the state of Florida was paying him, it was nowhere near enough.

For the next few minutes, there appeared to be a chaotic confusion of alligator tail, human legs, and splashing water—but Davis clearly knew what he was doing. He clamped the jaws shut with one hand and somehow managed, with Foss's assistance, to bull wrestle the gator onto the boat. Yelling at Foss to avoid the animal's powerful tail, Davis gently propped its head on his knee, dried it with a towel, and deftly taped it shut.

I went wild, jumping up and down and punching the air as though I'd just knocked out the heavyweight champion of the world. I was thrilled to have caught every detail of the capture on film. Florida was crazy: We had captured an alligator, but I was the one who was hooked. Early in 1967, soon after shooting the Everglades adventure, I bought a winter home for my family in Boca Raton—a piece of real estate sitting halfway between a beautiful stretch of ocean beach and the swampy wilderness of alligator country.

That first episode of *The Outdoorsman: Joe Foss* aired in January 1968, sponsored by Liberty Mutual in some seventy-five markets around the country. On many of those stations, the half-hour program ran on Sunday, January 14, the same day as Super Bowl II—the biggest of the made-for-television sporting events. Elsewhere that January, Apollo 5, an unmanned lunar module, took off for the moon; *Rowan and Martin's Laugh-In* premiered on NBC; Peggy Fleming won the US figure skating championship; and the Vietcong, as part of the North Vietnamese Tet Offensive, launched a surprise attack on the US embassy in Saigon.

All of those events, along with the alligator encounter in the Everglades, were captured on television. Satellites were beaming the images around the world. There was no escaping it anymore.

By the time that first episode aired, we had been traveling and filming *The Outdoorsman* for over a year and already had twenty-six programs in the can. With a few exceptions—hunting red stag in the highlands of Scotland and jaguar in the rain forest of British Honduras (now Belize)—Foss insisted that we confine ourselves to US soil. Sticking to the States, we still had more than enough wildlife to work with on *The Outdoorsman*. The American wilderness is as rich, diverse, and entertaining as its people. It accommodates all kinds. After corralling the gator in the Glades, we flushed out quail on Catalina Island off the coast of California; chased wild geese on the shores of Chesapeake Bay; shot episodes where the buffalo roamed, the deer and antelope played, and the American woodcock mixed it up with fat skunks and little foxes.

On the big island of Hawaii, I filmed Foss going after wild boar, descendants of the pigs brought over the ocean by Tahitians and Polynesians more than a thousand years before. On a different island, in a different world—Nunivak Island, Alaska, three times the size of Oahu but with a population of only two hundred—we came across a people who had never seen a pig, wild or otherwise. The Cup'it Eskimos lived for the walrus. They depended on its skin, meat, bones, blubber, intestines, and ivory for their kayaks, mukluks, meals, tools, artwork, and rain gear. I could relate. If the only thing that will keep your head dry is the gut of a walrus, cut it out and make a hat out of it. And if you're lucky enough to come across a wild pig, roast it and have a luau. I've been on both sides of the divide—feast and famine—and either way, you make do with what you've got.

But just when you think you've got it all figured out, you trip over a blade of grass. Foss had been pheasant hunting since he was ten, and I thought it would make a nice story to take him back to his roots in South Dakota. We drove out to where the cornfields met the prairie, released a couple of retrievers, and Foss, feeling right at home, plucked out a piece of corn silk to chew.

The shoot went fine. Foss knocked a few birds out of the sky, nothing spectacular, but I had enough to make a show out of it. But within a few days, Foss began to have stomach pains, which rapidly spread through his body and grew more severe by the day. He was losing weight, the strength in his legs was gone, and his doctors were stumped. Finally, desperate, he went to the Mayo Clinic for tests, which found arsenic in his blood—an arsenic then commonly used in pesticides. It was the corn silk that nearly killed him. We've managed to poison our food in order to make more of it—a Faustian bargain. The lesson: Be careful what you put in your mouth.

"From now on," Foss said, "I'm sticking to cigars." It took several weeks for him to recover his strength, but he refused to go off schedule. During his recovery we shot a segment at a Wyoming ranch. I had to strap him onto a horse a couple of times, but the work was done and the show went on.

Foss had the constitution of an ox, and within a month he was back at full strength, stomping on the ground and snorting out commands. But the real miracle through all our travels and treks was that Mark Dichter survived. Mark's strength—his laser-like focus on his work—was also his weakness. He'd get so wrapped up in the sound of things, he'd lose sight of where he was and where he was going.

We were in the Rocky Mountains, just across the border in British Columbia, searching for mountain goats and grizzly bears. We weren't having much luck, climbing up and down mountain trails most of the day, finding very little for Foss to shoot at or for me to film. It was just one of those days, and Foss was in one of his moods—pushing forward, determined to find something before the light faded. His frustration rising, he took off up one of those ridges as though he was a mountain goat. Several hundred feet up the ridge, I whispered for Foss to hold up. I'd spotted our first bear, a grizzly and two of her cubs splashing around in a stream at the base of the ridge looking for dinner. I turned to see if Mark was ready with his microphones—only to discover that he was no longer with us.

Our sound man was gone, and we had no idea where he was . . . until eagle-eye Foss nudged my shoulder and pointed to a spot in the trees about twenty yards from where the bears were fishing. Mark. He'd wandered off on the wrong trail and now was clearly lost. He was too far away for us to warn him, but we could see that if he continued on the path he was following, he was going to have a problem. It's not a good idea to disturb a hungry grizzly with two cubs to feed and protect. But that, as far as we could tell, was exactly what Mark was about to do.

But he was not eaten by the bear. Just before his path led him through the trees to the stream, his luck kicked in: The mama grizzly gathered up her cubs and climbed up on the opposite bank. She turned, looked at Mark, and stood on her hind legs. For a brief moment the kid from Brooklyn stared down the British Columbian bear, the two separated by some fifteen feet of white water. Mark beat a hasty retreat. He didn't lose his life, but he did use one of them up that afternoon.

Wherever we went to film *The Outdoorsman*, the running joke was, what would kill Mark this time? In Alaska he lost his footing and slid five hundred feet down a glacier. It took him the entire day to catch up with us. In Utah, it was a horse that threw him. In Wyoming, it was an avalanche that nearly buried him. In Montana, it was a fish that nearly drowned him.

We were on a mountain lake angling for trout, seven of us divided between two small boats with outboard motors. I was in one with Foss and a guide from a nearby fishing lodge; Mark was in the other with the owner of the lodge and two of his boys, a ten- and a twelve-year-old. The kids cast their lines, as did Foss, and naturally it turned into a competition: Which boat would catch a trout first?

Mark had grown up on a steady diet of New York sports teams, rooting with a passion for the Dodgers, then the Mets, the Knicks, Rangers, and Giants. He always wanted *his* team to win—and in this case, his team consisted of the two boys fishing in his boat. And what do avid sports fans do when their team wins . . .?

Sure enough, one of the boys was the first to hook a fish and reel it in, and I could see what was going to happen next. I yelled out, "Don't stand up! Don't stand up!" Mark stood up. And the boat capsized. He lost all his equipment but managed to help hold on to the boys until we could haul them up into our boat. When I shared the story with Robert Maddox at Liberty Mutual, he was so amused by the idea of the kid from Brooklyn plunging into a lake in Montana, he arranged for a ceremony to give Mark an award—the same piece of paper the company gave to companies with good safety records. Dichter framed it and hung it in his family's sound studio.

Mark was a brilliant sound technician, and to me that's all that mattered. If you're going to work in a collaborative business like moviemaking, there's nothing more valuable than talent. Write me a compelling script, perform a powerful scene, or capture it all on camera or microphone, and I don't mind if you rock the boat a little. It comes with the territory. Mark deserved every award he got.

One of the perks of producing a weekly outdoors show was free stuff. Hoping that I would feature their products on future episodes, companies sent me fishing rods, tents, snowshoes, coolers, heaters, sleeping bags, freeze-dried foods—it was a survivalist's dream. I didn't know what to do with it all, most of it piling up in my garage. The promotional items didn't all go into storage, though. One winter morning, a brand-new Ski-Doo showed up on our Pelham doorstep. My youngest son Billy wrecked it the first day. He was ten.

My kids loved to go fast. They had to if they wanted to keep up with me. I wasn't around much, but when I was, I made every minute count. It's simple economics: The less of something you have, the more valuable it becomes. Because of my work and travels, I couldn't give my kids much of my time, but I could give them the world. I wanted them to know that there was more to life than Westchester County. (My son Robi would later tell me, "I remember one trip, sleeping in a tent on the Kenya–Uganda border, the sound of gunshots in the distance, seeing the bodies in pools of blood in the morning.")

Every few months from the mid-'60s on, I made a point of taking one of my children to work with me, which meant pulling the kid out of school and flying off to Nairobi, New Delhi, the Badlands of North Dakota, or wherever my latest assignment happened to be. They came back with stories of riding elephants, roping calves, and dining on goat's brains for breakfast.

Back home in Westchester, there were no elephants to ride or goat's brains to eat, but that didn't mean we couldn't keep things interesting. Travers Island, which is no longer an island but a peninsula jutting out from Pelham into the Long Island Sound, is a suburban sanctuary of the New York Athletic Club. The "island" has restaurants, tennis courts, a yacht club and marina, as well as an Olympic-size saltwater swimming pool. It was an idyllic setting for some very fierce competitions—and back in the 1960s and '70s, we Halmis were in the thick of it.

In addition to self-reliance, another character trait that passed from my father through me to my children was the determination not just to excel but to win at whatever games and sports we played. My dad's duels in Budapest ended at first blood; in our duels at Travers, in which families would lock up against each other in "friendly" competitions, the Halmis were out for blood. My wife Eleanor, my sons Kevin, Robi, and Billy, and I were all good athletes and bad losers, but it was my daughter Kim who led the way. I could always count on her to lead us to victory.

When she dived into that pool, no one could keep up with her. Kim was a fish in water and was always looking for ways to swim longer and faster. Travers Island has a history of training and turning out American Olympic athletes, and there was a time when it appeared that Kim might be one of them. But it was not to be. The timing was off. At fourteen, she was too young to compete for the 1968 Summer Olympics, and by 1972 the times—and Kim—had changed. She spent a year studying languages at the Sorbonne in Paris, then went on to Rollins College in Florida. She had different dreams to pursue.

Looking back, those summer days spent on Travers Island—Eleanor and I and the kids framed by the sun and saltwater—all have a dream-like quality. It's a dream in which my kids never grow old—roller-skating down the sidewalk, gliding effortlessly through the water, sitting next to me on a plane headed god knows where, or just waiting for me at the door when I get home.

There were, of course, other times that were not so dreamlike. It was the '60s and early '70s, after all—not the easiest time to be raising teenagers. And I certainly made my share of mistakes. One of them was giving Billy, when he got his driver's license, a sleek, fast—and expensive—Jensen-Healey. I don't know what I was thinking.

Billy tells the story this way: "There was no upside to getting in trouble with Dad. One thing all of us had in common: We loved to drive fast, and I remember my first car, this great little British two-seater. Well, I think I may have been driving a little too fast, and I cracked that car up. I had to have it towed to the gas station. My dad went to see the mechanic. The mechanic looked at that poor little car and asked dad, 'Is Billy hurt?' 'Not yet,' Dad answered."

Rebellion is not a phase you go through or a set of beliefs you try on for size. It's a state of mind that puts you in direct opposition to the state of the society you live in. There's nothing vague or faddish or fashionable about it. I had rebelled first against the Fascist and then the Communist rulers in Hungary because I couldn't breathe. They were squeezing the life out of me, and the only way to break free was to go underground and fight my way out. I was driven by anger, desperation, and fear—and didn't get out from under it all until I stood on American soil. This was air I could breathe.

In the summer of 1966, I returned home from one of my last, and longest, assignments for *True* magazine: "A Camera Safari to Capture Africa's Big Game." I spent two glorious months trekking through Kenya, Uganda, Tanganyika, and Mozambique, shooting the wildlife I loved, without drawing a single drop of blood. But back in Pelham, things were not so pretty. My son Kevin, not yet fifteen, had hair down nearly to his shoulders and refused to get it cut.

I didn't want to overreact, but I thought my world had come to an end. I accepted shaggy hair and rock music as facts of life—just not in *my* life and not in *my* house. I urged Kevin to reconsider. He declined. I urged louder. But he was adamant: All his friends were growing long hair. I cut off the debate. I told him we'd work something out the next day. In the morning I suggested we get in the car, go for a drive, and talk it over—see if we couldn't find some common ground.

Six hours later we pulled into the parking lot of the Staunton Military Academy. Nestled in the Shenandoah Valley, in the shadow of the Blue Ridge Mountains, it would make a beautiful setting for the next four years of Kevin's life. It was also a good place for him to make some new friends, with shorter hair. ("Dad was a loving dictator," Kevin now says.) Staunton, I decided, was our common ground.

Just as my experiences at Sárospatak shaped the rest of my life, Kevin's time at Staunton would shape his. Following his graduation in 1970, he went on to attend Norwich University in Vermont, the oldest private military college in the United States. After Norwich, Kevin was commissioned as a second lieutenant in the US Army Air Defense Artillery and assigned to a NATO Nike Hercules surface-to-air missile battalion in Germany. This kid who ten years earlier had been ready to go to war over a haircut now stood on the same line as I had thirty years before—a soldier on the front line of the Cold War. The only difference was, all I had was words. Kevin had nuclear warheads.

Unlike Kevin, Robi in the late 1960s was too young to worry about how long his hair was or about asserting his independence from authority. Kevin was a rebel without a cause. Robi was just a kid full of mischief—and there were times I could've killed him. This is how he remembers it:

One evening after school in the fall of 1967—I was ten—my friend Mark and I were looking for something to do. Somehow we got our hands on a book of matches and went out into my backyard, getting as far away from the house as we could. Our neighbors were pretty wealthy and they had their own bowling alley. The building gave us cover, where no one could see us, a good spot to see what we could light on fire. It turned out, with just a few sticks and some newspaper, we could build quite a blaze—bigger even than we had counted on. We ran back to the house, grabbed a couple of buckets of water and doused the fire. Or so we thought.

Apparently we were better at building fires than at putting them out. The sirens woke me up in the middle of the night. The bowling alley had gone up in flames. The next day in school Mark and I agreed that no one had to know about our little backyard adventure. We'd take the story to our graves. I told him to come over to my house and act like nothing had happened. When we got there, my dad and mom were sitting in the living room with two detectives. They asked me if I had anything to do with the fire. I said absolutely not! Then they turned to Mark and asked him the same thing. "We did it!" he confessed. "We did it."

Not only had I set the bowling alley on fire, I lied about it. Except for going to school, I wasn't allowed out of my room for a month.

I decided not to kill Robi. It wouldn't bring the bowling alley back, and I doubt Eleanor would have gone along with the plan anyway. But at least he learned his lesson: If you're going to build fires, you better know how to put them out. He's become quite good at it, making a career out of playing with fire—financing movies and other forms of entertainment.

He starts with a few sticks and newspapers, and he lights up the sky. He's just better now at controlling the bonfires. He's only burned down the one bowling alley that I know of.

When it came to rebellion, the one real insurgent in the family was my daughter, Kim. As much as I love the company of women, I often end up driving them away. I demand a lot from them, sometimes more than they can give, and Kim was no different. ("What is it about family? You fight and you struggle and you alienate what you love most. It's a mystery to me," Kim says.)

As the only girl in a house full of boys, she had it rough, and I was tough on her. I wanted her to excel at school and at swimming, and yet I didn't want her to grow up. I gave her a hard time about putting on makeup, the clothes she wanted to wear, and the boys she wanted to see. But she was as headstrong and willful as I was, and we had our battles. Looking back, I wonder, what use is there in winning the battles when in the end you lose the war? When she finally broke away, she broke far away. Kim didn't burn down the neighbor's bowling alley, but she did burn her bridges. There's nothing harder or sadder than losing time with one's child. It's time you can never get back.

———

I gave as much as I could to my kids. Sometimes it was too little . . . and sometimes it was too much.

In 1970 we moved out of Pelham and into a new house we had built overlooking a golf course in Greenwich. I didn't move there for the golf, but it was a nice piece of land—certainly a step up from our first house in Connecticut, the one on a cemetery in Weston—and Eleanor and I had developed a circle of friends in the area.

We enrolled Kim in the Greenwich Academy, a prep school for girls, but she didn't get on well there—she was at odds with us, the school, the whole community, a square peg in a round hole—and only lasted a year. We finally agreed to send her abroad to complete her senior year at the Sorbonne, where she could pursue her love of foreign languages. She was lost in Greenwich, and we hoped she'd find herself in Paris.

Robi and Billy we sent to the Brunswick School for boys. Unlike

Kim, they fit right in. There was just one problem with Brunswick—and that was me. Every month the school held a father-son night—an opportunity for the fathers to invite friends and colleagues to come speak to the boys about the world outside the classroom. A program designed to contribute to the school's mission to "ably and generously prepare boys for life," it also led, in my experience, to simmering resentments, outrage, and ultimately to a full-blown scandal.

The soap opera originated with the people I knew. The boys listened politely—and sleepily—to the parade of doctors, lawyers, and stockbrokers who spoke, but they always looked forward to the nights my guests took the stage. Because of my work in magazines and television, I was able to invite sports figures like New York Giant Pete Gogolak—who introduced soccer-style kicking to American football—and basketball player Dave DeBusschere of the world-champion New York Knicks. How were the other parents supposed to compete with that kind of star power? I became the most popular dad with the boys . . . and the least popular with their fathers. But my reign as the king of father-son night was short-lived.

A guy goes into a diner and orders a hamburger. A few minutes later the waitress returns with a plate with a bun, but no burger. The waitress puts down the plate, reaches under her arm, pulls out a burger, and puts it on the bun.

The customer says, "That's disgusting," and the waitress says, "Just be glad you didn't order a hot dog."

This was Rocky Graziano's opening joke on the occasion of his appearance, at my invitation, at father-son night, at the Brunswick School.

And it all went downhill from there. Aside from a few giggles from some of the older boys—the audience included the school's entire faculty, administration, and student body, from the kindergartners to the seniors—the auditorium was dead silent. That changed with Rocky's next question: "What the f**k do you want me to talk about?" The festivities ended soon after that—it was the biggest disaster in the seventy-year history of the school—and I was invited never to invite anyone to speak at father-son night again.

Graziano had delivered the wrong material to the wrong audience at the wrong time in the wrong place. A similar issue was brewing in my work, behind the scenes on *The Outdoorsman: Joe Foss*. Liberty Mutual wanted to expand the program's appeal—and its ratings—but instead found the audience declining. And their marketing department had pinpointed the primary problem: *Joe Foss*.

I am, and always have been, a conservationist. To watch a wild animal in its natural habitat, moving and mating and surviving by instinct, is one of the most beautiful and exhilarating experiences I've ever known. But in the 1960s, nothing stood still. Everyone and everything was part of one movement or another, the whole country packing up and moving on, seeing things in a new light. The American conservation movement was no different.

It began as a movement of hunters, led by President, and big-game hunter, Teddy Roosevelt. They set out to save the country's natural resources from the encroachments of civilization—from the big lumber companies and mining outfits that were systematically grinding the wilderness down to dust. But sixty years later, the environment had changed. Hunters were no longer friends of the conservation movement; they had become its target. And it was television, shows like *The Outdoorsman*, that turned the tables—spilling the blood of the hunted animals into America's living room for all to see . . . and denounce.

I had moved on from hunting, using only a camera now, but those who stuck to their guns, men like Joe Foss who couldn't adapt and move forward, were bound to be left behind. Liberty Mutual didn't care about any of that—conservation or hunting or politics. All they cared about was selling insurance to the most people possible, which meant offending as few people as possible. *The Outdoorsman* was out and so was Joe Foss.

Liberty Mutual was still committed to a weekly half hour of syndicated action/adventure documentary programming. But they had one condition: They wanted a kindlier, friendlier outdoors—more travelogue than blood sport. It was up to me to find a kindlier, friendlier on-air personality to act as tour guide. I didn't have to look far.

Ladislas Faragó had a theory. "Everyone," he said, "is Hungarian." I wouldn't go quite that far, but it's true that there *are* Hungarians everywhere, and many in America. The evidence is all over the place: Harry Houdini's magic, George Cukor's movies, Edward Teller's bomb, Joe Namath's Super Bowl, Calvin Klein's jeans, Jerry Seinfeld's jokes, George Soros's money . . . the list goes on.

Some, like me, were born in Hungary. Others, though born here, carry the old country around in their veins. Either way, at bottom, we're all part of the circle. It was only natural, then, that I would ask golfer Julius Boros to host the program—and that he would accept. Why him? Because he was Hungarian. He may have been born in Connecticut, but he was a made member of the club . . . and in on the joke.

Julius was a very relaxed guy. He never rattled—*swing easy, hit hard* was his motto, and it served him well as winner of two US Opens and a PGA Championship. He had the hands of a violinist and the swing of a big-band leader, an easygoing style both on the golf course and in front of the camera.

He was the polar opposite of Joe Foss. Julius liked to play golf, go fishing, and go home. He hated to travel and often as not stayed behind when we went out for a shoot. He'd just tape a two- or three-minute-long introduction for the episode. He tagged along when there was golf or fishing involved, teeing off at the Himalayan Golf Course in Pokhara, Nepal; playing a round with Mickey Mantle in the Bahamas; or joining the king of Morocco at his Royal Dar Es Salam Golf Club—a round disrupted by the royal dachshund, which took golf for a game of fetch.

Even when he did play along, he was not all there. When we filmed one episode, fly-fishing in Montana, Mark Dichter would cast the line, handing it off to Julius when the trout bit and my camera started to roll. But it wasn't just him. More and more now, my heart wasn't in it either. The formula was wearing thin—I was running out of places to go and stories to tell. Reality, I found, can be very confining. I had devoted episodes to dog weight-pulling contests, snowshoe baseball in Alaska, kite flying, souped-up super sleds, and hot air balloons. And the truth was, I didn't much like golf. The only thing more tedious than hitting a little white ball around a field with a stick is filming someone else doing it.

Liberty Mutual's enthusiasm was fading as well. By the early '70s, the days of corporate-produced and -sponsored programs were going the way of drive-in theaters and black-and-white TVs. The company's ad agency, BBDO, said they'd be better off buying quick-hitting thirty-second spots on network programs like *Bonanza*; *Love, American Style*; and *The Flip Wilson Show*. As far as the *Outdoors* show was concerned, the end was near.

———

Piranhas have a voracious appetite. An indigenous guide leading my film crew down Brazil's Araguaia River claimed to have seen a drunken man fall into the water during the dry season. The piranhas, he said, stripped away his flesh in a matter of minutes, his skeleton floating to the surface downstream. True or not, it makes for a colorful story to tell tourists and filmmakers. I, however, was not there to hear or film it. I never made it to the Amazon basin. In fact, I never made it out of Rio de Janeiro.

The plan was for Julius Boros and me, along with Florida business-man and future billionaire Don Soffer, to head south of the equator, take in the Carnival in Rio, and then head north into the Amazonian water jungles for the fishing. But on our first night, in the hotel, I felt as though a school of those piranhas had somehow swum down into my gut and was attacking me from the inside out. In the streets below, Carnival was in full swing. The entire city was singing and dancing and drinking and making love, and I thought I was going to die—my skeleton picked clean and popping up downriver.

The pain was excruciating, and the only place I was going was to a hospital bed. The doctors said I had pancreatitis. Mark Dichter man-aged to get a call through to my family, and Billy—being Billy—dropped everything and headed for the airport. Within twenty-four hours he was at my bedside. I asked him to take my place and oversee filming on the fishing trip. He didn't hesitate, and everything went smoothly—three days on a boatel on the Araguaia catching razor-toothed dogfish and three-foot-long catfish. The trouble started when Billy came back from the expedition to fetch me back to the States. The hospital refused to let me go.

They claimed I owed them fifty thousand dollars in cash for my treatment, and they weren't going to release me until I paid them. I was too sick to put up a fight, but not Billy. Something he said—he told them that he was a doctor, that he *had* to get me back to the United States immediately, that he was in touch with the American embassy, and so on—turned the trick, and with tubes still coming out of me, he got me into a wheelchair, into a waiting limo, and onto a plane back to New York. Billy had just turned eighteen.

I survived. *Outdoors* did not. Liberty Mutual finally pulled the plug. It was just as well. I had produced and filmed exactly one hundred half-hour documentaries for them. I had traveled to every state in the union and had gone around the world twice . . . and the world was catching up. The show was killing me. And I had something big to fall back on—a hippopotamus.

The sultan of Zanzibar has a problem. A gang of cigar-smoking sharks has laid siege to the harbor, curtailing the lucrative clove trade. His solution: transport a dozen hippopotami from the countryside to do battle with the sharks. The plan works. The shark gang is destroyed. But that leads to another problem: the hippopotami. The sultan decrees that they be slaughtered, which they all are save one: little Hugo the Hippo.

To survive Hugo must run a gauntlet of corncob artilleries, pea-pod machine guns, an apple samurai, a banana octopus, a gun-toting cyborg-cowboy, and a wizard skilled in the art of hippo-notism. Ultimately, he is put on trial for scavenging for food from the gardens, but is redeemed and released, presumably to live happily ever after. . . .

That a children's tale filled with such horror, blood, and carnage was conceived in Hungary didn't surprise me. Hugo's story—his resiliency in the face of violence and injustice—was Hungary's story as well. What did come as a shock was that Hungary's Department of Cultural Affairs reached out to me to bring the animated feature to the screen. The very same government that twenty-five years before had declared me an enemy of the state and sentenced me to die was now giving me a movie to produce. Hugo's story, then, was also mine: persecuted, prosecuted, and ultimately redeemed.

This was also my first chance to deal in fiction, to create rather than capture a story, and I leaped at it. I worked with Pannónia Filmstúdió, the animation division of the Hungarian Film Production Company. We were producing two versions of *Hugo the Hippo*, one in Magyar, the other in English. It was up to me to cast the English-language version, assemble a lineup of singers and musicians to perform the soundtrack, and, most important, find an American partner to help finance the picture. George Barrie fulfilled two out of three of those requirements.

As a young man in the 1930s, Barrie knocked around Brooklyn playing the piano and saxophone. But with marriage came the need for steadier work and income—and a job selling cosmetics. Barrie started up his own company, based in a garage in New Jersey. Success was immediate, but his real breakthrough came with Brut, the premise of which was—real men could smell nice too. But what the cologne really reeked of was money. His original investment in that New Jersey garage ultimately led to the purchase of Fabergé, a $180-million-a-year business, a board of directors that included Cary Grant, a fleet of private jets, headquarters in Manhattan and Paris, a grand piano in his bedroom . . . and a piece of *Hugo the Hippo*.

I had worked with Barrie before on a couple of Fabergé advertising campaigns. One idea he had was to blow up a big rubber model of Brut and set it amid a pride of lions. We flew to Kenya on one of his Gulfstreams, found a suitable pride, and set up the shoot. It was all for nothing. For some reason the smell of the rubber sent the lions into a frenzy and they tore the model to shreds. We were lucky to get out alive. But as far as Barrie was concerned, it was worth a try. He was never satisfied and always eager to try new things. At heart, he was still a musician and wanted to entertain people. To that end, he formed Brut Productions.

Barrie arranged for Marie and Jimmy Osmond to do several of the songs for the soundtrack for *Hugo the Hippo*, and I put together the cast of voices, including Burl Ives, Paul Lynde, and Robert Morley. Nonetheless, for several reasons, Hugo never got off the ground in the States. For one thing, I suspect that the story's twisted imagination and nightmarish adventures didn't appeal to American sensibilities of the time. Not even Marie Osmond could save it. American audiences did catch up with

Hugo several decades later, however, and it has gone on to achieve cult status, as it is regularly screened on college campuses around the country.

Even if *Hugo the Hippo* had appealed to Americans in the early 1970s, they wouldn't have had a chance to find out. George Barrie was a sharp guy, but a novice moviemaker. He thought moving pictures were like perfume. You made it, then you went out and sold it. He had neglected to line up a distributor for the film, and it didn't stand a chance here. But Barrie didn't care. To him it was just another experiment. His next was to ask me to take charge of Brut Productions.

That experiment lasted two years. It wasn't a good fit; the chemistry wasn't right. I didn't know enough about making movies yet to be running a movie production company, and as for Barrie, with all his money, life for him was one big party. I had become part of his jet set, flying off to London, Paris, Rome, or Tel Aviv without any real destination in mind— running around, refueling, always on the go, going nowhere fast. All I did was collect a fat paycheck . . . and got fat in the process.

I quit. I wasn't cut out to run somebody else's company. I had proven I could make movies on my own, and that's what I was determined to do. I was nearly fifty—what *was* my next move? The answer came from a little kid—a boy in Budapest who had loved to read about adventure and imagine life in far-off lands, who had loved the circus and later the opera . . . a boy who, on special occasions, would go to the theater to sit in the dark and watch American motion pictures—stories about gangsters, cowboys, beautiful dancers, and giant apes climbing on skyscrapers. I wanted to make movies.

CHAPTER TEN

It's like World War II Every Day

Move forward and never retreat. And the first thing you do—day one on the set, once the boots are on the ground and shooting begins—is take all your schemes, strategies, and storyboards, put them in a nice, neat pile, and light them on fire. Because having brought all the pieces together, all you can do now is let the script play out—improvising, reacting, and rewriting along the way—and do your level best to keep casualties to a minimum.

Patrick Stewart has said that he came after me for the role of Ahab, but as I recall, I was the one who had to romance him. . . .

Late in 1996, around Christmas, I caught a flight to Los Angeles. I had a miniseries of Herman Melville's *Moby Dick* in development and had sold the idea to the USA Network. They had just one condition—I had to attach a major star to the movie. My first choice—and only choice—was Patrick Stewart. I had seen his work and could see that his approach to acting was comparable to Ahab's approach to the whale—relentless. The problem was, Patrick passed on the project.

His agent told me that between *Star Trek: The Next Generation* and playing *Othello* on stage in Washington, there was no room in Patrick's life for any great white whales. The answer was a definite no, and I took the man at his word. The trick, then, was how do I change the word from a no to a yes? I couldn't do it over the phone, I would have to look him in the eye and sell him on the role. I convinced him to give me thirty minutes, in his agent's office . . . in Los Angeles.

When the meeting took place, I just started talking . . . about Melville and Shakespeare, Ahab and Othello, obsession and opportunity, Gregory Peck and Patrick Stewart. Peck had played the role in the 1950s, and I told Patrick that he was the man to do it for the current generation. I don't know whether I talked Patrick into it or if he agreed simply to shut me up and get me out of his agent's office. Either way, I had my Ahab. Patrick would turn in his keys to the starship *Enterprise* and take the helm of the *Pequod*.

Not only did I have a star to lead my ship forward, I had one of the greatest actors in the English-speaking world taking on one of the greatest characters in American literature. With Patrick on board as Ahab, Henry Thomas as Ishmael, and Ted Levine as Starbuck, and shooting set for Point Cook in Australia, I rounded out the doomed *Pequod*'s crew with a cast of respected Australian actors—Bruce Spence, Hugh Keays-Byrne, and Dominic Purcell among them.

Now came the tough part: casting the Great White Whale himself. As far as I was concerned, there was no point in making *Moby Dick* unless I could *make* Moby Dick—a monstrous, moving, life-size sperm whale worthy of Ahab's monomaniacal obsession. Then I'd need a body of water large enough to contain the whale, the *Pequod*, and the "grand, ungodly, godlike man" that was its captain. Ultimately I settled for a Leviathan some forty feet long and a dozen feet across—not as big as the biggest whale, but large enough to pass—made of rubber, metal, wood, plastic, and a mess of tubes and wires.

Filming took place on a beach near Melbourne, where we had dug a deep pool—a good home for our mechanical Moby Dick during the several weeks we needed him on set. A network of tubes and cables emerged from the belly of the beast, connecting him to a control room. There, a crew of technicians, on command, could raise him out of the water, open and close his savage jaws, lift his titanic tail, and give everyone on set a good splashing. The pool itself overlooked the Tasman Sea, and camera angles would complete the magic, transforming the tiny patch of blue into our own piece of the open ocean.

Although the White Whale casts his dark shadow over the entire film—a fever infecting Ahab—his close-up, his moment of glory, doesn't come until near the end, the pursuit and climactic confrontation between man and beast. A year and a half of planning, writing, casting, rewriting, financing, negotiating, filming, cajoling, shouting, begging, and more rewriting had led to this moment and this scene that pitted Captain Ahab's mortal obsession versus Moby Dick's primeval power.

Ahab damns his ship, damns his entire crew save one, and damns himself in the fulfillment of his single passion. He casts his harpoon into the beast, is caught around the neck by his own rope, and lashed to the whale, his fate is sealed. *To the last I grapple with thee; from hell's heart I stab at thee; for hate's sake I spit my last breath at thee.*

There was only one proper way to film the scene—lash Patrick by the neck to *our* whale and send them both plunging to the bottom of the pool, the two of them rising once to the surface, bound together, then plunging once again.

I sensed a hint of misgiving, but Patrick didn't say a word. He is an actor's actor, and if that's what the scene required, that's what he would do. We had it timed out to the second. The average person who is in good shape can hold their breath for a little under a minute. But Patrick is a very fit man, a swimmer, and we discovered he could remain submerged under water for close to a minute and a half. We weren't going to take any chances. We timed the dive at forty-five seconds and tested the mechanism several times.

Finally we—or I should say Patrick and the whale—took the plunge, Patrick in his heavy coat and boots tied to the machine.

Fifteen seconds passed. Thirty. Forty. One minute. One minute ten seconds. Nothing. The whale was not coming back. Something had gone wrong. Somebody had panicked, pressed the wrong button. Wires were crossed. Almost the entire crew and a couple of the actors jumped into the pool, diving down to untie the poor actor and bring him up to the surface, gasping for breath—Patrick as blue in the face as the Tasman Sea.

When he was done spitting up water, he asked me if I was trying to kill him. I said no, the whale was. But the fact is, a few seconds more or a few feet deeper, and I would have gone down as the man who sent Captain Jean-Luc Picard to a watery grave. After giving him a few minutes to cool down and dry off, I asked Patrick to do another take. The crew jumping into the pool to save him had ruined the shot.

A month later over dinner in London, I apologized to Patrick once again for the screw-up with the whale and offered him an olive branch—a role in another production I had in development. Did he want to play Napoleon? He practically dropped his fork. *That* was one role he had always wanted to play. At which point I informed him that I only needed his voice. I was making *Animal Farm*, and Napoleon was a pig. For the second time in a month Patrick gave me a look that could kill. But instead of me killing him in Australia, or him killing me in a London restaurant, it was the beginning of a great friendship. And he took the role of the pig.

After the pig, we did Shakespeare together—in the Wild West. Patrick was the *King of Texas*—a 2002 adaptation of *King Lear* set on a nineteenth-century American ranch. He played the patriarch John Lear with Marcia Gay Harden, Lauren Holly, and Julie Cox as his daughters. His scene near the end, when Lear goes mad, is the single finest performance I have ever personally witnessed.

But back to the Great White Whale. *Moby Dick* was nearly finished, but there was one last piece of the puzzle, one more scene to film—Father Mapple's sermon, which stands, full of foreboding, at the beginning of the story, pointing like a harpoon at the inevitability of the ending. I had yet to cast the crucial role, but I knew exactly whom I wanted to fill it. Once more, I flew out to Los Angeles and, in his Beverly Hills home, I screened the all-but-finished movie for Gregory Peck, the star of John Huston's 1956 version of *Moby Dick*. Greg told me that he had always disliked Orson Welles's portrayal of Mapple in that film, and thought that he, too, had been miscast—that he had been too young at the time to play Ahab. So here was an opportunity for him to put the ship right, I said, to kill two birds with one sermon.

A halo of white hair and beard surrounding that famously handsome face, Greg delivered six minutes of Golden-Globe-Award-winning fire and brimstone—six minutes that made the picture. When it was over, smiling and exhausted, he climbed down from the ship's prow, which stood as his pulpit, and the entire cast and crew and all the extras gathered around him and reached out as though to touch the pope's robes.

I saw Greg one more time after *Moby Dick*. I met him at the Ritz in Paris. He owned the movie rights to *To Kill a Mockingbird*, and I wanted to remake it. I didn't stand a chance. He was kind, pleasant, apologetic, and totally adamant. The rights were his, and they would stay his. Gregory Peck would always be Atticus Finch, and Atticus Finch would always be Gregory Peck.

Father Mapple was Gregory Peck's last role. His final words on film, as the camera cuts from the church pulpit to the sea as the *Pequod* sets sail, are these: "Here we die. We leave eternity to thee."

Call me Ishmael is how the story begins. Ishmael is the survivor, the narrator, the one whaler who rides out the storm, clings to a coffin as the ship goes down, and lives to tell the tale. It was a hell of a ride . . . and I'm still on it, clinging to the box that has kept *me* afloat: my camera.

The first story I had to tell—and sell—on film came to me in the early '70s when I was moving away from documentaries into drama. It was a natural next step. I had been telling stories my whole life. Turning to drama gave me the freedom to create rather than capture them. Finally I could let my imagination run wild. I could join the circus.

The idea I had was to fictionalize and film the story I had done for *Life* magazine a decade earlier in Africa—"I Go Visit a Chief's Son." But I had no idea what to do with the *idea*. So I turned to the Yellow Pages. Under "movie studios," I found that United Artists had offices in Manhattan. I dialed the number and asked to speak to the president. I can be a very persuasive fellow, and through pure Hungarian bullheadedness, I talked my way into the office of CEO David Picker and pitched the story directly to him. His first question was how much I would need to make the picture. Pretending I had a clue, I said one million dollars. His eyebrows shot up. "You can do it for *that*?"

"Yes," I said without hesitation. Remember: *Say yes to anything*. We signed the contract within half an hour. The problem was, now I had to make a picture.

Another lesson I quickly learned in the business of moviemaking was that a million dollars doesn't go very far. It might get me to Mount

Kilimanjaro, but I might not ever get back. By the end of the shoot, I'd have to start breaking into piggy banks. The credits at the end of the movie include the following:

Technical advisor: Kevin Gorman [my stepson]

Makeup: Kim Gorman [stepdaughter]

Still photographer: Robi Halmi [son]

Animal keeper: Billy Halmi [another son]

The more members of the crew I could pay an allowance in place of a salary, the farther my million dollars would go.

On my first shoot, I learned fast how to be a producer. It meant that I had to do everything, including the catering—the crew having rebelled over the lousy food and leaky tents. Every few days I'd jump into my Piper Cub and fly off to Nairobi on a grocery and liquor run. To this day, whether shooting on a shoestring or a seventy-five-million-dollar budget, the key to keeping cast and crew happy is good food and drink.

Without that Piper Cub—I had learned to fly back at school in Sáro-spatak—the movie never would have gotten off the ground. In one scene I needed a hyena, but as it turned out, even in the shadow of Kilimanjaro, hyenas are not easy to come by. I contacted the owner of the Nairobi Zoo, who agreed to lend me one. All I had to do was pick it up, so off I went. But as we discovered when I landed in Nairobi, there wasn't a cage small enough to fit into my Cub. I didn't have time to waste—in this business minutes are money, and I had neither—so we quickly came up with a solution. A tranquilizer. A couple of animal handlers came out with a syringe, and after a few minutes the hyena drifted off. We hustled him into the backseat of the Cub and I took off.

Unfortunately, five minutes away from my landing strip—five minutes that seemed like an eternity—the tranquilizer wore off. And the hyena was hungry. Hyenas, I suppose, are always hungry, but I didn't have the foresight to arrange an in-flight meal for him, so in lieu of a zebra or wildebeest, he started to gnaw on the back of the leather seat I was sitting in. I managed a quick white-knuckle landing, jumped out of the plane, and slammed the door shut before my passenger found the fresher meat on the back of my neck.

Call *me* Ishmael. Or Ahab, for that matter. Because in telling the stories, I often ended up in the middle of them, fending off hyenas, lashing myself to whales. Times have changed. Nowadays I find I have very little to do on set. There are twenty people running around doing what I did alone when I first got started. Once the shooting starts, now all I have to do is make sure there's a nice wrap party when it's over. Food and drink. Times may have changed, but the whales haven't—and neither have I. They keep coming, and I keep diving in with them to see where they'll take me. It's the nature of the beast, the nature of moviemaking—my kind of moviemaking, anyway. Call me crazy.

The whales aren't always mechanical. I've discovered that they can swim around in bottles of whiskey and ride around in big black cars with tinted windows. They can break down hotel room doors and punch out directors. And sometimes the whale is simply an idea that takes hold in my head, which I'm determined to bring to life, come hell or high water.

━━◆━━

After wrapping *Visit to a Chief's Son*, I tried my hand at several feature films with the Hollywood studios. For instance, *The One and Only*, a comedy about wrestling starring Henry Winkler, Kim Darby, and Hervé Villechaize, the little guy from *Fantasy Island* ("The plane! The plane!"). The standout moment for me was a dinner scene during which my biggest challenge was keeping the flirtatious Villechaize from coming on a bit too strong to the actress playing Kim Darby's mother. Thankfully, I failed. The unscripted moment ended up in the film and got the movie's biggest laugh.

For the most part I found the process of making features unrewarding—both creatively and financially. I'd have better luck a decade later, in 1990, producing *Mr. & Mrs. Bridge*—starring Newman and Woodward as opposed to Darby and Winkler made all the difference in the world—but by the late 1970s I was done with features. The studios controlled everything—from casting to catering—and in the end I came out with nothing. The studios assigned their most creative people to the accounting department—they were cat burglars, profits vanishing across the studio rooftops in the dark of night.

Flying back and forth to Los Angeles, walking into the studio offices hat in hand and walking out without a dime . . . there had to be a better way. Determined to bypass the studios, I realized that the solution was right before my eyes: television. I had made television documentaries without ceding control; why not make television movies?

As a photographer working in advertising, I had plugged into connections up and down Madison Avenue. I turned to a couple of ad execs at Benton & Bowles—Jeff Grant and Michael Letner—whose client, General Foods, was hungry for programming to sponsor.

I went to Grant and Letner with *My Old Man*, a Hemingway short story I had come across about a father, a son, and a horse race—a story of love, loss, and redemption.

They asked if I could do it for nine hundred thousand dollars.

Yes.

Could I change the teenage boy in the story to a girl to appeal to a female audience?

Sure.

Could I get John Erman, who had just done several episodes of *Roots*, to direct?

No problem.

And could I get Kristy McNichol to star?

Absolutely.

I was in. Now all I had to do was figure out who the hell this Kristy McNichol person was. Turned out she was one of the biggest teen stars of the time. But getting McNichol to sign on was child's play compared to landing John Erman to direct. Going after Erman meant going into the lion's den—I had to go back to LA and the offices of the Creative Artists Agency.

Erman's agent was Bill Haber, one of the five founding members and owners of CAA. Over the next several decades, Haber, along with partners Michael Ovitz and Ron Meyer, would hold the keys to the kingdom. CAA changed the way the game was played, bundling its clients together—actors, writers, and directors—and selling them as a package in high-profile blockbuster deals that turned into blockbuster movies. In the eyes of many, the agency had co-opted and become more powerful than any single Hollywood studio.

I admit to a bad case of the jitters walking into his big, open office with the blinding Southern California sunlight streaming through the windows. I needed John Erman, and Haber knew it.

The first thing he did was to come out from behind his desk, put his arm around my shoulder, and give me a tour. I was impressed. In the bathroom in his office, in the middle of the entertainment capital of the world, the man had his own bidet. There it was—he was in the driver's seat. What I didn't know at the time was that Haber went completely against type. He might be a Hollywood agent, but he also happened to be one of the nicest guys in the world. Ultimately he would guide me through all nine circles of Hollywood—lust, greed, fraud, treachery, etc.—and we would become the best of friends, ballooning in the South of France and yachting off the coast of Majorca. But there on that day, in the presence of the bidet, we cut a deal. No doubt Haber got the better of me, but John Erman would direct *My Old Man.*

The stars in place—McNichol, Warren Oates, and Eileen Brennan among them—it was time to make a movie. Occasional problems came up, like when a couple of wise guys in camel-hair overcoats appeared at my office, asking why I wasn't using Teamsters. I told them because I couldn't afford it. They showed me the guns under their coats and said I couldn't afford *not* to hire them. I tried reasoning with them, explaining that I had survived Nazi camps and Communist trials, and that there was no way I was going to let them push me around. It was a matter of principle. And money. Whether or not they scared me—and they did—didn't matter. The point was that if I was going to start paying for Teamsters, I might as well shut the whole production down. Say yes to anything, but sometimes you have to say no. To my relief, they were reasonable men. Or lazy ones, anyway. They left and never came back.

Other than a few other hiccups, the process went smoothly. I had a script, I had chosen a location—Saratoga Springs in upstate New York—I had no studios breathing down my neck, and I was doing exactly what I wanted to do. It seemed as if there was no limit to what I could do on television; the possibilities were endless. It was the perfect medium for all the stories I wanted to tell. I was on top of the world. And then I was knocked off my perch.

My wife Eleanor had fallen ill.

We had a winter house down in Manalapan, near Palm Beach, on the Atlantic coast of Florida. Late that spring, as we were closing the house down for the season, Eleanor began to have trouble breathing. She had been sick with what we thought was a bad cold, but her doctor ran some tests and said her arteries were clogged. She needed a triple bypass, and the sooner the better.

My son Billy was in medical school in Philadelphia, working in the hospital where Dwight Eisenhower's onetime cardiologist was affiliated. I flew Eleanor to Philadelphia, where Billy met us. It all happened so fast that my other children couldn't get there. Kim was working as a tour guide in Guadeloupe, Kevin was in the army, serving in Germany, and Robi was away at college in Syracuse. June 4, 1979, Eleanor went into surgery. Billy arranged to go in with her, as an observer. He watched his mother die on the table.

For the first time in my life, I was lost.

I'd never been much of a husband, and when it came to Eleanor's disappointment in me, her frustration and anger, I was always on the move, never there when it mattered. Still, I loved coming home to her, and I counted on Eleanor in ways she could never count on me. Twenty-five years before, when my first wife Marilyn left, I was hurt but not surprised. But I took for granted that Eleanor would always be there when I got home. I was wrong, and now she was gone. Up until this moment, I had never figured out what to do in the face of death. Strange, because I've seen so much of it. Maybe that's why I keep moving.

I turned for support to our kids. My father had ingrained in me the importance of self-reliance, and I had passed that lesson on to my children. But sometimes self-reliance is nowhere near enough. The pain of loss brings into focus the power of family. We huddled together like a clan around a fire.

Robi, who had just graduated from Syracuse, accompanied me to Saratoga Springs—and in a sense he hasn't left my side since. From that time on, my dream became Robi's, and his dream became mine—and for the next thirty years we pursued it. We became partners in a shared future. We built a company—an empire of movies. It was Eleanor's legacy, her death forging a bond between Robi and me that changed both our lives. I create the stories, he creates the financing—through good times and bad. Whether calling up one of his banker friends for an emergency line of credit or disappearing for a few hours and returning with a suitcase full of money to keep the cameras rolling for a few days, Robi's always found a way to make sure the lights don't go out.

We filmed the final scenes on location—the Kristy McNichol character riding her horse to victory while her father, listening to the race on the radio, quietly dies in a hospital bed. We sent the cut to the head of General Foods for approval. He said he couldn't stop crying. Neither could I.

In December 1979, just in time for the holidays, *My Old Man* ran on CBS. Beyond all expectations, it earned a twenty-nine share. I was off and running, pitching ideas to General Foods, Procter and Gamble, and Liberty Mutual. Once I'd sold a story to one of the big sponsors through my ad agency contacts, selling it to a network was a piece of cake. I was guaranteeing that the finished picture would bring in advertising revenue to the network while retaining creative and financial control over the production.

Television was my world now—a three-ring circus, a pot of gold, and a Pandora's box all rolled into one. The best toy a kid could ever ask for. I was starting over. I was fifty-five years old.

And the last thing I wanted to do was go home. In fact, I sold both my houses—in Westchester and in Florida. They were filled with too many ghosts. I took an apartment on East 56th Street.

———

Bruce Learned worked for the OSS in postwar Austria. I knew him from my time in the Hungarian resistance and had watched his daughter, Michael Learned, grow into a strong, sensitive, intelligent woman and actress—the perfect lead for *Nurse*. With Eleanor's death in the operating room still haunting me, I charged right back into the heart of a hospital—conjuring up a nurse who might help save the Eleanors of the world. Michael was fresh off her success on *The Waltons*, making the project an easy sell to the sponsor, General Foods, and CBS. The movie turned into a great ratings success, leading to my first television series.

The network offered to build me a hospital on a soundstage in Queens. But I'm allergic to movie sets. There's no sense of adventure working in a studio, no risk and little reward—shooting models under hot lights is like shooting fish in a barrel. Camera in hand, I preferred to walk through a building on fire or ski down a glacier. Moviemaking is no different, all fire and ice.

I said to CBS, why build a hospital when there are already dozens in place all over the city? They said there was no way a working hospital would allow me to walk in with a cast, crew, and cameras—and film a television series while they're patching up the city's wounded. Twenty-four hours after my conversation with the CBS execs, I came back with a contract to take over an entire floor of the Metropolitan Hospital in East Harlem.

The arrangement made for some unusual challenges, unexpected shots, and unscripted scenes—which was the beauty of it. With cameras rolling, we captured life-and-death emergencies, panicked improvisations, real blood and broken bones, crazy people wandering in and out of frame.

It was not much different from any other movie location I've ever been on . . . or, for that matter, my life.

The Hungarian Countess Esther Szirmay wandered into the frame of my life in the summer of 1980. But I wouldn't know how crazy she was until after I married her.

I was in Montreal scouting locations and met up with some expatriates from Hungary, one of whom insisted that I meet his visiting sister: the countess. We had a glass of wine, which led to another glass of wine, which led to dinner. And then another dinner and breakfast. I was alone and didn't like being alone and found it refreshing to be talking—and making love—in Hungarian again. She invited me to visit her castle outside of Budapest. I asked her to marry me.

There was just one problem. Her Hungarian passport allowed for travel to Canada, not to the States. But I had never let a piece of paper or passport stand in my way before, and I wasn't about to now. This was my future wife, after all.

Back in New York, at my favorite Hungarian restaurant, I had a talk with a fellow I knew from the old country who worked there as a waiter/bouncer. I asked him if he'd like to make a little money, and he agreed to the plan I laid out for him. Then I went to Hertz and rented the biggest car they had available, one with a trunk large enough to accommodate both Esther and her luggage. It was like the old days when I crossed from Hungary into Austria hidden in a potato truck, except that Esther enjoyed the relative luxury of a Chrysler, even if she did spend thirty minutes of the trip in its trunk. A couple of days later, Esther and I were uncorking a bottle of wine on 56th Street. I was an American citizen now, and by marrying her, the passport problem would be solved.

On location down in Savannah, *When the Circus Came to Town*, a Movie of the Week for CBS, was about to go into production. It starred Elizabeth Montgomery as a woman in a small town, bored and sheltered, who decides to break free from her lackluster life and join the circus. Christopher Plummer plays the rake who leads her on, seduces, and finally falls in love with her. But I had business in Los Angeles, so I sent Robi down to Georgia to stand in for me as producer. Conveniently, I also had business in Las Vegas: a twenty-five-dollar wedding on the Strip. Esther was joining *my* circus. Or perhaps I was joining hers.

Robi, who has always had a flair for the dramatic, hired a skywriter to draw a heart in the skies over Vegas during the ceremony. What he couldn't have known was that, in the end, my marriage to Esther had all the substance of that puff of smoke in the sky. She loved her wine and her vodka chasers, loved to drink more than she loved me. Or she needed it more, and after an intoxicating start, the marriage dissolved into one long hangover, the price of a different kind of intoxication. It didn't take me long—several months—to realize my mistake, but it took me several years to act on that realization.

A new wife meant a new, and even bigger, house. Esther had acquired a couple of komondors—huge, white, shaggy Hungarian sheepdogs that would have each required his own parking space in Manhattan—so it was back to Westchester. I bought a place in Bedford, then went back to work. As luck would have it, I was headed as far away from Esther as geographically possible. I was off to the other side of the world—China and the Forbidden City.

I was in negotiation to film the first American movie to be shot entirely on the Chinese mainland since the Communist takeover. August 1981, just when the air controllers' strike began, I managed to fly into Beijing five weekends in a row, meeting with party officials and cultural committees, hammering out the details of the cast, shooting schedule, and filming locations—every location requiring an additional license.

Finally, after I had attended all the necessary banquets and acquired all the necessary permits, I could move forward with *Peking Encounter*. It was a simple story, part travelogue, part love story: A young man working in the American embassy falls for a Chinese girl, but ultimately their romance is stymied by the cultural and political divide. Cast in the role of the girl was Chen Chong, an actress unknown in America but hailed by the People's Republic as "the Chinese Elizabeth Taylor." She later emigrated to America, changed her name to Joan Chen, and has gone on to put her own stamp on the film industry as an actor, director, and producer.

Moviemaking is nothing new to China. In terms of size and scope, the film industry is second only to India's Bollywood. But back in the '60s, '70s, and '80s it was a different animal. Every movie made in China at the time was an industry in itself, employing hundreds and taking a year or more to make. I had twenty-one days. It was a challenge, climbing a mountain no one had ever climbed before—or moving one.

Day one, early morning, the Forbidden City, all the pieces in place, cast and crew and a Chinese handler for every American, the cameras ready to roll under the watchful eye of the ubiquitous Mao Zedong posters, and a big black car pulls up to the set, right in front of the Imperial Palace, where no cars are permitted. An exception was made for the Minister of Culture. He introduced himself with a little bow and said, in perfect English, that he loved the script. He just wanted to change one little thing. He didn't like that the American guy was screwing a Chinese girl. His thought was: It should be a Chinese guy screwing an American girl.

Twenty-one days, and the clock was ticking. I had no choice. I knew if I didn't go along with his "suggestion," I'd be the one who was screwed. I rewrote and recast the movie on the spot. The Chinese guy had his way with the American girl, and everybody was happy.

You can't control everything. In fact, you can't control much of anything. If you think you can, stay out of the movie business. The best you can do is put your harpoon into the whale and hop on and influence the direction it takes.

I certainly couldn't control the changing of seasons or the speed with which a network green-lights a project. But I was a master at working around them. And believe me, there were a few network executives into which I would have gladly put a harpoon.

After China I took off for northern Canada to film *Cook and Peary: The Race to the Pole*, a movie inspired by an article I read in *National Geographic* that explored the controversy over which man reached the North Pole first. But thanks to CBS and its dithering delays, we arrived on location too late. Spring had sprung, and the snowpack was gone. We were chasing ice. I chartered a plane and flew the entire cast and crew—including stars Rod Steiger and Richard Chamberlain—to Greenland. If we didn't hurry, we might have to follow in Cook and Peary's snowshoes and film the damn movie on the North Pole. But our luck held . . . until the last day of shooting, when the ice broke, taking Chamberlain—Dr. Kildare and the king of the miniseries—with it.

Chamberlain was bonding with some Alaskan huskies as the platform of ice he was standing on broke off and began to drift off into the Greenland Sea. The dogs were barking, the crew was shouting, and I was on the phone calling for a helicopter. After fifteen minutes of Chamberlain and the dogs hopping from floe to floe as the ice continued to break up, the chopper arrived and plucked them all to safety. The water out there, Chamberlain told me later, was as black as night.

Aside from the politburo in Beijing and the ice in Greenland, another aspect of moviemaking I can't—and, in fact, don't want—to control is the acting. The best actors are those who are beyond your control. And I don't mean that they show up five hours late and throw tantrums on the set. I mean that they possess an independence and creativity that adds to the script and their role in ways you never imagined. A great actor brings to a picture a sense of surprise and serendipity that can strike out like a wildcat. That's not something you want to control even if you could. You unlock the cage, stand back, and let it go.

Whenever I find such an actor, I'll go to any length to work with him or her again. And there have been many over the years, actors like Peter O'Toole.

When I first worked with Peter on *Svengali* in 1983, it wasn't a question of the ice breaking under the actor's feet; it was a matter of what he was having *on* ice the night before. It's no secret that in his day, Peter was not only a legendary actor, he was a legendary drinker—a man who, by his own account, once went out for a drink in Paris and woke up in Corsica. During the filming of *Svengali*, he was hanging around with a couple of Irish guys. Every morning one of them would give me a call, letting me know whether Peter was standing up or not, and thus I would know when I could start shooting that day.

Jodie Foster, who plays Zoe, the singer entranced by the Svengali's hypnotic and charismatic power, was entranced by Peter's hypnotic and charismatic power. She hung on his every word and gesture—and what young actor wouldn't? But like his character, Peter could be a bit of a devil. The Svengali is a singing teacher who takes Zoe on, pushing and twisting and bullying her into becoming a better singer. "Art," he says, "is a form of bondage"—and Peter played the role to the hilt. In the middle of a scene, he'd twist Jodie's ears or flick her nose to see how she'd react. Jodie, a good sport and a good actor, always stayed in character. She stood her ground, passing Peter's acid test. After all, he was only human. All actors are. Some are just more human than others.

That same year, 1983, I worked for the first time with another of my favorite actors, George C. Scott. And you don't get any more human than George. He was a force of nature, an instinctive actor, and a volcano of a man. I remember reading a magazine article comparing him to "Moby Dick thrashing in a minnow pond." That description alone, even if I had never seen him take command and go to war in movies like *Dr.*

Strangelove, Patton, and *The Hospital,* would have convinced me to reach out to Scott.

By that time I was working on three, four, five projects at any given moment—editing my last picture, casting my next one, developing ideas for the one after that. I was reading scripts, pitching networks and sponsors, scouting and heading out to locations. My heart was in my work, and I had very little left for Esther—no time or energy to write a proper ending to our marriage. It baffles me. I've loved and lost so many women, and it gets me into so much trouble. You'd think I'd learn. But my philosophy in love has always been damn the torpedoes; the potential rewards outweigh the risks. The same goes for working with an actor like George C. Scott.

In the winter of 1983, I was back in China—Hong Kong and Macau—having cast Scott as an American businessman looking for his long-lost son, and Ali MacGraw as the American embassy employee serving as his interpreter, in *China Rose.* But I had a situation.

The production was going over budget and we were running out of money. That was the bad news. The good news was that I was in Hong Kong. And so was Tommy Quinn, alias Georgios Samaras, Robert Dzigi, Tasos Douros, and Pele Lechien. Tommy was an Irish kid from Brooklyn who had made good—or bad, depending on what it was you were measuring. When they arrested him in 2010, the authorities estimated that he had swindled over the years some five hundred million dollars in Florida land scams and various insurance, stock, and security frauds.

I knew Tommy from New York, and to me he was just a smart, funny guy who also happened to be one of the most generous. He could afford to be.

I met him in the Peninsula Bar and asked if he wanted to buy the foreign rights to *China Rose.* He asked how much. I said a hundred thousand dollars, we shook hands, and he took me to a bank, where he withdrew the cash and officially became an investor in the picture. I didn't know where the money came from, and I certainly wasn't stupid enough to ask. It looked like I might actually get *China Rose* in the can before something blew up in my face. . . . Then, the final night on location, there came the explosion. I got a call in my room from the hotel manager.

As near as I could piece it together, George C. Scott, for whatever reason—he was a volatile man with an eye for pretty women and a predilection for vodka—had burst into a room not his own, breaking down the door, scaring the living daylights out of a couple of Japanese tourists. Whatever, or whomever, he was looking for was not there.

Thanks to Tommy, I had enough cash on hand to pay for the damages and offer the couple an upgrade to a suite. Best, I thought, to get George out of town. He was due in Vienna to start filming *Patton II*, and there was no way I was going to let him travel alone. On the plane, the vodkas kept coming, and at one point he got up and headed for the emergency exit, which I thought he was trying to open. I jumped out of my seat and grabbed his arm. He said, "Bob, there's a problem. The elevator isn't working." Even eight miles high, cruising somewhere over the Himalayas, Scott was a hard man to keep down.

Depositing Scott in Austria, I took a left turn and headed for my home away from home—Africa. Bill Holden had owned a huge estate near the Kenya Safari Club, and when he died in 1981, the place was broken up and sold. I bought a nice piece of it, including the guesthouse, and started adding on, including a dining room with a huge rotating table, where for several years my whole family and various friends gathered for Christmas.

The place was a dream come true, waking up on the slopes of Mount Kenya with a backyard full of zebras and rhinos. It was as though I had built my own private Városliget. I came to the house in Kenya whenever I needed to catch my breath—for a couple of minutes—before diving back into the world to go after the next whale.

❦

Some actors require special handling, and as producer I've played many roles—ringmaster, psychiatrist, and enforcer among them.

Sometimes it was a question of personality. I cast Maximilian Schell, winner of the 1961 Academy Award for Best Actor in his role in *Judgment at Nuremberg*, as the phantom in *The Phantom of the Opera*, and, as great an actor as he was, he was not an easy man to work with. I shot the movie in an old opera house outside of Budapest, and the fact that we were in Hungary played into my hands, as I knew exactly where to go to hire a couple of tough guys to make sure he stayed in line. I never worked with Schell again.

Other times, the issue was history. When I was developing *Izzy & Moe*, based on the true story of a couple of New York Prohibition cops who became famous for donning outrageous disguises to shut down speakeasies, I was determined to get Jackie Gleason and Art Carney to play the pair. Both were wonderful actors and gifted comedians. The problem was they hated each other's guts. Shuttling back and forth between Gleason's mansion in Miami and Carney's house in Westchester, I acted as diplomat, devil's advocate, and marriage counselor, convincing each that the other took the blame for the divorce and wanted to kiss and make up. Once I got them on the set, it was as though they'd never stopped working together. Whatever had come between them in the past evaporated before the camera.

Often enough, however, it's the biggest challenges that lead to the most compelling work, like pouring your heart—and money—into a movie starring an actor who can't walk and can barely talk.

The trouble began with Katherine Hepburn. *Terrible Tess*, the story of an aging former tennis star, had been written for her, but she had to withdraw when she injured herself in a fall. Losing Hepburn put a large, potentially fatal, hole into the project. But I liked the script too much to give up on it, and I set out to find a star big enough to fill the void. Remarkably I found one, a short drive away from Bedford, living on a farm in upstate New York. I would deliver the script myself. First, though, I had to have a talk with the writer. If the People's Republic of China could do it, then so could I—turning the former tennis star into a former boxer, and *Terrible Tess* into *Terrible Joe Moran*.

When the script was ready, the actor read it and said he always wanted to be a professional boxer, so in a way it could be the story of his life. He took the part. But the truth is, I got lucky. The actor was Jimmy Cagney, and Jimmy's doctors had been telling him to get out of the house and do something, which was when I showed up with *Terrible Joe Moran*. Making the movie was just what the doctor ordered. But getting the picture done turned into a real fight, and Jimmy took the first blow when he suffered a stroke.

The stroke knocked Jimmy off his feet and into a wheelchair. Although he was as sharp as ever, his speech was not, the words slurred and melting into each other until he could barely read his lines. The CBS executives voiced their concerns, but they were paid to worry, as was the insurance company, which upped the premium on working with Cagney to two hundred thousand dollars—a sizable bite out of my budget. But with the doctors' okay, and Jimmy's heart set on playing the role, I ignored the network and pushed the production forward. I installed the star in a suite at the Carlyle on 76th Street, in and around which most of the shooting would take place. The picture featured Art Carney and couple of younger actors—Ellen Barkin and Peter Gallagher.

Like an old racehorse, the moment the clapboard snapped, Cagney's eyes opened wide, and he was ready to run. We did, however, have to pull a few rabbits out of our hat to move the show along. The stroke had not only put him in a wheelchair, it had rendered his hands too weak to maneuver it. So we rigged up a series of ropes and pulleys that enabled us to move him from mark to mark and room to room. As for the king's speech, by the time we showed the first cut to CBS, they were thrilled and amazed by how clear and crisp his line readings were. I told them we had developed a miraculous new sound technology that allowed us to take each word he spoke, shape it, polish it, and put it back into context. The executives bought it. What I had actually done was hire a Cagney impersonator to dub every line he spoke.

I needed one more trick to wrap the film. The story put Jimmy on an emotional roller coaster, and several scenes required him to break down and cry. Cagney had smashed grapefruits in girls' faces and gone up in a ball of fire, but I don't believe he had ever cried on screen before. But I learned that he was a very patriotic guy, a true Yankee-Doodle dandy. When my wife Esther got her American citizenship, Jimmy invited all our friends to a restaurant in Greenwich, had the place filled with American flags, and told the band to play the national anthem . . . at which point I noticed that his eyes welled up. I had my ticket—the national anthem. I could make Jimmy Cagney cry on cue.

Of all the actors I've ever worked with, Cagney awed me the most. I think I fell a little bit in love with him. He told me once, with a kind of sadness and regret, that acting was just a job. He didn't know how to do anything else. And all it was, he said, was hitting your marks and telling the truth.

Two years later, in the spring of 1986, Floyd Patterson, Mikhail Baryshnikov, Milos Forman, and I were among the pallbearers at Jimmy's funeral. A fighter, a dancer, a director, and a producer bore him up the steps of the small church on the Upper East Side where as a kid he had been an altar boy. Ronald Reagan, actor and leader of the free world, read the eulogy. All that was missing were the fireworks. Carrying him out of the hearse and across the street, one of us—I won't say which—stumbled on the curb, nearly sending the coffin crashing to the pavement. It was Jimmy trying to hit his mark one last time.

Around the time of Cagney's funeral, I got mixed up in a prostitution ring.

Producers came out of the Hollywood woodwork vying for the rights to *Mayflower Madam*, the tell-all bestselling book by Sydney Biddle Barrows in which she opened up about her high-end Manhattan call-girl service catering to businessmen, politicians, and Saudi princes. I couldn't outbid Hollywood, but I could out-talk them, and Sydney realized that I was the only potential suitor who saw the humor and hypocrisy in her story. What is it about sex and successful women in America that brings out the arrest warrants and handcuffs?

To me it was not so much a story about what happens in the privacy of the bedroom, but about an independent woman who breaks out of the male-dominated corporate world and manages to come out on top—only to face the perversity of a justice system that's determined to bring her down. If a crime is victimless, is there really a crime? And that's exactly what I asked the judge, testifying on Sydney's behalf. In New York State criminals are not supposed to profit from their crimes, and the court was out to strip Sydney of her ill-gotten gains, both from the book and my movie. "Who got hurt?" I asked the judge. "Is there any proof anyone fell out of bed and broke a leg?" The case was ultimately dismissed.

Sydney and I hit it off—we were birds of a feather, both of us experts at casting actors, costuming them, and giving them a script, creating and marketing fantasies. We were fellow members of the oldest profession in the world—storyteller.

Casting Sydney, I chose the most clean-cut, grown-up girl-next-door I could think of—Candice Bergen. Candice was so clean-cut—raised a strict Catholic—that even though she had just turned forty and was married with children to French director Louis Malle, she still had to call her mother to ask permission to take the role. She played the role of a yuppie madam as if she was born to it. It was a fun set to work on. Sydney herself had cast her own call girls in the movie, and they were all savvy and funny, good company—a real pleasure to work with.

But in my business, people are falling out of bed and breaking their legs all the time—and the bigger the business, the harder the fall. So when it comes to mergers, partnerships, and suitors, you have to be careful whom you sleep with. Which brings us to *Trouble in Paradise*.

A sexy, sophisticated socialite and a not-so-sophisticated but very handy and handsome sailor are stranded on a deserted island. At first she rejects his advances, but over time she succumbs to his rugged charm. They fall in love. Complications ensue.

It's an old story and a good one, but there was definitely *Trouble in Paradise*. Working and dealing with difficult stars—alcoholics, egotists, and bad midgets—is part of every producer's daily regimen. It comes with the territory—monitoring and managing the theatrics both on-screen and off. But on location in Australia, Raquel Welch pushed the envelope. As an actor, she believed in *authenticity*. But as a producer, I often found that *authenticity* translated into *overtime* and *cost overruns*. It's a common area of disagreement between actors and producers that I suspect goes back to the dawn of Greek tragedy. Raquel wanted *truth*; I wanted to tell a story. The result was *Trouble in Paradise*.

But Raquel was the least of my problems. And they were all about to come to a head. Not long after *Trouble in Paradise* premiered, in the spring of 1989, my company crash-landed. And the complications that ensued very nearly buried it for good. All of our money vanished into thin air. Our bank accounts were empty. We were broke.

Robert Halmi Inc. (RHI) came into being in 1979, and from the beginning we were always scrambling for cash. The company almost immediately went public—on Denver's notoriously wild and woolly penny stock market—to raise a little money, and a very little it was. Robi went out on the road to hustle up investors, knocking on doors, selling 2 percent of the company here, 3 percent there. It wasn't the banks in New York that kept us going; it was the money Robi brought in from an investment banking company in Pittsburgh.

Like his father, Robi's a magician, managing to keep RHI alive—even if it was on life support—meaning that I could keep on making my movies, which was all I cared about. By the mid-'80s, all our hard work began to pay off. The business started to hum. The company expanded, buying into the Hal Roach studios in LA. We were making good money and building a reputation as a solid investment. And that was our undoing.

The newspapers in Australia called Christopher Skase the next Rupert Murdoch. He started out as a stockbroker and journalist, then in 1975 bought a small Tasmanian company called Qintex. He started to borrow and buy, and borrow some more. By the time Skase started sniffing around RHI, Qintex was a one-and-a-half-billion-dollar Melbourne-based monster. Owner of five high-end Australian resorts and a major investor in Australian television and football, Skase was looking to expand operations into America. He was building an empire.

Robi hammered out the details, and in 1987, just as *Trouble in Paradise* was about to go into production, Skase and I sealed the deal on legal pads while on safari at my ranch in Kenya. RHI merged with Qintex, and millions of dollars and unlimited opportunities were on the table. But once the transaction was consummated, I wondered, what the hell did I just do? It was like the first night after my marriage. I knew something was wrong. It was only a matter of time before I fell out of bed and broke something.

Skase's next big move in America was a game changer. In 1989 he went after MGM/UA, and Kirk Kerkorian agreed to sell the studio to the Australian for something in the neighborhood of a billion dollars. Skase immediately installed me as MGM's president—a position I held for about an hour, as the deal fell through before the ink was dry on the contract. Skase had bought the company with money he didn't have. The emperor had no clothes, and I had no standing as president.

Back in Australia, Qintex had already begun to melt down. Skase couldn't even manage to come up with the first thirty-million-dollar down payment for the studio. The creditors were coming for him and what turned out to be nearly $750 million in debt.

Part of Skase's problem was plain bad luck—Qantas went on strike, turning his resorts into luxurious, empty money pits. But from the beginning my gut told me that there was less to Skase than met the eye. I just refused to listen.

Skase vanished, turning up several months later on the island of Majorca in Spain. For a decade the Australian government fought to extradite him. His creditors put a bounty on his head and drew up plans to kidnap and bring him back to Melbourne. But Skase was too slippery. The only thing he couldn't outsmart or outrun, after ten years, was the stomach cancer to which he succumbed in 2001.

As for my company, by the end of 1989, the Qintex disaster gutted it. When we made the deal with Skase, both Robi and I had taken Qintex stock as payment, which was worth about as much as the Hungarian pengö in 1946—nothing. I had no money to pay my mortgage, let alone meet my payroll. But I wasn't worried. I'd seen worse. The work would come and the money would follow. I was going to keep on making movies, and Robi was already up to his old tricks, coming back from meetings in London with two million dollars—the first investment in the new RHI, rising from the ashes of the Qintex stock.

◆

Robert Duvall. Tommy Lee Jones. Danny Glover. Diane Lane. Robert Urich. Frederic Forrest. Anjelica Huston. D. B. Sweeney. Chris Cooper. Steve Buscemi. One thousand extras. One hundred horses. Fifteen hundred head of cattle. Thirty wranglers. Ninety crew members. Six cameras all rolling at once. Sixteen weeks. Countless anxious phone calls from the president of CBS. Eight hours. Four nights. A thirty-eight share. Seven Emmy awards.

1989. The same year Qintex turned into a black hole, I came home to a small Texas town called *Lonesome Dove* and buried my dead. This was the America I loved and dreamed of as a kid, cowboys and cattle drives, fiercely independent men and women risking everything for a piece of something, braving the elements for the possibility of love. The cast carried the picture because they lived it. They were professional actors, and I didn't need to touch them to know they were real. They all hit their marks and told the truth, and in this business *truth* is a rare gem.

~~

I loved life in Kenya. But as much as it went against my grain, I knew that I was fighting one battle I could never win: age. By the time I was in my late sixties, I had to give some ground and make the occasional tactical retreat. My house in Kenya stood at an altitude of seven thousand feet—it was a good life there, but not an easy one. In addition, politics had taken a turn. Conflicts among the Somalis and Sudanese were beginning to leak into Kenya, and there was a sense of impending anarchy and dark doings. I'd had enough of that in Hungary and didn't like the idea of having to carry a gun wherever I went. As much as I loved the place, I knew that I couldn't call East Africa home for much longer. But before leaving the country, I'd embrace it.

Ivory Hunters (originally *The Last Elephant*) stars Isabella Rossellini, John Lithgow, and James Earl Jones. It explores the poaching and slaughter of elephants for their ivory, which epitomized for me the self-destructive forces unleashed across that part of the world. Isabella, who has dedicated herself to wildlife conservation, was a natural for the female lead and, as anyone who has ever worked with her will tell you, she has an uncanny magnetism—an allure that goes far deeper than her famous beauty and that evidently extends far beyond the confines of her own species.

There were several scenes in the film that featured an orphaned baby elephant, and as soon it spotted Isabella, the little elephant—which wasn't really all that little—took to her as a child to his mother. He followed her wherever she went, knocking down tents, crashing into food-service tables, leaving no stone—or latrine for that matter—unturned in his determination to remain close by her side. He was another George C. Scott—except that he weighed half a ton.

Near the end of the picture, we had to shoot a climactic elephant stampede with Isabella and John Lithgow in the middle of it. I went out into the bush with some locals and corralled, as best we could, a herd of the wild animals. I'd been around elephants for years, hunting, photographing, filming, and simply marveling at them. I knew that, despite all those old Tarzan movies to the contrary, even in the midst of a stampede, an elephant is one of the most graceful creatures on earth. He'll go out of his way to avoid—and step around—anybody in his path. I assured my two stars that all they had to do was stand still. The elephants would go around them.

But we'll never know. We spooked the herd, and off they charged. The animals held nothing back, and they hit their marks at about fifteen miles per hour—and all my assurances to John and Isabella were ground into the dust under the elephants' feet. The two of them yelled bloody murder and ran like hell, diving for their lives behind a jeep. They later told me they loved it—the adventure, the excitement and adrenaline—which was good, because I had to reshoot the entire scene. This time they stood in the jeep as the elephants charged past them.

The Last Elephant was over, and within a few years my time in Kenya would be too. That baby elephant was on his own—but a little bit of him rubbed off on me. I've been close to Isabella Rossellini for more than two decades and have cast her in more of my movies and miniseries than any other single actor.

Giving up my retreat in Kenya—I donated the buildings and land to Save the Children—compelled me to face up to my problems in Bedford. I had to get my house in order. The trouble there wasn't political, it was marital.

Over the years Esther's drinking had gotten progressively worse. We tried psychiatrists, clinics, drugs, and residential treatment programs, but after a few days or weeks of abstinence, she'd invariably fall off the wagon—drinking alone and doing her best to hide it, but the binges and blackouts would inevitably come. One evening in the summer of 1990, I came home to find every light and television in the house on, all the kitchen cabinets and the refrigerator door open, and no sign of Esther. Either the house had been robbed and ransacked by a television-watching thief, or my wife had lost track of her liquor stash—and herself in the bargain.

I found her in the backyard, cowering in the komondors' big dog-house, with two empty bottles at her side. I told her this couldn't go on. She said that I had never been there for her, and it was hard for me to argue the point. We agreed that the best thing was for her to go back to Hungary and stay with her family. We said that we'd reevaluate later, but I knew there was nothing to reevaluate—this was simply a way to smooth her exit out of the picture. The marriage had been over for a while, and now I was just beating another tactical retreat.

Esther was happy to get away from me. She went back to being a countess in her castle outside of Budapest, and three years later we divorced. Several years after that, Esther finally succeeded in drinking herself to death. I began to doubt that I was cut out for marriage. Were there any women out there willing to take me on?

One I would gladly have asked was Joanne Woodward, and that's exactly what I told her over dinner in Paris. I said that she was lovely, intelligent, and independent, and if she ever wanted to get rid of that husband of hers. . . . Her husband, sitting next to her, just gave me one of those million-dollar smiles of his. Paul Newman, half Hungarian, knew a Budapest bullshitter when he saw one—and I don't think he was worried about losing Joanne. He wanted to talk about race cars.

I had sent Ruth Prawer Jhabvala's screenplay of *Mr. & Mrs. Bridge* to Joanne, thinking that the Mrs. Bridge character—with her mixture of compassion, isolation, and repression—could have been written for her. I also thought that the story of a middle-class American marriage and family would resonate with a television audience. But Paul, who read the script and loved it, had a different idea. Not only did he think Joanne should take the role, he wanted to play opposite her as Mr. Bridge. But not on television. He wanted to do it as a feature, so I called Harvey Weinstein at Miramax, James Ivory signed on to direct, and the stage was set, which was how I came to be in Paris, on location, flirting with Joanne and talking race cars with Paul over dinner.

When it comes to moviemaking, I know what I'm good at—bringing everything together. I'm not an editor, I'm not a writer, and I'm certainly not a director. I tried that once, on a movie that no one has ever heard of, thankfully, and discovered that I didn't have the temperament for it. An actor would come up to me and ask how to do a scene, and I'd say I don't care, just do it fast. As a producer, I bring things together, and with a movie like *Mr. & Mrs. Bridge*, all I have to do is stand back and let the talent go to work.

The problem was, Harvey Weinstein didn't know *how* to stand back. He wanted to change the ending. Mrs. Bridge dies, and he wanted her to live. But Joanne wanted to die. Paul wanted her to die. Everyone wanted her to die, and we all got mad at Harvey for trying to change it. In the end, Mrs. Bridge died, Joanne Woodward got an Oscar nomination for Best Actress, and the only one who was mad was Harvey.

But sometimes dying is good for you. It worked for RHI.

Thanks to Qintex, RHI had entered the 1990s barely breathing. But coming out of its coma, the company was stronger, more agile, and more creative—both in our filmmaking and our financing—than ever before. We were making more and better movies and lining up more and bigger investors. In 1992 RHI went public again, with a valuation of $200 million. Two years later, in 1994, Hallmark Cards bought the company for $460 million. It pays to die when it gives you an excuse to start over.

In the early '90s, the business of financing, making, marketing, and distributing television movies and miniseries changed. In some ways the shift was slight, but in others it was seismic. America wasn't the center of the world anymore. It was a matter of percentages.

Before the shift, when calculating how much any particular movie would make, the rule was that America comprised 60 percent of the market, while Europe and the rest of the world—the aftermarket—made up 40 percent. But the times, and television, had changed overseas. Many channels in Europe that had been owned by their government had been privatized and were hungry for commercial programming. The result was that America had shrunk to 40 percent of the market, and the aftermarket had grown to 60 percent.

Robi and I were well positioned to exploit the expanding market-place. We took frequent tours of the investment capitals of Europe; from England to Germany, Italy, Switzerland, and France, we followed the money. Robi talked return on investment, and I spoke their language, my multilingual education at Sárospatak paying dividends. And although I was American by choice, I was a citizen of the world by nature. I had had a house in Africa, and later on, another one in Spain and a 110-foot yacht floating around the Mediterranean. And so not only did I know their language, I knew their history, culture, and favorite wines—a little bit of charm served with a nice Cabernet going a long way in this business.

Another development back in America that helped put RHI into overdrive was the proliferation and growing strength of the cable channels. Many of the well-established brands like HBO, Cinemax, and Showtime had been around for a while, but the '80s and '90s ushered a whole new crowd into the home television theater—Lifetime, TNT, and the Sci-Fi Channel (now Syfy) among them. And they needed content. But that wasn't all. In their attempt to outflank the start-ups, which were draining market share, the networks introduced the idea of "event television," creating a *you have to see this* buzz around their movies and miniseries—which translated into bigger stories, bigger productions, bigger budgets, and more money for us. It was like Christmas in July. The networks were going to war with the cable channels, and we were selling ammunition to both sides.

We demonstrated the willingness to work hard, take risks, and never say die. We had the proven ability to move quickly, adapt to changing circumstances, and seize the day. And we had the good fortune to be in the right place at the right time with the right people. Put it all together, and that's how RHI went from zero to 460 million in four years. In the interim, however—between the zero and the 460 million—I still had occasion to scramble for cash.

In one case in 1991, I nearly broke the bank over a woman. I wanted her so badly that money was no object. Her name was *Scarlett*, and there wasn't a hotter property around. I didn't need to read the book to know I had to have it.

Bidding for the film rights to the *Gone with the Wind* sequel started at two million dollars. Robi and I quickly lined up investors here and in Europe to cover a $5.5 million bid. But before submitting it, Robi called me to say that he'd heard a rival producer was going in with a bid over six million, and it looked like we were sunk. But this was one whale that I wasn't going to let get away. Go in for eight, I said, we'll worry about making up the difference later. The Margaret Mitchell estate accepted our bid. I had my *Scarlett*.

A friend of mine at William Morris, which represented the book, called to congratulate me. He said the eight million had broken records, was making headlines, and everyone in the industry was talking about it, but he had one question for me: "Do you have the money?" I told him I would by the next day. I hung up and started calling all of our contacts in Europe, selling them on a new idea: The Search for Scarlett. Each country would conduct its own audition for the role—and from those auditions we would produce and deliver an additional hour of programming. They bought the concept. Now not only did I have *Scarlett*, I had the money to pay for it.

Before it was over, I had hundreds of videotapes. Everyone wanted to be Scarlett—black, white, Asian, German housewives, Italian fashion models, and English schoolteachers. They were some of the worst actors on the planet, but it made for some great reality television and free publicity.

The coveted title role ultimately went to British actress Joanne Whalley (then Whalley-Kilmer), with Timothy Dalton as Rhett, and a supporting cast that included Sean Bean, John Gielgud, Julie Harris, and Ann-Margret. As wonderful as Whalley proved to be as Scarlett, she brought some heavy baggage along to the London set. She and her husband were going through a rough stretch, and his presence proved problematic.

One of my biggest problems with television was that it had pushed aside and taken the place of great literature. It had stifled our imaginations and stolen away our dreams of adventure. One of the first miniseries I developed in partnership with Hallmark Entertainment was *Kidnapped*—the beginning of a string of classics I intended to bring to the small screen in a big way.

Robert Louis Stevenson had been one of my favorite writers as a kid, and now I was as excited as a kid to be bringing one of his stories back to life. Adding to my anticipation was the casting of the picture's lead. We landed Christopher Reeve, formerly known as Superman, an actor I considered comparable to Cary Grant—equally adept at light comedy, action/adventure, and serious drama. We arrived on location in Ireland in the spring of 1995. As we would be prepping prior to shooting, Christopher asked if he could come a few days late. He was an avid horse rider and had been invited to train in Virginia for an upcoming dressage event.

I've been around all kinds of animals, photographing and filming polar bears, Bengal tigers, and great white sharks, but of them all, I've never seen a more capricious or misunderstood animal than the horse. Perhaps the danger comes from the illusion that we have trained them and have them under our control. But I've seen rodeo horses throw men around like dolls, and cowboys working on *Lonesome Dove* walk away from a horse just from catching a crazy look in its eye. A rider is only in control of a horse until the horse decides differently.

Christopher never made it to Ireland. His horse refused to take a small, simple jump, and the momentum threw Christopher over. The fall crushed several of his vertebrae, severing the connection between his body and his brain. He had mastered comedy, drama, and adventure; now he would be tested by tragedy—a role he handled with courage and resolve. Although he didn't make it to Ireland, Reeve finally made it to my set, three years later—cast in the Jimmy Stewart role in my remake of *Rear Window*. Like Cagney before him, a broken body didn't break his spirit. Both men were artists to the end.

Armand Assante stepped in to take Reeve's place in *Kidnapped*. He's a tough but sensitive guy with forceful opinions and a formidable right hook to back them up. In the hundreds of pictures I've made, this is the only time I've had a star punch out his director, and a director threaten to sue his star. But at the end of the day, egos soothed and compresses applied, we overcame the bad blood and artistic differences and gave my childhood companion, Robert Louis Stevenson, some well-deserved airtime.

———————

Hidden away beneath London's Stafford Hotel there is an old bomb shelter, used during the war by American and Canadian officers, which has since been converted into a wine cellar. A huge table runs the length of the vaulted space, decorated with framed newspapers, maps, and other World War II memorabilia. Late in the spring of 1995, I invited Ted Danson, Mary Steenburgen, Peter O'Toole, Omar Sharif, Alfre Woodard, John Gielgud, Geraldine Chaplin, James and Edward Fox, Kristin Scott Thomas, Isabelle Huppert—along with the ghost of Jonathan Swift—to join me in the bomb cellar for a candlelit dinner. It was an ideal spot—beyond the reach of all the Yahoos—to kick off *Gulliver's Travels*.

A producer is an alchemist. I bring all the elements into one place, stir them up, and, in a process that defies logic, summon a moving picture out of the strange brew. Critical to the process is creating a chemistry that binds all the elements together. The cast and crew of a picture will often stay together for weeks at a time. Daily dramas unfold, laughs are shared, secrets revealed, insecurities exposed, and occasional fights break out (see Armand Assante above). In other words, they become a family, and I sit at the head of the table—negotiator, counselor, confidante, disciplinarian, referee, godfather, bartender—whatever the clan requires. . . .

Whether it was uncorking a bottle of champagne in New Guinea with Pierce Brosnan when he learned that his ship had come in—*Robinson Crusoe* becoming the next James Bond before my eyes. . . .

Or feeling Neil Simon's pain—we all did; he drove everybody nuts on the set of *London Suite*—as he rewrote line after line, scene after scene, day after day, never satisfied with what he had written the night before. . . .

Or doing what I could to protect Caroline Thompson, director of *Snow White: The Fairest of Them All*. It was those bad midgets again—my hands full keeping their hands off her. She'd written some wild stories—screenplays for *Edward Scissorhands* and *The Addams Family*—but nothing could have prepared her for the insanity on the set of *Snow White*. . . .

But that night at the Stafford, peace was at hand, and I relished every minute of it. I was in my element, at the head of the table in a man-made cave telling stories and drinking wine. That's where all great stories and good chemistry begin—over good food, in good company, in a nice setting.

Peter O'Toole and Omar Sharif, as you might expect, took center stage. It's where they belonged. The conversation came around to the first time they'd worked together, in 1962's *Lawrence of Arabia*—two young men stuck in the middle of the desert, living in tents, four hundred miles from the nearest water or women. All they had to amuse themselves was a radio and a few cases of whiskey. One evening, passing a bottle back and forth, they heard the news of a dance craze spreading from America to Europe: the twist. It wasn't long before the two of them were gyrating together under the desert stars . . . and now here they were again, picking up where they had left off thirty years before, writhing hip to hip around the dinner table, everyone in the room cheering them on like belly dancers. Everyone, that is, except for Ted Danson. Ted was scared. How was he going to keep up with these guys? They were the giants, and he was afraid he was going to come across as the Lilliputian.

Ted more than held his own as Gulliver, taking over at center stage as soon as filming began and dominating the screen in a movie that won an Emmy as the best miniseries of 1996. And not only that, if pressed, Ted could dance circles around Peter and Omar and every one else in the bomb shelter that night.

Gulliver's Travels changed a lot of things. It was the first television movie to rely on the extensive use of CGI—computer-generated imagery—special effects. The story had been adapted for the screen numerous times before, but always in miniature form, focusing on one small section of Swift's narrative—Gulliver's journey to Lilliput. But I wanted to tell the whole story, and London's Framestore, which later did the CGI in the Harry Potter movies, made it possible. They shrunk the Lilliputians down to size (no midgets to tie me down this time), blew the Brobdingnagians all out of proportion, made horses into talking Houyhnhnms, and engineered and launched the floating island of Laputa. CGI puts one more trick up a storyteller's sleeve. It's what makes carpets fly and dinosaurs run, and it's why I believe every great story should be retold and remade every forty years or so. The technology changes and so does the audience.

Another thing *Gulliver's Travels* changed was me. It had more of an impact on my life than any other movie I've made before or since. Every book I consider making into a movie, and every script that will potentially end up being a movie, I send out to readers to analyze and break down. Are the characters defined enough, the conflicts strong enough, and is the arc clear enough? While *Gulliver* was in development, I read a report on one of the early scripts that had been prepared by a London reader. Although the report found and identified flaws in the script, I was struck by how empathetic and respectful the report's author was to the writer. I asked to meet the reader. Then I asked her to dinner. Then I asked her to join me on location in Portugal. And then I asked her to move in with me.

Caroline Gray was born in Singapore thirty-five years after I was born in Budapest, and when our paths crossed in London, the arc of *my* life took a sharp turn. But this time I vowed to steer clear of marriage. It was a vow I kept for some seven years until Caroline and I tied the knot in 2003 at my New York apartment. After all, I was older and wiser now, and for the first time in my life I found that I preferred being home to being away. Caroline has made my story a happy one.

⌁

Unfortunately CGI was of no use to me when I built my house in Spain. Before giving away my place in Kenya, I had started looking for a suitable spot in Europe, preferably on the Mediterranean, to spend family vacations, entertain friends, and conduct business. The nicer the setting, the easier it is to close deals. I had been out on safari with Jock Anderson, who had been my safari guide and organizer from the beginning. He, too, was looking to get away from the turmoil in East Africa and had bought some land on the Costa del Sol, north of Málaga. He painted a picture of paradise—a subtropical climate similar to Kenya's, but overlooking the blue waters of the sea. The plot was huge, he said, and he offered to sell me half. I agreed on the spot.

Perhaps this is one time I should have looked before I leaped. The land was situated alongside a sheer drop down into the Mediterranean, and the first architect I brought out to look at it said that there was a reason a house had never been built there—it was impossible. *Impossible* had never stopped me before, though, and I kept at it until I found a builder willing to take the plunge. And it did turn out to be a paradise, a spectacular home with a wine cellar, a pool in the courtyard, and a gorgeous southern view. It didn't faze me that one of the reasons I had given up the house in Kenya was its location on the side of a mountain, and here I was living on the edge of a cliff.

But that house turned out to be one of the best investments I've ever made—paying off in a way that had nothing to do with money. A sad reality of the business I'm in is that friendships tend to be fleeting, lasting as long as it takes to make and market a movie. Because they are so rare, when a lasting friendship does develop, it is that much more valuable.

In 1995, after shooting *London Suite* in England, I invited its extraordinary cast to join me at my house in Spain. Among those who accepted was the man known by millions as Dr. Frasier Crane. As gifted, funny, and articulate as he is, Kelsey Grammer has overcome more than his share of tragedy and trouble to achieve his success—something I could easily relate to. He's also a marvelous and versatile actor, capable of doing Shakespearean tragedy on Broadway, comedy on *Frasier*, and everything in between. But more than that, he's one of the nicest guys I've ever met, warm, generous to a fault, with a mischievous wit. One morning, on a whim, Kelsey and I took off from Spain for Morocco, where we spent hours meandering through the bazaars in Casablanca. It was the beginning of a wonderful friendship.

Nearly a decade later, knowing how much Kelsey loves to sing, I offered him the role of Scrooge in *A Christmas Carol: The Musical*—a movie that still airs every December. We re-created the nineteenth-century London winter in the Budapest summer, and Kelsey transformed himself into the miserly main character, giving voice to Scrooge's dreams, nightmares, and ghosts. A good voice—and a good friend—is hard to find. I was lucky enough to find them both wrapped up in one package. The house in Spain is long gone, but Kelsey remains a valued part of my life.

All my life, I've had a gift for making something out of nothing, and with my new toy, CGI, I could build virtually anything I wanted. In 2002, with the help of CGI, I built on the back lot of England's Pinewood Studios a continent populated and shared by humans and dinosaurs—*Dinotopia*. The eighty-million-dollar budget—the largest for any television miniseries up to that point—also helped the cause.

But no matter how advanced the technology, or how much money you have, the key to building a successful movie will always be a good script, and one of my greatest challenges as a producer is finding writers whose vision agrees with mine. I get a picture in my head of what a movie should be—but transferring it out of my head and onto the page can be a delicate, drawn-out operation. I never dictate or confine a writer to a particular path. Once a story is in a writer's hands, it belongs to him or her. When a script fails, more often than not, it's my fault for not clearly expressing a framework for the screenplay. But when it succeeds, it's as though I'm reading the story for the very first time, the writer taking my ideas and creating something entirely original.

Playwright and screenwriter Peter Barnes, who'd written the features *The Ruling Class* and *Enchanted April*, always surprised me. Ensconced in his booth in a McDonald's near his London home, armed with a yellow pad, pen, Big Mac, and fries, he'd pick a story apart and put it back together, dreaming up scenes that could be part Shakespeare, part Groucho Marx, and pure Peter Barnes. He had the ability to read my mind and then improve upon it. In the late '90s, crumbs all over his shirt, Peter helped me bring magic to *Merlin*, put *Alice in Wonderland*, and, as the millennium drew to a close, build *Noah's Ark*.

Building the boat was easy. Flooding the world took some work. On location in Australia, we constructed a dam, created a body of water, and put an entire village in its path. Knowing we had to shoot the pivotal scene in one take, we put cameras all over the place to make sure we got it from every angle. The night before, I had dinner with the cast and crew— Jon Voight, F. Murray Abraham, Mary Steenburgen, and James Coburn among them—and offered a single piece of direction for the scene. *Just survive.* The next morning we blew the dam up, and, without benefit of rehearsal, the actors were all swept away. And they all lived.

The only casualty, according to several religious scholars, was the Bible. They criticized the movie for playing fast and loose with the gospel truth. But to me scripture is just another script, on which to make notes in the margins—the overall story more important than its particular elements. Adding scenes, subtracting them, or moving them around is part of the process. After all, the original authors weren't writing a movie. And they got some things wrong too. Somewhere in the Bible it says, "The wolf shall dwell with the lamb, and the leopard shall lie down with the kid." But not in my experience. Even more challenging than manufacturing the deluge for *Noah's Ark* was keeping the animals from eating each other. There were no lambs lying down with lions on my set.

Alice
I don't want to meet mad people.

Cheshire Cat
But you can't help it. Everyone here is mad. I'm mad. You're mad . . .

Alice
How do you know I'm mad?

Cheshire Cat
Because you're here, and everyone here is mad.

And so is director Nick Willing. Mad, that is—in the best sense of the word.

Not long after I talked Patrick Stewart into going after a White Whale, I convinced Nick to chase a White Rabbit, to dive down a rabbit hole—together with Martin Short, Whoopi Goldberg, Miranda Richardson, Ben Kingsley, Christopher Lloyd, and Peter Ustinov, among others—and make *Alice in Wonderland* (1999). He was just the man for it. Nick Willing puts performers at their ease, and thus gets the best out of them. If being pleasant and smart and engaging is a strategy, Nick has mastered it. The people on his set—from the gofers to the big stars—don't want to let him down. He's tricky that way, being so nice.

Another reason I like working with Nick is that his imagination runs wild. When he makes a movie, he creates a mythology—a world of meaning and metaphor behind the world on-screen. As a result, our collaboration has taken us far and wide—from the fantasy worlds of Alice's Wonderland, *Tin Man*'s Oz (2007), and Peter Pan's *Neverland* (2011) to the very harsh reality of *Baby Sellers* (2013). Nick has breadth as well as depth; he's a natural born storyteller.

Getting back to *Neverland*: As in every artist, there's a bit of Peter Pan in Nick—a refusal to grow up entirely, his sense of wonder and play mixed with a touch of darkness and danger.

How do I know he's mad? Because he's here, and everyone here is mad.

———

Brutal heat, poisonous snakes, and blinding dust storms were just a few of the plagues visited upon us during our forty days and nights in the Moroccan desert filming *The Ten Commandments* (2006). Strangest of all, coming near the end of our stay, was the freak hailstorm that severely damaged our lavish Egyptian palace but left the Hebrew slave quarters untouched. It brought an eerie air of unintended authenticity and urgency to the shoot. Even God was hitting His marks. But as arduous as our time in the desert was, aside from the snakes and storms, I had 1,500 extras and 1,000 snakes to corral—the hard part came later.

I went back to Hungary, my childhood home, where I had set up a CGI facility. I had to get the climactic scene on film. It was seven months of work for five minutes of film and a single miracle—the Hebrew exodus across the Red Sea. Cecil B. DeMille's version always bothered me, two walls of water flying up, a paved highway down the middle. I wanted the sea to recede, leaving behind a rocky, muddy, marshy mess. You can find your way back home, but it's never easy.

It starts with an idea, which leads to a story, which grows into a world. You find writers to realize it, directors to run it, actors to inhabit it, and money to make it all go round. As a producer, that world is in your hands.

And when it all works out—when the stars are aligned, the light is right, and your vision clears—you can part seas.

⌐━━⌐

Spotlights cast columned shadows across the ancient sanctuary. The lights dim as the moon rises over Athens and the Acropolis, and the screen comes to life. Penelope is in pain, screaming. Odysseus is running across the hills, racing to her. "Take me home," she says. She is giving birth, and Odysseus has his son.

The Odyssey premiered at the Parthenon. The government officials, businesspeople, and assorted Greek dignitaries in attendance treated me like I was Zeus, but it was a trick of the eye. I had cast Irene Papas in the picture, and now she was on my arm—Irene Papas, the Greek goddess of film, star of *Zorba the Greek*—and her aura had simply rubbed off on me. I may have hurled a few thunderbolts in my day, but mostly, I'm the guy dodging them. Odysseus is more my speed, running across those hills.

In Hades, the blind prophet Tiresias tells Odysseus, "You do not see that it is the journey itself that makes up your life." And now, after all these years, after all the miles I've covered, I've discovered that the whale I'm chasing—the one I'm determined to catch, tame, and bring to earth— is me.

CHAPTER ELEVEN

Kid with a Camera

The Chain Bridge has played a profound role in the life and history of modern Hungary. Built in 1849, after the failed revolution of the previous year, it was one of the first permanent spans across the Danube, linking Buda with Pest, the east with the west, the past with the future. On a warm afternoon in May 1967, I walked past one of the lions carved in stone that guard the entrance, continued out to the center of the bridge, stopped, and poured my father's ashes into the river.

This was my first time back in the city since my father engineered my escape, after the show trial twenty years before, during a prison transfer. But on this visit I barely made it out of the airport.

I don't know exactly what motivated me to make the trip to Budapest at that particular moment, in that particular spring. The urn had sat under a desk in my studio, and then under a workbench in my basement, for five years, and could have stayed there forever. But it was weighing on me, one of those things you tell yourself you have to do; it's on your list, but there's no deadline or urgency, and finally you just do it. I went down to the basement, saw the urn sitting there amid the half-empty paint cans and broken chairs, and decided it was time for him to go. He had freed me; it was time for me to return the favor.

I arrived at the Budapest Ferihegy International Airport without any luggage, carrying only a little bag with the brass urn in it. The customs official took the urn out of the bag and inspected it at arm's length, as though fearing it might go off at any moment. He asked me what was inside. "My dad," I said.

He didn't seem to like my answer, narrowing his eyes and shaking his head in a way only civil servants can. He put the urn down on his table and took out a knife. He said he had to open it. I told him if he did that he'd be very sorry, because something bad would happen to him, which he took for a threat—which it was. Voices were raised, security was called, a supervisor was summoned, and I found myself, if not surrounded, then certainly the official center of attention. *Yes,* I thought, *now I am back in Hungary.*

But matters were sorted out. I was an American citizen and a bereaved one at that. The supervisor called his supervisor, and they settled on a compromise. I would be allowed to proceed into Budapest, my urn unopened, with one proviso: I would have to finish my business in twenty-four hours, then leave the country. They never specified what exactly the consequences would be if I overstayed my welcome, but I thought it best not to find out.

I took a taxi into the city, asked the driver to drop me at the bridge, walked out over the water, and gave my dad back to Budapest. Then I turned around and came home.

———

In 1925, at the Spring Trade Fair in Leipzig, Germany, Oskar Barnack, manager of research and development at the struggling Leitz Company—a manufacturer of microscopes and other optical equipment—introduced a new camera to the market. Most of the company's investors and financial advisors argued against the move: What did Leitz know, they asked, about the camera business? But Barnack convinced the one man who mattered—his boss, Ernst Leitz II—to move forward with the project, and after that spring in Leipzig, photography and photojournalism in particular would never be the same.

The compact, lightweight 35-mm Leitz camera—the Leica—with its collapsible lens was hailed as an *integral part of the eye* and an *extension of the hand*. It freed the photographer from the box camera and tripod, took him out from under the black cloth, and took him out into the world, to work in outdoor settings with natural available light.

That same spring, in March 1925, at Selfridge's department store on London's Oxford Street, Scottish inventor John Logie Baird turned a switch, adjusted some dials, and gave the first public demonstration of electromagnetic televised images in motion. Within two years, twenty-one-year-old American Philo Farnsworth, who grew up in a house without electricity, made his first transmission with his invention, the image dissector, in his San Francisco laboratory. "There you are," he declared to his assistants, "electronic television." When one of his backers asked Farnsworth when they'd see money from the invention, he promptly broadcast his first image: a dollar sign. It was prophetic, a sign of things to come.

The development of the compact camera and the experimental transmission of televised imagery were both in their infancy in the 1920s—and so was I. Born in 1924, I am in fact the oldest invention of all three. But that's splitting hairs. I would grow up with the two new technologies—a coincidence, but in my case, as it turned out, a very happy one. Like everyone in Europe then, I was born to uncertainty. It was our lot. Timing was—and is—everything.

But the instant I put a Leica to my eye and snapped my first shot, life came into focus. I was hooked.

When I came to America, except for what I carried in my head and in my heart, I had to leave Europe in the dust. Officially, I did not exist—I had no passport, no identification whatsoever. But I did have my identity; it was bound up in the one little piece of Europe that I had brought across the ocean: the Leica hanging around my neck.

The camera wasn't enough for the civil authorities, however. They couldn't have some anonymous displaced person wandering the streets of America taking pictures without proper identification. So they gave me a piece of paper, which was duly witnessed and notarized—an affidavit of identity and nationality. The problem with the piece of paper was, no one knew what to make of it. What exactly did this affidavit entitle me to?

Over the next few years, when I traveled overseas on assignment, the paper became a source of puzzlement. Customs officers would look at it and ask, "What the hell is this?" But they never turned me away. I can be very persuasive, and no matter what country I was in, when I explained that I was a photojournalist there to take pictures for an American magazine, the gates opened. The camera was my passport.

By the time I came to America, I was twenty-seven years old, and I had seen a hell of a lot. But until my first night in the hotel on Madison Avenue and 31st Street in Manhattan, one thing I hadn't seen was a television. The television and I might have come into the world at around the same time, but until I came to the States, we had traveled in different circles. Now, here we were in the same room, together for the first time, staring each other in the face.

I didn't even bother to take off my jacket. I turned on the TV, sat on the bed in the dark, and watched the *Texaco Star Theatre*—Milton Berle in drag. It was mesmerizing. I couldn't take my eyes off the black and white light in the box until the network signed off and the "Star-Spangled Banner" was done.

In bed that night, the end of my first day as a free man in America, I barely slept. My mind was going in all sorts of directions. One thought I had was—this television thing could be a dangerous weapon. It took control of me, and I couldn't break away until it let me go. The next day I wrote my first letter to Sy Bourgin in Vienna. In it I wrote:

Television is, I guess, the number 1 public enemy to the American people. It has a hypnotizing power that when you turn it on, you cannot do anything else until you turn it off.

Through my work with Radio Free Europe in Austria, I knew how powerful, persuasive, and insinuating the airwaves could be. There was no defense against them. And now, with television, the airwaves could take the ears *and* eyes by storm—a flank attack. Milton Berle in a dress packed more energy and force than a roomful of atomic bombs.

Even in those early days, everyone was watching. At the conclusion of the most popular programs, like *Texaco Star Theatre*, the water pressure in some major cities dropped dramatically, toilets flushing all over town as viewers held their water until the show was over. And that was when there were a mere six million TV sets in America. Now there are close to three hundred million—one for every man, woman, and child in the country.

1951, the year of my arrival, saw two other eye-opening developments in the wonderful world of television: a college football game was broadcast in color, and NBC became the first network to send its signal nationwide. Television was on the march and growing bigger and stronger with each step—a conquering hero to some, a mortal threat to others.

To Hollywood, it was a monster. The studios decided that the dimensions of the screen itself—and thus of the moviegoing experience—was their one and only advantage. Bigger, they declared, *is* better, and they pulled out a whole bag of tricks to prove it. Cinerama, CinemaScope, VistaVision, Panavision . . . these were the weapons that would knock the little runt in everyone's living room down to size. The studios even tried to introduce a new, third dimension into the theaters, handing out special glasses at the door. But it was all smoke and mirrors—gimmicks that might sell a few tickets but weren't going to save the industry.

What Hollywood, in its panic, didn't realize was that it didn't need saving. People have been gathering together in the dark since the invention of fire to hear a good story. Ultimately, the studios survived because they did what they did best—turning down the lights and telling a good story. Instead of fighting the phenomenon of TV, Hollywood joined—and took advantage—of it. From the beginning, television has had a voracious appetite. There was always more time to fill, and the studios realized that they could crank out content for both the big and small screens.

The marriage between the television and movie industries was just the beginning of an ongoing evolution—and occasional revolution—in the very nature of entertainment over the last fifty years. It is an unfolding, unrelenting drama in which this kid from Hungary has been fortunate enough to play a part. Little did I know, back in that hotel room when I wrote in a letter about the hypnotizing power of television, that several decades later I would become one of the hypnotists.

━━⌣⌣━━

Television has been called a lot of things—a vast wasteland, idiot box, glass teat, the boob tube, and on and on—and over the years it has certainly found ways to stoop to new lows. But it has also given us *Mad Men* and *Frasier*; has brought us the Olympics and the tearing down of the Berlin Wall; and has taken us all on a trip to the moon. The TV set has been—and always will be—home to the good, the bad, and the ugly. It depends on how you use it and what you watch.

For me, television has been the bearer of my own American Dream—one more box full of dynamite for me to climb into, light the fuse, and see what comes out the other end. All I've ever wanted to do is tell stories, and I couldn't ask for a bigger, better, or more receptive audience than the one at home eating dinner, lying in bed, or simply sitting back at the end of the day to enjoy an evening of entertainment. The challenge has been to keep up with the changing face of the medium.

The Greek god Zeus in his day had a knack for altering his appearance and his nature as a way to approach, attract, and seduce prospective lovers. A swan, a bull, a shower of gold—it didn't matter, whatever the situation called for; he just wanted to have his way. And television, a supernatural being in its own right, is every bit the shape-shifter that Zeus was, which means that, having survived in the business for over forty years, I've had to do some shifting of my own—four decades of adapting, adopting, rolling with the punches, following the money, keeping current with the technology, and staying one step ahead of those behind the money and the technology.

It was, in short, like this:

First came the advertisers. In the beginning, it was not unusual for entire programs to be sponsored by a single company. Back then there were only a couple of minutes of commercials per hour, but the sponsor was also an integral part of the show itself, spreading its logos and products around the set and sometimes getting top billing—*Kraft Theatre*, *The Colgate Comedy Hour*, and *The United States Steel Hour* were just a few of the viewing options. And if the hour belonged to US Steel, so did the final word on script, casting, and content.

But then the networks got wise. They owned the airwaves, and as those airwaves spread, reaching into more homes, finding and creating more consumers, they became infinitely more valuable. Owning a TV set was no longer a luxury; it had become one of life's bare essentials—in a league with a toaster or washing machine, except more intimate and pervasive. Nobody put a *toaster* in their bedroom. Television changed everything—how people spent their time, their votes, and their money. The pie was getting bigger and bigger, but it was still cut into just three fat slices: ABC, CBS, and NBC.

A half hour became twenty-five minutes and then twenty-two, the rest of the time eaten up by commercials. And rather than selling by the hour or half hour, the networks now found it more profitable to sell thirty- or sixty-second spots. Television had become a three-ring circus, and the three networks were the ringmasters.

Then, television went underground . . . and into orbit. Cable had been around for decades—an overregulated, unprofitable alternative to antennas—and it wasn't until Ted Turner set up a satellite feed so he could sit in the Hood Yacht Club in Marblehead, Massachusetts, and watch his Atlanta Braves baseball team that the concept of a "superstation" was born. But even then, cable television was a backwater, a home to local talk shows and televangelists, retreads and reruns. When I developed a project, it would only go forward if I could sell it to one of the big three networks; I could then turn around and sell it at a discount to one of the fledgling cable outlets for rebroadcast later.

But the backwater was starting boil, small revenue streams turning into tidal waves. The cable networks began to multiply and grow and expand. HBO, TNT, Lifetime, Showtime, SyFy . . . where once there were three choices, now it seemed there were three hundred. And the new, young networks had seen the light: Not only could they rerun movies and series, they could also create their own. Unlike the big three, they didn't have to worry about appealing to the broadest possible audience, and although they were in the same game, they were playing by a different set of rules. Censorship, for one thing, was optional. As a result, cable had the capacity to be smarter, sexier, and more provocative.

The earth was moving, and ABC, CBS, and NBC were having a hard time standing up, let alone keeping up. Enter General Electric, Capital Cities, Disney, Westinghouse, Viacom, and Comcast. Suddenly the original three networks were no longer the big guns; they were the targets, taken over and swallowed up by companies that used to buy thirty seconds of their time to advertise washing machines. And yes, broadcast television had always been about the money, but now it was *really* all about the money. Reality shows like *Survivor*, *Who Wants to Be a Millionaire*, *Big Brother*, and *The Bachelor* were cheaper to produce, and I found it virtually impossible to sell the big three an original movie or miniseries.

So once again I turned in a different direction, shifting the shape of my motion pictures to appeal to a newer, younger audience.

The ever-more-profitable and more daring cable networks were in the market for darker, edgier stories. I had been pushed to the edge, living through the darkness at the heart of the twentieth century—World War II—and brought that sense of turmoil and turbulence into my twenty-first-century moviemaking. *Human Trafficking* delves into the international underground trade in sex slavery. *Tin Man* reimagines *The Wizard of Oz*, as it unfolds across a futuristic, apocalyptic landscape. And then there's *Alice*, in which a girl grown up descends into a Wonderland of repression, revolution, torture, redemption, and love—a very adult twist on a childhood classic.

That is very much like the Wonderland in which I have grown up. The world changes around you, and if you don't change with it, you are left behind. Television keeps changing too. Antennas, and the notion that the airwaves are as free and available as oxygen, are relics. It's all digital now, and everyone pays for it. The original big three networks and the throng of cable networks are now intertwined and interconnected in a complex of entertainment empires.

Television isn't just television anymore. It's streaming video, Amazon and Netflix and YouTube, hundreds of options—news and sports, comedy and drama, reality and fantasy, available twenty-four hours a day, on demand, freed from the constraints of time and space—and it's all available on your smartphone. The possibilities are endless.

Television can be great and often is, but it can also still be that vast wasteland. Who hasn't, at one time or another, picked up a remote, surfed through four hundred channels, and found nothing worth watching? Television can take you places you've never been and always wanted to go, or it can be a journey to nowhere. But like it or not, it's where the world lives.

Television and I were born at the same time, and in many ways we have grown up together. The difference is, I have grown old, and it hasn't. The medium is still in its adolescence, and like a teenager impossible to predict where it will go, what kind of trouble it will cause, what wonderful things it might accomplish.

Over the last few years, either television has left me behind or I have left it. We have grown apart. I have always had a love/hate relationship with the medium. Television gave me financial and creative freedom, but it could also leave me cold. Early on, in one of my first pitches, I went to an executive at one of the networks and described the movie I wanted to make. It was about three brothers driven by faith, yearning, and passion—a story about love, lust, madness, and murder. He wanted to know the title. I told him *The Brothers Karamazov*. "Is there a book?" he asked.

I recently turned ninety, and as I look forward to a new decade in my life, I also look forward to taking a new direction. Instead of television, I'm going to make features—pictures on a smaller scale for people who still like to gather around a fire and enjoy a good story. But I'm kidding myself. I haven't broken away from TV; I'm just appearing before it in a different form. Because sooner or later, in some way or another, those features are bound to find their way onto a television screen. You'll be able to Google the titles and get them, on demand, on your smartphone. Just as when I first sat in front of a TV set in my hotel room when I arrived in New York, I can't tear myself away from television.

On March 26, 1984, I went to the White House. Jimmy Cagney had invited me to join him as President Reagan presented him with the nation's highest civilian honor—the Presidential Medal of Freedom. Jimmy cried throughout the ceremony, then swapped stories of old Hollywood with the president and his wife Nancy. As luck would have it, I was seated next to the secretary of state, George Shultz, and the subject of Hungary came up. The country keeps following me around. The secretary said he was contemplating whom he should name to replace the current US ambassador to Hungary, and brought up the name of a man who, like me, had been born and educated in Budapest but was now an American citizen.

I shook my head. Nominate an American-born ambassador, was my advice. The Hungarians, I said, would never listen to another Hungarian. Shultz chuckled at my geopolitical insight—or lack of it—but the next ambassador to Hungary was born in Michigan and went to school at Yale.

Four years later, in December 1988, at the Waldorf Astoria in New York, the American Hungarian Foundation honored me with their George Washington Award. Aside from the fact that there is documented proof that Washington had Hungarian blood in him—or so every Hungarian will tell you—we Hungarians have a deep respect and reverence for America's founding father. He led an underdog revolution against a far greater power and delivered his country into freedom and independence—something our country had been trying unsuccessfully to do against various greater powers for nearly a hundred and fifty years.

Our time was about to come.

On June 19, 1991, the last of the Soviet troops crossed the border out of Hungary, into Ukraine, and into a ghostlike past. Six months later, the day after Christmas, the Union of Soviet Socialist Republics ceased to exist. Communism had been dead in Hungary for a while, but now, with the Soviets out of the picture, they finally got around to burying the corpse and getting rid of the stink. In its place came democracy, a free economy, and membership in the European Union. The transition wasn't easy; in fact it was a bit of a mess, but it was a mess in the right direction. Things have to fall apart before they can be put back together. It had taken several thousand years and countless casualties, but Hungary had finally stumbled onto the right side of history.

As a kid roaming around Városliget, the big city park in Budapest, one of my favorite places to visit was Vajdahunyad Castle. Built at the turn of the twentieth century to commemorate a thousand years of Hungarian history, it is, like the country and history it celebrates, a visual puzzle of an edifice. It is, in fact, a fusion of twenty-one different structures, each representing an already existing building in the Kingdom of Hungary. Depending on how you approach it and where you stand, your experience of the building is completely different. Is it built in a Romanesque style? Gothic? Renaissance? Baroque? Yes, yes, yes, and yes. It is all things to all Hungarians. But back then, to me as a boy, it was just a castle, a place where knights once battled with swords on the parapets, fair maidens looked out on the world from tower windows, and dragons breathed fire in the air.

Several years later, after the war was over, I returned to bombed-out Budapest to find most of it in ruins, but the great pretend castle, untouched by the violence, towered over the rubble, still vigilant and standing guard over the park and the city. Hungary, it seemed to say, would survive—as would the memories of my childhood and the powers of my imagination. For several days I slept—and ultimately found comfort in the embrace of a woman I didn't know—in the shadows of Vajdahunyad. A thousand years of Hungarian history was my bed.

In the spring of 1994, fifty years after I slept in the park, I returned once again to the castle. The minister of culture and the mayor of Budapest had invited me to join them and assorted other dignitaries for dinner beneath the vaulted ceiling of the Knights' Hall at Vajdahunyad. The Nazis were long dead and buried, the Communists had faded away, and, for whatever small part I had played in slaying those fire-breathing dragons, I now sat at the head of the table. Special guest Isabella Rossellini said some nice words about me, and the Hungarians roasted some pigs, clinked their glasses, and gave me a medal.

I'm not sure exactly what the medal was for, but it came as a great honor. The boy from Budapest—activist, rebel, criminal, fugitive, freedom fighter, insurgent, tour guide, interpreter, Emperor of the Night, enemy of the state, dead man walking, escapee on the run under a ton of potatoes, Cold Warrior, hothead, American picture-taker and moviemaker . . . the kid with a camera—had come home.

~ ❦ ~

Every life is a production: Some big, some small; some seen as major achievements, others as major flops; some doomed from the start, others entertaining from start to finish. And you can never completely control how the production turns out—if you could, what would be the point? It would be like reading the last chapter of a mystery first. All you can know for sure is that, sooner or later, it will come to an end. Until that time comes, the best you can hope for is that life takes you by surprise . . . and that you take life by storm.

By that measure, I've led a charmed life—a story in three acts.

The first act was all about *survival*.

I learned from my father how to take care of myself. He insisted that I study the mechanics of boxing, fencing, and chess—all of which require focus, discipline, and, even more important, the ability to look without fear into your opponent's eyes, take his measure, and anticipate his next parry and thrust. My father also sent me to Sárospatak, making sure that I knew my way around a classroom as well as a boxing ring. Literature, language, geometry, geology, and physics—once I got all that into my head, I had a map of the world and a manual to how it worked. But the knowledge and experience I gained from sports, games, and books was only the half of it. My father taught me the ropes. My mother taught me how to circumvent them.

In the short time I spent with her, I came to appreciate the art and power of performance—having the resources to adapt to circumstances, play a part, and move on. She brought out the opera in me. It's an intuitive, instinctive thing: I could write my own story, take center stage, or blend into the scenery, depending on what life threw at me.

Whether it was on purpose or it was just in their nature, my parents both gave me a strong sense of independence. They had their lives, and I had mine. They sent me off to school, and even when I was at home, they left me to my own devices. I was compelled to rely on myself and to form strong friendships. Without that ability, I never would have gotten by.

But all of that—physical and mental conditioning, self-possession and self-confidence—would have come to nothing if not for one thing. Luck. Anyone in Europe, Asia, or North Africa who survived the first half of the twentieth century had to be lucky. Every day was a throw of the dice. Some lost their lives; others lost their souls. The rest of us washed off the dirt and moved on.

I emerged relatively intact. I took what I needed from the experience, left the rest behind, and took off for America and my second act. Survival was still part of the equation, but that was more by choice. I put myself at risk because every fiber of my being—and the lens of my camera—was focused on *fun and adventure*.

No one appreciates his freedom more than someone who has had it taken away, and now that I had mine back, I took it for all it was worth—and took it to extremes. I was a young man of great appetites, and I had no intention of keeping them in check. I went crazy. There's no rational explanation for voluntarily walking through fire, playing with dynamite, hanging from hot air balloons, or seeking out close encounters with polar bears and Bengal tigers.

Poets and psychiatrists would say that, after what I'd been through during the war, the closer I came to death, the more alive I felt. But I say, it was just fun. Women are dangerous because they are beautiful. Or is it the other way around? It's the same with the world. The more beautiful something is, the more dangerous it becomes. And it's always worth the risk to pursue it. Just me, my camera, and one more gorgeous abyss to snap pictures of . . . that was my life, and I was never happier.

There are two words I hate, because they scare me to death. The first is *security*. Physical, financial, or spiritual—whatever forms it comes in, I want no part of it. Security is a nice warm bath that drowns ambition, stifles creativity, dulls the senses, and puts you to sleep. The second word is *retirement*. Strap my corpse to a golf cart, and I'll go out and do all eighteen holes, but until then, I'll pass. I'd rather keep working. I prefer to live until I die, which brings me to act three: *making movies and making a family*.

If my intent has been to avoid complacency, flirt with danger, and court disaster, then I have chosen the right business. No script, no star, no director, no producer, and no movie is ever a sure thing. Every day is a gamble. Every shot I take and every scene I compose requires that I take another risk. Because as much as I've learned from the past, the one thing I know for sure is that I can't predict the future. I never know how a story will turn out until it's done. Making a movie is a game of chance . . . as is raising a family. It's the same thing. You put your heart into it and hope it all comes together.

My luck has held. I've managed to make hundreds of movies that have won a room full of awards. And I have Caroline, four children, Kevin, Kim, Robi, and Billy, and twelve grandchildren whom I love. But luck is never enough all by itself. I have also been willful. Throughout my life, whenever I've put my mind to something—whether it's coming to America, making a movie about a whale, or throwing my father's ashes into a river—I've usually found a way to do it. There has been plenty of suffering and pain and heartbreak along the way, but they have only served to make the pleasure and love and success that followed that much more sweet. Now

I can savor my achievements and accomplishments in the same way that I once savored a taste of my grandfather's smoked cheese or a spoonful of my mother's cold cherry soup—both in the moment and in memory.

Now I have come full circle. The one advantage to getting old, living into my nineties, is that it has given me the time to get back to the kind of work I wanted to do in the first place.

The company that I founded forty years ago, the company that bore my name—Robert Halmi Incorporated, RHI—is no more. And it's just as well. It had grown too big and burdensome, and it was holding me back. The work I was doing didn't belong to me anymore. There were too many cooks in the kitchen. In the end, RHI was nothing but a name—just three trademarked letters that popped up on the credits at the end of a movie. I don't need it anymore. The names that really matter to me—Caroline, Kevin, Kim, Robi, and Billy—are mine forever.

Even in my tenth decade, it's time to take another chance. I'm going out on my own. I've got a head full of ideas, a list of new projects, and a circle of good friends and fine actors to help me turn the pictures in my head into movies on the screen. Once again, as it should be, I answer only to myself. I'm about done with this memoir, but as for my life, I still have another chapter to write, and more stories to tell.

—◦—

As *Merlin* the movie draws to a close, the title character, played by Sam Neill, dismounts from his horse—the same horse that he rode at full gallop out of the trees and into the twilight as the movie opened. But now the wizard walks forward slowly and deliberately. Age has caught up with him, and his eyes reveal more apprehension and uncertainty with each step he takes.

Old Merlin is back in the forest of his youth, approaching a thatched hut in a small clearing. Years ago, the Lady of the Lake stole some of the wizard's magic and cast a spell over him—a spell that placed him at the center of history, but separated him forever, he believed, from Nimue, the woman he loved.

In his time, Merlin has stood witness and had a hand in the birth of Arthur—and thus the birth of a new world. Through his wit, artifice, and sorcery, he created the stage upon which young Arthur would lay his hands on the sword Excalibur, build Camelot, and form the Knights of the Round Table. But Merlin would also live to see the destruction of the world he helped create and watch helplessly as King Arthur is slain by his own son Mordred. Ultimately, though, Merlin manages to defeat his enemies, simply by turning his back on them and leaving them to the past.

Over the decades that followed, he wandered from village to village, telling his stories, seeking to entertain and enchant his audiences in exchange for a few coins. But now his journey has led him into these woods. Excalibur and the Lady of the Lake have vanished into the mists, and the spell is broken. Merlin has found Nimue. Played by Isabella Rossellini, she emerges from the hut to reunite with her lover.

"You've grown older," Nimue laughs.

"You, too," Merlin says.

"Does it matter?"

"No," he says, "not anymore. But . . ."

"What?"

"I think I have one last trick."

Merlin passes his hands over her face and then over his own, and they are transformed and transported—young again, beautiful and virile, as if no time has passed.

"No more," he says. "That's the end of magic."

But there *is* more. There is always more. And a man like Merlin always has something up his sleeve, knowing that the end of one story is the start of another. The real trick is to live to tell it—and to live every day with a passion.

That is show business.

Index

ABC (American Broadcasting
Company), 186–87, 258–59
abortion, 43
Abraham, F. Murray, 248
adventure magazines, 120
advertising, 133, 136, 141,
158–60, 258
Africa, 129–32, 202, 230
Alaska, 107–10, 111, 112, 117–18
Albans, Bill, 158
Alice in Wonderland (movie), 248,
249–50, 260
Allied Control Commission, 51,
53, 76
Allies, 26, 30
alligator hunting, 194–96
Alpine Rally, 150
American Army intelligence, 134
American Broadcasting Company
(ABC), 186–87, 258–59
American Geographical Society,
107–10
American Hungarian
Foundation, 262
American International Rally,
150–51
American Press Club, 63–64
American Sportsman, The (TV
show), 187, 188
Anderson, Jock, 246–47

Animal Farm (movie), 216
Ann-Margret, 242
Araguaia River, 208
Arctic Circle, 116–18
Argosy magazine, 112–13
Arledge, Roone, 187
Arrow Cross Party, 25, 28, 54
Arrow Shirt company, 158
arsenic, 197
Assante, Armand, 243–44
Attila the Hun, 22
Austin, Bill, 113–16, 121–22
Australia, 68, 214
Austria, 21, 62
Austrian National Socialists, 21
authenticity, 234

Baby Sellers (movie), 250
Baden-Baden, 11–12
Baird, John Logie, 254–55
Bárdossy, László, 21–22
Barkin, Ellen, 232
Barnack, Oskar, 254
Barnes, Peter, 248
Barrett, Peter, 160, 177
Barrie, George, 210–11
Barrows, Sydney Biddle, 233–34
BBDO, 159, 208
Bean, Sean, 242